"What Georges and Baker have done in this wonderfully helpful volume is unprecedented. They have plumbed the depths of current scholarly discussions on honor and shame from multiple sources (biblical studies, theology, anthropology, and intercultural studies) and have made such information wonderfully accessible for the practitioner. Intelligent, informed, and culturally perceptive, this resource will impact the theory and practice of missionaries and local leaders in unprecedented ways. Throughout, the writing is critical yet engaging. The appendixes ('Key Scriptures on Honor-Shame' and 'Biblical Stories Addressing Honor-Shame') will prove to be exceptionally helpful resources. Those working in the global world of today must read this book. To not do so would be a true shame!"

Christopher Flanders, Abilene Christian University

"Georges and Baker have taken the seeds of previous work on honor and shame in the environment of the biblical world and in modern cultures and cultivated them into fruitful insights and guidance in the areas of theology, crosscultural engagement and, especially, missions. They provide a culturally sensitive reading of Scripture and of modern non-Western situations, significantly advancing the question of how awareness of this dimension of the texts and our global community can improve our interactions with people living from a decidedly different axis of values and in our thinking about the contextualization of the gospel."

David A. deSilva, Ashland Theological Seminary, Trustees' Distinguished Professor of New Testament and Greek

"I was so glad for this book to stretch my heart and mind. Baker and Georges gave me new tools and hope for ministry, not just in a Majority World context, but in Western contexts that are increasingly both secular and globalized. Their experiences and thoughtfulness as missionaries give particular power to their call for us to love and care for people in 'old' ways."

Mako Nagasawa, director, New Humanity Institute

"An exceptional book on this timeless worldview and timely topic. The authors interweave real life stories to help us rediscover a biblical worldview and see how to apply the living Word of God today."

Samuel E. Chiang, president and CEO, Seed Company

"Although Jayson Georges has written on the important topic of honor-shame in the past, this book, coauthored with Mark Baker, takes an understanding of honor-shame dynamics to another level. Every message bearer working in non-Western cultures needs to read and apply the insights and principles of this book if they are to avoid the typical cultural blunders too often committed by too many. Within are crucial insights for effective crosscultural ministry."

Marvin J. Newell, senior VP, Missio Nexus, author of *Crossing Cultures in Scripture*

MINISTERING

in

HONOR-SHAME CULTURES

BIBLICAL FOUNDATIONS *and* PRACTICAL ESSENTIALS

JAYSON GEORGES *AND*
MARK D. BAKER

IVP Academic

An imprint of InterVarsity Press
Downers Grove, Illinois

InterVarsity Press
P.O. Box 1400, Downers Grove, IL 60515-1426
ivpress.com
email@ivpress.com

InterVarsity Press® is the book-publishing division of InterVarsity Christian Fellowship/USA®, a movement of students and faculty active on campus at hundreds of universities, colleges and schools of nursing in the United States of America, and a member movement of the International Fellowship of Evangelical Students. For information about local and regional activities, visit intervarsity.org.

Scripture quotations, unless otherwise noted, are from the New Revised Standard Version of the Bible, copyright 1989 by the Division of Christian Education of the National Council of the Churches of Christ in the USA. Used by permission. All rights reserved.

While any stories in this book are true, some names and identifying information may have been changed to protect the privacy of individuals.

Cover design: David Fassett
Interior design: Beth McGill

Images: desert landscape: © mycola/iStockphoto
white paper background: © tomograf/iStockphoto
crown illustration: © Varijanta/iStockphoto

ISBN 978-0-8308-5146-1 (print)
ISBN 978-0-8308-9330-0 (digital)

Printed in the United States of America ∞

Library of Congress Cataloging-in-Publication Data

Names: Georges, Jayson, author.
Title: Ministering in honor-shame cultures : biblical foundations and
*   practical essentials / Jayson Georges and Mark D. Baker.*
Description: Downers Grove : InterVarsity Press, 2016. | Includes
*   bibliographical references and index.*
Identifiers: LCCN 2016036462 (print) | LCCN 2016037193 (ebook) | ISBN
*   9780830851461 (pbk. : alk. paper) | ISBN 9780830893300 (eBook)*
Subjects: LCSH: Christianity and culture. | Honor--Religious
*   aspects--Christianity. | Shame--Religious aspects--Christianity. |*
*   Missions--Theory. | Church work. | Evangelistic work.*
Classification: LCC BR115.C8 G37 2016 (print) | LCC BR115.C8 (ebook) | DDC
*   261--dc23*
LC record available at https://lccn.loc.gov/2016036462

P	24	23	22	21	20	19	18	17	16	15	14	13	12	11	10	9	8	7	6	5	4	3	2
Y	36	35	34	33	32	31	30	29	28	27	26	25	24	23	22	21	20	19	18	17	16		

CONTENTS

ACKNOWLEDGMENTS

THE IDEAS IN THIS BOOK CANNOT be separated from the community I shared in Central Asia. Thanks to the team for being our family. And thanks to those Central Asian believers who, amid various trials, live as though no other glory matters. This book has described God's honor; your lives embody it. I wish I could mention your names here, but they are already written in another book.

Over the last eight years I've been encouraged and sharpened by conversations with hundreds of people about honor and shame. Thank you for those invaluable discussions. But overall, the sustained conversations with close friends have been the most meaningful. So thanks to Ted, David, John, Wayne, Colin, Cy, Werner, Larley and Jackson for being friends and partners in this effort.

I wish also thank Mark for coauthoring this book and mentoring me through the writing process. I have learned much from your long-standing passion to overcome the tyranny of shame, and your strategic ways of doing so. Also, thanks to our IVP Academic editor Dan Reid for your insights and encouragement from beginning to end. We have benefited tremendously from your experience and enthusiasm.

And finally, my wife deserves immeasurable thanks for her encouragement and patience. You, my dear, are far more precious than jewels and clothed with dignity. Sharing life with you is a great honor.

In the process of writing this book, my own emotions halted progress at times. I have been overcome by the reality of my own shame (a reality faced by anyone who writes about shame), but also captivated by the splendor of God's honor. For example, reading Mark's paragraphs on the saving significance of the cross in chapter five prompted a powerful and transforming time of worship for me. Glory and praise to the only one who saves from shame and restores honor, Jesus Christ.

Jayson Georges

First and foremost I am grateful to Jayson for inviting me to write this book with him. I have learned much from his deep knowledge on the subject. His passion for the topic added to my already strong convictions of its importance.

I am grateful to Doug Frank for introducing me to the theme of shame years ago. More importantly, he led me to experience freedom from burdens of shame through Jesus. Norman Kraus, through his writings and personal conversation, first led me to sense the importance of this topic for communicating the gospel in honor-shame cultures. Grace May reinforced that. New Testament scholars Kenneth Bailey, David deSilva, Joel Green and Ryan Schellenberg have taught me valuable insights on honor and shame. I have used those insights in countless Bible studies in many places, including Honduras, seminary classrooms and the Fresno County Jail. I have been enriched by the opportunity to proclaim the gospel through the lens of honor and shame and by the opportunity to learn from many in those studies who shared their stories with me.

I have taught at Fresno Pacific Biblical Seminary (formerly Mennonite Brethren Biblical Seminary) since 1999. I have learned a great deal on the topic of honor and shame from international students and students who have been missionaries in honor-shame cultures. I am especially grateful for the privilege of teaching a number of students from the Japanese Mennonite Brethren Church. They have taught me much and fueled my conviction of the importance of this theme in global mission.

This is the third time I have worked on a book with IVP Academic editor Dan Reid. I am grateful for his skill and wisdom as an editor and for our growing friendship. Jayson and I benefited from Dan's years of editing experience, but we were especially fortunate to have an editor who grew up in Japan, who was a child of missionaries and who taught in the Philippines for two years. His firsthand knowledge of the subject and passion for the importance of this book was an extra gift.

Jayson and I would like to thank those who read parts or all of the manuscript and gave us valuable feedback. Some cannot be named because they are missionaries in sensitive areas. Those we can mention include Robert Brenneman, David deSilva, Sandra Freeman, Yoshio Fuji, Mathieu Gnonhossou, Karen Huebert-Sanchez, Ryan Schellenberg, Yuritzy Villasenor and an anonymous reviewer arranged by InterVarsity Press.

Finally, I thank Lynn, Julia and Christie for their love and for their support of this project. I am honored to have them as my wife and daughters.

Mark D. Baker

1

A WORLD *of* SHAME

*There is nothing in this entire world that you
need to protect more than your honor. Because you're
nothing without your honor. You'd be dirt, just dirt and
nothing else. If someone tried to take my honor, then
I'd do anything to get it back. Literally anything.*

A MUSLIM IMMIGRANT TO GERMANY

What is more sacred than honor?

DIO CHRYSOSTOM, *ORATIONES*

*A*ISHA ACTIVELY LIVED OUT HER FAITH as a mature Christian. From the time she trusted Christ as a university student, Aisha was a fruitful disciple maker in her campus ministry. After that season, Aisha and her husband joined a local church-planting team. To assist them, my (Jayson's) team hosted a weekend of training. Over the previous months I had begun exploring honor and shame in the local culture and in Scripture with increased intensity. The training time with Aisha and her teammates provided an opportunity to dialogue with national Christians on the topic. We examined the biblical story through the lenses of honor and shame for over an hour. Reading the Bible in honor-shame terms came easily to them since their Central Asian culture mirrored the social world of the Bible in many ways. They became increasingly animated as the study progressed. Aisha grasped the implications full well. She spoke with wonder and joy, but also with sadness and confusion. Her eyes watered up, and she begged to know, "Why has nobody told me this before? I have shared with my sister many times that God forgives her sins, but she just says her shame is too great for God." Her understanding of the gospel, similar to that of many Christians, did not address shame. The consequences of that reality upset her and filled her with sorrow. What was lacking in Aisha's explanation of how Jesus saves? Why did Aisha's theology say so little about the very forces of shame that defined her sister?[1]

Mike ministered to refugees in the United States by sharing life together and helping them get settled. He would often visit Abdul's house and be regaled with generous hospitality. Being from Iraq, Abdul maintained Middle Eastern values of hospitality and eating. Visits to Abdul's house would extend for hours. Good conversation and food were guaranteed. One day, Abdul came to visit Mike. But when he arrived, Mike was busy preparing to leave for a scheduled meeting. Upon opening the door, he greeted Abdul, but explained he was busy and closed the door. Mike's actions offended Abdul. Though polite on the surface, internally he left angered and confused by Mike's not welcoming him into the home. Mike continued on his way out the door, unaware that his actions might be offensive to Abdul. Why did Mike assume he acted appropriately? Why was Abdul offended? What cultural values influenced Mike's actions?

Enrique was an eager disciple, soaking up all the theological input I (Mark) gave him and earnestly seeking to live it out. I invited him to go with me to a conference on holistic mission in a nearby Honduran city. Aware of his limited finances I offered to pay for 75 percent of the cost, including meals and an overnight stay at the retreat center, if he would pay the rest. He enthusiastically accepted my offer, and gave me the amount of money I had requested. Enrique later asked me if Francisco, a young man he was discipling, could come as well. I agreed that Francisco could come under the same financial arrangement, and asked Enrique to explain that to Francisco. The day came to leave for the retreat. Enrique had not given me Francisco's portion, and neither did he mentioned anything about it. I assumed he would give me the money before we registered.

We got off one bus, and took a local bus to the retreat center. The closer we got the more concerned I became. I wanted to talk to Enrique alone about the money, but had no opportunity. Finally, just a few steps from the door of the building where we would register, I stopped in the middle of the path and directly asked Francisco, "Could you give me your portion of the registration fee now, so that we have the money straight before we have to actually register?" They both looked very uncomfortable; Francisco turned away, and Enrique looked at me, his expression communicating, "I can't believe you just did that." But all he said was, "He was not able to get the money." I asked, "Why didn't you tell me? We had an agreement." They said nothing. They simply bowed their heads slightly and looked down. I alone walked to pay the fee for all three of us. Although I tried to mend the relations, the damage done in that moment hung over us the whole event. Why was our sense of the right thing to do so different? Was I wrong to have asked? Why did Enrique not mention the lack of finances beforehand?

Q: Why did Aisha's sister not welcome the gospel?

Q: Why was Abdul offended?

Q: Why did Enrique not communicate about Francisco's finances?

A: Honor and shame. They all interpreted their circumstances through the lenses of honor and shame.

The values of honor and shame guide most of life in Majority World cultures: how you hear the gospel, how you relate to others and how one should communicate. For Aisha's sister, Abdul and Enrique, their cultural compass directed them toward honor and away from shame. Avoiding shame and maintaining honor was the default operating system of their culture.

Most of the world thinks and lives according to the cultural values of honor and shame. Christians ministering among Majority World peoples encounter this reality in many ways. For this reason, we must use an "honor-shame missiology"—a biblically rooted approach to Christian ministry among the nations that proclaims and mediates God's honor for the shamed.

A foreign culture is like the night sky—initially fascinating, but quickly daunting without a configuration to meaningfully connect the dots. Amateur stargazers see stars, but miss the constellations. Honor-shame is like the lines between stars; they give meaning and structure to life. Westerners rarely get honor-shame dynamics; they seem foreign. When we fail to connect the dots, we experience cultural frustration and miss kingdom opportunities. In light of the prominence of honor and shame for shaping life in many cultures, too much is at stake to not account for them in Christian mission.

The Depth of Shame

On April 15, 2013, two pressure-cooker bombs exploded at the Boston Marathon. The tragedy and ensuing manhunt for the Tsarnaev brothers fueled a media frenzy. As the media dug into the bombers' background, they interviewed people whose lives intersected with the Tsarnaevs. Their American friends and classmates expressed mostly disbelief and sorrow about the tragedy. Meanwhile, their Chechen uncle lashed out at them, outraged over the social repercussions. Listen to his words: "You put a shame on our entire family—the Tsarnaev family. And you put a shame on the entire Chechen ethnicity. . . . Everyone now puts that shame on the entire ethnicity."[2] When the Boston Marathon bombing occurred, we suspect most Americans did not think all Chechens are shameful, yet that was the Chechen uncle's primary response. He interpreted the event as fundamentally shame inducing. Americans grieved the loss of safety, but the Chechen uncle feared the shameful actions of two members would infect the whole group.

The testimony of international Christian apologist Ravi Zacharias reveals the powerful force of shame in many cultures. As a young boy in India, he lived to play cricket but was a jokester at school. This conflicted with cultural values. Zacharias explains, "Indian children are raised to live with books and get to the top of the class, or else face failure and shame."[3] His subpar report cards from school reflected poorly on his parents, and led to humiliating thrashings from his father. As a teenager Zacharias made a halfhearted commitment at an evangelistic rally, but his life of failure at school continued to haunt him. He decided to end his life to escape the shame. At age seventeen

Zacharias reasoned to himself, "A quiet exit will save my family from further shame." Zacharias's attempt to end his own life was motivated by shame, not depression. His family's reputation was more important than his own life. (His attempt to overdose on drugs was unsuccessful, and he eventually recommitted his life to Christ while recovering in the hospital.) When social reputation is the basic foundation of life and identity, people's pursuit of respect, honor and status frames every facet of life.

In 2014 a group of militant Muslims overtook regions of war-torn Syria and declared themselves the Islamic State of Iraq and Syria—ISIS. Interestingly, they interpreted those political events as the liberation from disgrace and restoration of status. Note the honor-shame language in their propaganda magazine:

> Soon, by Allah's permission, a day will come when the Muslim will walk everywhere *as a master, having honor, being revered, with his head raised high and his dignity preserved*. . . .
>
> The time has come for those generations that were drowning in *oceans of disgrace*, being nursed on the *milk of humiliation*, and being ruled by the vilest of all people, after their long slumber in the *darkness of neglect*—the time has come for them to *rise*. The time has come for [the Muslim world] to wake up from its sleep, remove the *garments of dishonor*, and shake off the *dust of humiliation and disgrace*, for the era of lamenting and moaning has gone, and *the dawn of honor has emerged anew*.[4]

As morbid and evil as the ISIS ideology is, it reflects an inescapable reality—humans crave honor and abhor shame. The desire for honor and glory cannot be dismissed as a byproduct of sin or some cultural abnormality, but an innate part of being human, somehow rooted in God's creation. God created every human in his image, and "crowned them with glory and honor" (Ps 8:5). According to recent scientific research, the pursuit of honor and avoidance of shame appears hardwired into the human brain. The limbic system within our brain senses social threats (e.g., shame) the same way as physical threats. Both types of imminent danger trigger the same self-preservation instincts and share a common neural basis in the brain.[5] The human brain, and soul, was designed for honor. C. S. Lewis notes,

Glory, as Christianity teaches me to hope for it, turns out to satisfy my original desire and indeed to reveal an element in that desire which I had not noticed. . . . Apparently, then, our lifelong nostalgia, our longing to be re-united with something in the universe from which we now feel cut off, to be on the inside of some door which we have always seen from the outside is no mere neurotic fancy, but the truest index of our real situation.[6]

Though designed to experience God's true glory, our honor was exchanged for shame in the Garden of Eden. As a result, humans crave honor and grasp for it in warped and destructive ways, apart from God's original design.

In World War II the American military faced an unprecedented problem. For the first time a Western nation was warring with a modern military not from the Western cultural tradition. So in June 1944, the US Office of War Information assigned the American anthropologist Ruth Benedict to investigate and explain Japan's "exceedingly different habits of acting and thinking."[7] Benedict had gained renown for her ability to explain world-views. To help Westerners understand the anomalies of Japanese culture, Benedict highlighted the unique role of honor and shame. She explained the basic cultural difference as follows: "Shame cultures rely on external sanctions for good behavior, not, as guilt cultures do, on an internalized conviction of sin."[8] With Benedict's analysis, American policy in Japan during the war and subsequent occupation accounted for the realities of shame. In the same vein, contemporary scholars in a variety of fields—diplomacy, crime, ethics, psychology, community development, politics and social reform[9]—now recognize that honor and shame must be considered before developing practices and policies for catalyzing social change.

Despite heightened attention to honor and shame among social scientists, honor and shame play a negligible role among Christian theologians and missionaries. As the US Office of War did during World War II, those in-volved in global mission would also do well to examine honor and shame at a cultural level. In this book we turn, however, not just to anthropology for insight, but to the Bible itself. Just as Westerners fail to adequately observe cultural underpinnings of honor and shame in today's world, Western Christians also often overlook the prominent role of honor and shame in the Bible, though it comes from an honor-shame context.

A BIBLE COVERED IN SHAME (AND HONOR)

Nurdin and I (Jayson) became friends through an English club. One weekend I visited his family. After lunch we strolled through his village, in part so Nurdin could introduce his American friend to neighbors. Every person I met seemed to be a relative of Nurdin—a cousin, an aunt, a nephew and so on. So I jokingly asked, "Does the whole village consist of just one family?" He chuckled, and then explained an important feature of his culture—all children must know seven generations of ancestors. Village elders would even stop children at play and require them to recite their family lineage back seven generations.

Nurdin's explanation helped me understand the importance of genealogies in cultures like those found in the Bible. Genealogies, overlooked by modern Western eyes as irrelevant, are essential in group-oriented societies.[10] They determine identity, define family, confer status, identify potential spouses and establish social rank. Genealogies function as a manual for life by defining the boundaries of honor and shame. I heard of one young Middle Eastern man who, upon trusting in Jesus, first memorized the genealogy of Matthew 1:1-18. He wanted to know his family ancestry, the lineage he was born into spiritually. As in many contemporary cultures, people in the world of the Bible thought a person's identity comes from the family they are born into. So honor, in essence, is inherited from one's kin. For this reason, the New Testament opens, "An account of the genealogy of Jesus the Messiah, the son of David, the son of Abraham" (Mt 1:1). Genealogies are just one aspect of honor-shame that Western readers overlook in the Bible.

From genealogies to Jesus' confrontations with Pharisees, from the exile to the crucifixion, from Ruth to Romans and from the psalms of lament to Jesus' parables, honor and shame are presupposed furniture in the minds of biblical authors and their original audiences.[11] The pervasive concern for honor and shame in biblical writings gives a precedent for addressing honor-shame dynamics in contemporary ministry. The Bible consistently reveals God's heart to honor the shamed.

The Greco-Roman culture into which the early church expanded exhibited particular concern with honor. Aristotle said honor is the greatest of all goods after which important people strive.[12] Cicero, the Roman philosopher-politician, explained that ancient Roman life "was lived

under the constant, withering gaze of opinion, everyone constantly reck-
oning up the honour of others."[13] Roman philosopher Dio Chrysostom
asks rhetorically, "What is more sacred than honor?"[14] Honor and shame
prevailed throughout the ancient Mediterranean Society. In fact, one of
the premier virtues in the Greco-Roman culture was *philotimia*—the pre-
occupation and pursuit of honor. The *Oxford Classical Dictionary* explains,
"*Philotimia*, literally the love of honour (*time*). The pursuit of honour(s),
tangible or intangible, was a constant of elite behavior throughout Greco-
Roman antiquity; all that changed was its context and the extent to which
it was given unbridled expression or else harnessed to the needs of the
community at large."[15]

The apostles wrote to Christians socialized in a Greco-Roman world that
perceived life as "a ceaseless, restless quest for distinction in the eyes of one's
peers and of posterity."[16] New Testament professor David deSilva tells us,
"The culture of the first-century world was built on the foundational social
values of honor and dishonor."[17] As we train our eyes to see the dynamics of
honor and shame in the biblical world, we glean insights from the apostles'
ministry in contexts marked by honor and shame. The Bible provides
guidance for kingdom ministries among the many honor-shame contexts in
today's world.

GLOBAL REALITIES

For the church to fulfill her mandate to "make disciples of all nations"
(Mt 28:19) and "present everyone mature in Christ" (Col 1:28), a biblical
missiology for honor-shame contexts is crucial, due to several global realties.

Honor-shame is the predominant culture type for most people in the
world. As we will explain in more detail in chapter two, "honor-shame cultures" refers to *collectivistic* societies where the community tends to shame
and exclude people who fail to meet group expectations, and reward loyal
members with honor. In contrast, an "innocence-guilt culture," as commonly encountered in Western, Anglo contexts, is more *individualistic*.[18] It
relies on conscience, justice and laws to regulate social behavior. The third
cultural orientation Christian missiologists speak about is "power-fear
culture." This refers mostly to *animistic* or *primal* contexts where people fear
the unseen world of spirits, curses, ancestors and so on, and so act to gain

the power of the spiritual world. The three types of cultures are not isolated silos; all three dynamics interact and influence every culture to some degree, but usually one is more predominant in a given culture. So the term "honor-shame culture" is akin to "right-handed person"—it doesn't suggest the person never uses their left hand (or does not have a left hand!), but simply indicates their primary preference.

In 2014 Jayson developed TheCultureTest.com—an online questionnaire to assess a group's culture type. The initial nine thousand results from around the world have confirmed what anthropologists and missionaries commonly observe—non-Western cultures are most influenced by honor-shame values. Figure 1.1 indicates the degree to which each cultural dynamic (i.e., guilt, shame and fear) shapes "Majority World" and "Western" cultures.[19]

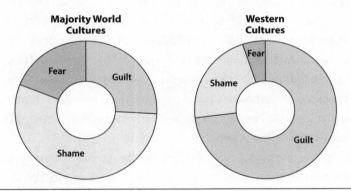

Figure 1.1. Comparing culture types

This data suggests that approximately 80 percent of the global population (i.e., Asians, Arabs, Africans and even Latin Americans) runs on the honor-shame operating system. Westerners (i.e., North Americans and Western Europeans) not familiar with honor and shame, globally speaking, are the odd ones out. Western society is like a computer running Linux—its cultural "operating system" has a minority share of the global market.

A person's culture type significantly shapes his or her worldview, ethics and identity, even more than individual personality. And more significantly for Christian witness, cultural context influences how people experience sin (i.e., as guilt, shame or fear) and conceive of salvation (i.e., innocence, honor or power). The global influence of honor and shame requires Christian theology and mission to account for their reality. Failing to biblically address them leaves significant aspects of people's daily life and worldview outside of the realm of God's salvation and truncates the gospel.

The accelerated rate of global migration also makes the topic of honor and shame crucial for ministry in Western countries as well. The face of the Western world has changed quite significantly over the last seventy years. Waves of international students, refugees and immigrants from honor-shame cultures have entered Western countries. As of 2010, forty million people in America are foreign-born immigrants. Since 1965 most immigrants to America have been from non-European backgrounds, resulting in significant demographic and cultural shifts.[20] As a result of this migration, Americans now regularly encounter people from the honor-shame cultures of Africa, Asia, Latin America and the Middle East. As a simple example, Mark's two immediate neighbors in Fresno, California, are Mexican and El Salvadoran; Jayson's immediate neighbors in Atlanta, Georgia, are Iraqi and Nepali. Understanding honor-shame is vital, at the very least, for living as Christians in today's multicultural world. An honor-shame missiology is not only for foreign missionaries fulfilling the Great Commission among the nations (Mt 28:16-20) but also for Christians in the West desiring to fulfill the Great Commandments among their neighbors (Mt 22:39).

While these two global realities (i.e., culture types and immigration) influence Christian mission in today's world, an even more significant reality about the changing face of the global church calls for an articulation of the gospel in honor-shame terms—Christians globally are increasingly from honor-shame cultures. Researchers have documented how global Christianity is shifting away from the West (i.e., Europe and America) and toward the South (i.e., Latin America and sub-Saharan Africa) and East (e.g., Philippines, Korea, China). In 1900, 82 percent of all Christians were white; by 2050, about 80 percent of all Christians will be *non*white.[21] This rapid shift in global Christianity toward the Majority World mandates fresh theological and missiological reflection. While some movements of Christianity have received and retranslated the gospel into cultural modes fitting their worldview and daily needs, that is hardly the global norm. Most expressions of Christianity in the world continue to be predominantly Western, in both liturgy and theology. The global church must articulate a biblical message for the pivotal values of honor and shame in order to help Majority World Christians love, obey and follow Jesus in their own sociocultural context marked by honor-shame realities. We hope over time more and more "honor-shame natives"[22] from the Majority World will themselves develop Christian theology and embody Christian mission for their honor-shame contexts. In the meantime, Western Christians, as they begin to note the honor-shame themes of Scripture, can encourage and foster this process of self-theologizing.

Though people of honor-shame cultures are following Jesus more than ever, the fact remains that most people in honor-shame cultures remain unreached for the gospel. Most of the ethnic groups with limited or no access to the gospel (i.e., unreached people groups) are predominantly honor-shame in their cultural outlook. The region of the world including North Africa, the Middle East and Asia (commonly referred to as the "10/40 Window") is predominantly honor-shame and contains

- 64 percent of the total global population,

- 85 percent of the people living in abject poverty (less than two dollars per day),

- 90 percent of the world's unreached/unengaged people groups,

- all four major non-Christian religions (Islam, Buddhism, Hinduism and Taoism), and

- a "Christian" population of only 8.5 percent (compared to 70 percent in the global West and South).

The lostness of people and the significant missional opportunities in this global bloc summons the church to consider how they could best engage this unreached region. Perhaps a reason for the church's limited presence in the 10/40 Window is a lack of biblical reflection on the core values structuring life. A biblical missiology in honor-shame terms may be strategic for fulfilling the Great Commission of making disciples of all nations.

The predominance of honor-shame in global cultures, the surge of immigration into Western contexts, the southward shift of global Christianity and the persistent reality of unreached peoples in honor-shame contexts all

highlight the need for a more relevant theology, and a corresponding missiological approach to address honor and shame.

Theology in a World of Shame

The process of contextualizing the forms and content of the Christian faith
for various cultures is commendable and essential. Yet many attempts at
contextual evangelism "assume the gospel."[23] That is, many Christians
tacitly presuppose a Western gospel with its emphasis on the legal aspects
of salvation. For them the very question, how do we communicate the
gospel? assumes a priori that "our" particular theology is the absolute and
complete truth.

However, one must realize even Western theology is itself *contextual*. In
the words of Lesslie Newbigin, "Every interpretation of the gospel is embodied in some cultural form. The missionary does not come with the
pure gospel and then adapt it to the culture where she serves: she comes
with a gospel which is already embodied in the culture by which the missionary was formed."[24] All Christian theology is embedded in the values
and language of a particular culture. Western theology has skillfully applied God's truth to the needs of its specific cultural milieu—characterized
as individualistic, rationalistic and guilt-based. For example, Augustine
and Luther, significant voices in Western theology, wrestled through
seasons of introspective guilt. So their experiences of individual pardon
and forgiveness shaped their theological formulations and subsequent
Western theology.[25]

Because of its inevitable cultural constraints, Western theology does not
exhaust the full meaning and application of biblical truth. Western theology
itself is not "wrong," but simply incomplete and limited by cultural blinders.[26]
There remain areas of biblical truth that Western theology has not yet examined because cultural conversations have not yet prompted such a theological inquiry. One such "blind spot" in Western theology is honor and
shame. The topic remains in the shadows of Christian theology and mission
because shame has been a secondary concern in Western culture (although
that seems to be changing).

The neglect of honor-shame in Western theology ultimately leads to
shallow forms of Christianity, as people trust God for one component of

salvation (i.e., forgiveness of sin's guilt), but then bypass Christ's work for absolving sin's shame. Western theology, in effect, keeps one hand of God's salvation tied behind his back, only allowing him to save in one arena of life.

Our objective is not to replace or correct Western theology, but to complement it. Hence, you will read the phrases "not only . . . but also" and "both . . . and" throughout the book, particularly in the theological sections. The gospel is a many-sided diamond, as we have outlined in our previous books.[27] But despite the multidimensional nature of salvation in Christ, Western theology's emphasis on one aspect of salvation truncates other facets of the gospel. So we aim to "rotate the diamond" to examine often-neglected aspects of Christian salvation so that readers can see (and proclaim) the gospel in a fuller, more complete manner.

Imagine that Joe was a builder who built homes with nails. So his main tool was a hammer. Every year Joe upgraded to the latest, strongest hammer. Then one day, Joe traveled eastward where people built homes with screws. But because Joe always built with nails, he instinctively pounded the screws with his hammer. No matter how hard he hammered, or how many hammers he used, he labored in vain. Then Joe discovered the screwdriver. Though it operated much differently than a hammer, the screwdriver was clearly the tool of choice when building with screws.

We cannot blame imaginary Joe for trying his best with the hammer. It was all he knew, and it worked so well in his home region. Likewise, our aim is not to criticize people for using hammers in a land of screws (i.e., rehashing theology and practices developed in the guilt-based, individual-oriented Western culture for ministry in Eastern, shame-based cultures). Rather, we want to share about screwdrivers, so you can work more effectively. This book broadly addresses the topic of honor and shame with applications for various aspects of ministry, such as spirituality, relationships, evangelism, conversion, ethics, discipleship and community. We offer not just one screwdriver but a broad set with different sizes and heads. To bear witness to God's kingdom and build Christ's church where honor and shame are the dominant values, we need a new set of tools—a reality we both realized as missionaries.

JAYSON'S FLOOD

I first encountered the topics of honor and shame as a biblical studies major in university. We learned about the ancient Mediterranean cultures to better interpret Scripture. My view of honor-shame cultures was mostly cerebral and generally positive, especially when contrasted to Western narcissism and individualism. But then two years later I encountered honor-shame in person as an expatriate missionary in Central Asia.

One afternoon, Nargiza came to visit our home. She was my wife's friend who regularly attended an investigative study of Jesus' life at our house. But on this visit she explained she could no longer attend, even despite her personal preferences. Her neighbors had noticed she visited us regularly, and began gossiping that Nargiza was becoming a Christian. Her association with us threatened her family's reputation, so her parents demanded she stop visiting our house. Through my relationships with Nargiza and other locals, I experienced the underside of honor-shame cultures: fear of others' opinions, rejection by family, gender inequality, gossip, nepotism and cronyism, hiding weaknesses, pressure to marry, focus on externalities, unquestioned obedience and public shaming.

As our work continued, two recurring episodes highlighted the cultural prominence of honor and shame. First, unbelievers hardly sensed personal guilt nor desired forgiveness of their sins. They disregarded my traditional evangelistic presentations as illogical or unintelligible. Somehow, my two plus two did not equal four in their minds. Second, the cultural forces of honor and shame regularly influenced Christians. They commonly faced persecution from family, pressure to marry unbelievers, strong expectations to conform and the inclination to mask shameful aspects of their lives. Although honor and shame dictated Christians' lives Monday through Saturday, they were hardly discussed on Sunday morning. To successfully engage nonbelievers and disciple believers in that context, our ministry team needed to understand honor and shame biblically.

Anthropology publications helped me understand honor and shame culturally but not theologically. How is Jesus good news to people mired in shame and seeking honor? I first explored biblical verses about honor and shame, and then noticed a larger theological motif—the removal of shame and the restoration of honor lies at the center of God's salvation. Shame is not just a social issue plaguing human relations, but a spiritual reality separating us from God as well. Ever since the fall, humans have been in a state of shame. But in Christ, our honor is restored as we enter God's family. God cares greatly about restoring honor, so much that he willingly bore the ultimate shame of the cross. Jesus is the solution for shame.

With this realization in hand, our team adjusted various aspects of our ministry—our business platform, relational bridges, evangelism methods, discipleship content and so on—to best account for the honor-shame realities. The exploration of these ideas in ministry, training seminars and publications[28] has been akin to an unplanned hike—the ascent of one peak revealed further peaks to explore. The stories of that journey, both the frustrations and breakthroughs, will be recounted throughout.

MARK'S STREAMS

Using water analogies, we might say a wave of honor-shame realities hit Jayson when he went to Central Asia; my experience is more like two streams that have joined into a growing river. Although honor and shame are secondary cultural drives in most contexts in North America, a growing number of authors are exploring people's experience of shame.[29] The first stream began when a professor introduced me to some of these writings. He helped me become aware of shame I carried and guided me to experience release from that burden through Jesus' loving embrace. The stream grew; with greater awareness of shame I began to observe the burdens of shame of many Hondurans. I had observed how they viewed God as a distant, angry and accusing figure. Rather than alleviating shame, their concept of God increased it. Kenneth Bailey's books *Poet and Peasant* and *Through Peasant Eyes* heightened my awareness of the themes of honor and shame in the New Testament.[30] Leaning heavily on Bailey, I developed a number of Bible studies and sermons to invite people to bring their shame to Jesus and to form their concept of God based on the Jesus they encounter in the Gospels. The great need and the depth of appreciation expressed by people who met Jesus through these Bible studies compelled me to write a book, in Spanish, that wove together these Bible studies and stories of shame and release from shame.[31] I continue to passionately proclaim release from shame through encounters with Jesus, most commonly now in Bible studies at the Fresno County Jail.

The second stream flows from a book I coauthored with Joel Green, *Recovering the Scandal of the Cross.*[32] In one chapter we summarized Norman Kraus's work contextualizing atonement theology in Japan. Kraus's experience introduced me to the reality that Jayson described above. Japanese people struggled to understand common guilt-oriented explanations of the cross's saving significance. That chapter on shame and the cross received the most comments from readers. Missionaries working in and people from honor-shame contexts have been especially appreciative. This fed my desire to better understand honor-shame dynamics and to look for examples of people taking them into account in their evangelism, discipleship and theology.

As these two streams joined I began realizing that the honor-shame dynamic was much more prevalent than I had thought. This new, and growing, awareness flowed into and enriched all realms of my life and ministry in Honduras and now as a seminary professor.

THE ROAD AHEAD

An honor-shame missiology serves as a compass helping Christians fruitfully navigate the terrain of Majority World cultures. To equip readers for ministry among Majority World nations, we address these issues.

Cultural anthropology (chapters two and three). In chapter two we explore the nature of honor and shame, and how they function in society. What is the difference between guilt cultures and shame cultures? What are the various types of honor-shame cultures? In answering these questions, we aim to unfold the inner workings of honor-shame cultures.

Then in chapter three we discusses the various ways cultures encode honor-shame values into daily life. How can we recognize honor and shame in cultures? Why are hospitality, indirect communication, purity regulations and patronage common features of honor-shame cultures?

But more importantly, once we see the dynamics of honor and shame playing out, what is a biblical response to them? Without understanding the cultural language of honor and shame, Westerners can feel culturally frustrated. When Nargiza's parents prohibited her from visiting us, I (Jayson) was appalled and outraged they would decide on her behalf. A series of negative cultural experiences in my first year prompted me to *replace* the prevailing honor-shame culture with Western values (e.g., egalitarianism and individualism), not *transform* or *redeem* it with kingdom values. We'll propose that the Bible, rather than dismissing honor-shame as inherently negative, advocates a balanced approach to honor-shame cultures, which notes both strengths and weaknesses. An informed cultural understanding of honor and shame can catalyze kingdom breakthroughs in our relationships and ministries.

Biblical theology (chapters four and five). A grasp of honor and shame aids our reading of Scripture as well. We can better understand why Adam and Eve "hid themselves" (Gen 3:8), or why the actions of the prodigal's father were so scandalous (Lk 15:11-32). Awareness of honor-shame allows us to rightly grasp the full weight of biblical words (e.g., *curse, scorn, reproach*), images (e.g., slaves, sons, thrones, feasts) and motifs like God's promised blessing or psalmists' yearning for vindication from shame.

Yet the values of honor and shame help us understand not just the *culture* of the Bible but also the *theology* of the Bible. In chapters four ("Old Testament") and five ("Jesus") we examine key biblical narratives in order to reframe theology in the key of honor and shame. What does the Bible say about honor and shame? What is the relationship between sin and shame? How does God save the shamed?

Honor and shame are not merely cultural themes laced through the Bible, but are foundational elements to rightly understanding biblical salvation. The mission of God has always included removing shame and restoring honor. God pursues glory for himself by honoring and welcoming people from all nations, as we will explain.

Practical ministry (chapters six–eleven). The work of God to remove shame and restore honor must inevitably redefine our conception of Christian mission. How can we, as the body of Christ, embody and express the kingdom of God in the various honor-shame contexts of today's world? Unpacking the nature of Christian mission in honor-shame cultures is the focus of chapters six–eleven.

In chapter six we reflect on the nature of shame in Christian spirituality, especially for you the reader. Before Christians proclaim God's honor to the nations, we must first possess and embody it ourselves. As we have taught Christians about honor-shame in theology and ministry, students note the degree to which shame influences their own identity and relationships. Shame is a defining aspect of human existence, but rarely addressed in churches or ministry. When is the last time you heard a sermon addressing shame? Most people have *never* heard such a sermon. Salvation from shame is not just a theological doctrine or ministry tool, but fundamentally a spiritual reality to be appropriated by faith. For these reasons, in chapter six we analyze the nature of shame in Western culture and guide readers toward salvation from their personal shame.

In chapter seven we propose eight "commandments" of relationships in honor-shame cultures so Christians can *relationally* communicate God's honor in culturally relevant ways. What are honoring ways to resolve conflict and reconcile relationships? What is a culturally appropriate (and God-honoring) way to share resources and help materially as a patron? How should Christians handle situations of hospitality and gift giving to bless people? When (and how) should we transform the sinful elements of honor-shame cultures? What is a good way to "give face" to people? Living out kingdom values in these nitty-gritty aspects of everyday relationships forms a vital element of Christian witness. So we offer practical tips for honoring people through relationships.

Building on the foundation of honoring relationships, chapters eight and nine explore the nature of evangelism in honor-shame cultures. To help define the "gospel," we examine two primary aspects of salvation in the Bible—status reversal and group incorporation. Then we propose practical ways to communicate those aspects of the gospel. Since evangelism is a process, one must also be aware of how the conversion process works in group-oriented contexts, at both social and spiritual levels. In honor-shame cultures the community plays a central role in the process of evangelism and conversion. We offer theological reflection and various examples of evangelism to help readers lean into more fruitful evangelistic approaches for their respective contexts.

In chapter ten we set forth a biblical ethic for collectivistic cultures. When people feel mostly shame instead of guilt when doing wrong, what is the best approach to moral transformation? What is the basis of morality and ethics in shame-based cultures? Following the example of 1 Peter, we note the New Testament presents a new honor code—a new paradigm of evaluating what is truly honorable and shameful—to guide Christian morality. A new honor code focused on glorifying God reshapes all of life, especially Christian leadership, as we examine.

Finally, in chapter eleven we explore honor and shame in the life of Christian community. What is a biblical vision for the local church in an honor-shame context? How can Christians resist the social pressure to conform, especially during shaming persecution? How can we address sin without destroying the relationship and causing the sinner to lose face? Is there a way to shame people biblically? How can Christian leaders successfully overcome shame and serve with genuine humility? We examine how Jesus' disciples in collectivistic cultures can live as true community.

SOME QUALIFICATIONS

This sort of book presents several challenges for us as authors. For one, we use terms such as *Western, honor-shame cultures* and *Majority World* to label complex cultural realities. Categorizing all seven billion people into a few groups obviously sacrifices nuance for clarity. We do realize that *Western* includes countries as geographically separated as the United States and Australia, and that *Majority World* is an umbrella term including diverse cultures from Honduras to Kenya to Japan. These terms, along with others such as *individualistic* and *collectivistic*, or *shame-based* and *guilt-based*, are rather imprecise and broad, but they are convenient and widespread terms that help clarify complex realities. The terms are simply generalizations (which always have some exceptions); so we ask readers to read accordingly.

Also, we as authors are Anglo-Americans. We do not sense a need to apologize for that fact, but we do acknowledge it. Our years of living in non-Western countries have in fact made us "bicultural" in some ways. This means at times we feel more comfortable in an honor-shame context than in Anglo-American culture. But nevertheless, honor-shame is not our birth culture; we are "adult immigrants." So our take on honor-shame cultures is ultimately that of bicultural outsiders. While recognizing the limitations of such a perspective, we try to play to the strengths of this vantage point in writing for fellow English-speaking Christians.

Finally, this book is not a magical key to unlock the door of ministry success. The vast diversity of global cultures, even honor-shame cultures, makes it impossible to offer a one-size-fits-all method or program for ministry. This does not mean we steer away from the practical. Along the way we offer many stories and positive examples of Christian mission in various honor-shame cultures. Our aim is to lead you in a paradigm shift—to see God's world and God's Word through a new lens. As you see honor-shame in both culture and Scripture, we pray God's Spirit will lead you to apply God's salvific honor to various cultural contexts in creative and redemptive ways for the glory of his name.

DISCUSSION AND APPLICATION QUESTIONS

1. What are some obstacles that keep people in Western cultures from understanding honor-shame cultures?

2. Can you identify how the pursuit of honor (or avoidance of shame) might be influencing any current events in the world?

3. Based on your experiences, what are the consequences of not having a biblical view of honor and shame?

PART ONE

CULTURAL
ANTHROPOLOGY

2

THE HEART *of* HONOR-SHAME CULTURES

Honor is the good opinion of good people.

SENECA

*Shame: A painful feeling of humiliation
or distress. . . . A loss of respect; dishonor.*

NEW OXFORD ENGLISH DICTIONARY

WE INVITE YOU TO IMAGINE the following scenarios in a North American context. A high school teacher, respected by her students, asks one of them, "Was my lecture today clear?" The student responds truthfully, "Well, actually I couldn't follow it. I did not get the point." Or another scenario: while putting his purchases into the car, a man realizes he inadvertently walked out of one store without paying for an item. He walks back into the store and pays. What is going on in these scenarios? Why does the student tell the truth? Why does the man make the extra effort to return and pay? Both scenarios display a high commitment to obeying rules—even when no one else would know if they had broken the norm or not. The motivation for right behavior comes from within.

Now picture another scenario: a grade school teacher briefly steps into the hallway. While the teacher is out of the room two students take something off the teacher's desk. You see them. The teacher comes back in and says, "Who took this? I know someone did this, or saw someone else do it. Tell me who." What do you feel? Your internal rule-orientation urges you to do the right thing and tell the teacher. At the same time a feeling of group loyalty and peer pressure compels you to be quiet and not say a thing. In this scene we observe two different approaches of how societies influence how we behave. One is rule/guilt based, oriented toward internalized principles. The other is community/shame based, focusing on preserving relationship.

Imagine a student trying to solidify her place in a group and one of the most popular group members asks, "Did you like my party?" Though she did not like the party, she does not say, "No, it was a lousy party!" Why might the same student who responded honestly to the teacher about the lecture give an evasive answer to a popular classmate about the party?

Think back to high school. Think of the group you were in, or a group you were trying to be in. How did your group's behavior or appearance differ from students in other groups in the school? Take a moment to recall how your group got you to do those things. How do they get you to behave, look and talk a certain way?

When I (Mark) was in high school in the 1970s the dress code to be "in" was simple but strict. We all wore Levi's and Converse sneakers to school every day. Before high school I had worn cheaper Wrangler jeans and off-brand sneakers. I still had some and would wear them at home after school or on the weekends. While I can recall going back to a store and paying for something that I had inadvertently not paid for, I never "confessed" to my friends at school that I sometimes broke the dress code and wore Wranglers. In the first case my internal sense of right and wrong compelled me to act; in the second I had no sense that I had done anything wrong since no one from my group had seen me wearing Wranglers.

We begin the chapter with these scenarios from North America for a number of reasons. First, to highlight that even if you are from a more guilt-oriented, rule-based society, you have had some experience with the honor-shame dynamic. Of course to have had some of your actions shaped by peer pressure is not the same thing as living in a context saturated by honor-shame. But keeping your experiences of behavior shaped by group expectations in mind will aid you as you read this chapter.

Second, we hope that the contrasting scenarios will help you recognize how behavior that is considered normal and appropriate can shift depending on what framework you operate out of. The example of informing a peer group that one had worn the "wrong" clothes at home likely strikes you as far-fetched—ridiculous. Yet one of Mark's Japanese students found the first scenario of directly answering a teacher as far-fetched, even ridiculous. He recounted that he hesitated to even ask a question in class because that would dishonor the professor by implying the lecture was unclear. For him to directly tell a teacher the lecture failed was unthinkable.

Third, we start with examples from North America to reiterate the point made in the previous chapter that these categories are not nice and neat. Rather, as Timothy Tennent explains, "Virtually every culture in the world contains concepts of both guilt and shame, including the pressure to conform to certain group expectations as well as some kind of internalized ideas about right or wrong. The difference is not in absence of shame or guilt, but rather in how dominant these tendencies are."[1]

Scholars often prefer to avoid such general labels, but we use the term *honor-shame culture* for ease of communication and in line with conventional discourse.[2] In this book, "honor-shame culture" refers to a context where the honor-shame dynamic is dominant. No group of people would self-identify as an honor-shame culture. Rather, the classifications "honor-shame culture" or "shame-based culture" are etic (i.e., outsider) terms for describing social groups that utilize public reputation to control behavior.

SHAME VERSUS GUILT

Gulzel was a young Christian who attended university in the city. On most weekends, Gulzel traveled back to the village to help her family tend the land and host guests. One particular Sunday Gulzel prepared to return to the city for Monday-morning classes. This meant finding a vehicle in the village center heading to town. Gulzel arrived at the taxi-stand lot and found a car waiting for a final passenger. Gulzel got in and the vehicle departed on its one-hour trek through the hill range—four men and young Gulzel.

After a short while the men began propositioning Gulzel and inviting her to their homes for tea. As a young girl she felt uncomfortable and tried to downplay the situation with a minimal response. After a while, the men stopped along the road for a round of vodka shots. Being intoxicated, the men became more assertive toward Gulzel. Their comments became harsher, and they were becoming physically aggressive. Gulzel feared what the men might do next. Just that moment, Gulzel noticed her uncle in an oncoming car. What would you do if you saw your uncle in that situation? How did Gulzel respond to the sight of her uncle? Instead of jumping onto the road and flagging him down, she turned away and hid—even though she had done nothing wrong!

This incident confounds Westerners. How could Gulzel shy away from an uncle who would surely protect her? For Gulzel, social shame trumped physical dangers. When I (Jayson) learned about this incident, my knee-jerk response to such injustice was anger. I wanted to file a police report so the perpetrators would be punished and justice served. But that would have only compounded the incident by exposing the shameful situation. Shame guides behavior much differently than guilt.

In shame-based cultures, acceptable behavior is defined by ideals from the community. You must be the person others expect you to be. For a young female like Gulzel, chastity is a primary expectation. The community expects her to remain sexually modest to ensure that her children are legitimate descendants of the family. So in the roadside situation, the community ideal of a pure, undefiled girl directed Gulzel's behavior. She acted so that her personal reputation matched the group expectation. Gulzel would have learned this expectation throughout childhood as she heard neighbors gossip about those who deviated from the ideal. The pressure to meet social expectations, and threat of shame for those who failed, outweighed her concern for physical safety. Being seen was more dangerous than being hurt, regardless of who was right and who was wrong.

Because shame leads to exclusion and rejection, the primary response is to hide or cover the shame. If others are not aware of the issue, then shame does not exist. This explains why Gulzel hid from her oncoming uncle at the roadside. And Gulzel's mother later assisted in hiding the potential shame, knowing her own reputation as the mother was also at stake. People contain shame to avoid alienation and rejection.

In contrast, guilt-innocence cultures define what is acceptable through rules and laws. Governments, corporations, schools and even families establish rules to guide our behavior; people expect those rules to apply universally to all people at all times. A mature person is a "law-abiding citizen" with a strong internal sense of right and wrong. Guilt-oriented cultures do not simply emphasize rules and laws, but socialize people to internalize them into a person's conscience. They rely on people's internal conscience (not external social pressure) to keep them from doing wrong.

One of my (Jayson's) earliest childhood memories is of a guilty conscience for stealing a Hot Wheels fire truck from preschool. Even though no one witnessed me, my young conscience tormented me until I returned it the next day. Guilt needs no audience because it results from breaking an internalized code. Note the wording of the above sentence, "my young conscience tormented me." The punishment came from within, not from the involvement of others. In a shame-based culture, this internal sense of self-torment is rare; consequences are external—you are shamed by others. Since shame means falling short of the opinion of others, it requires an audience. Gulzel avoided shame by staying out of her uncle's sight.

The difference between the culture types is *not* "Western cultures believe in right and wrong. Majority World cultures believe in honor and shame." That statement falsely implies honor-shame cultures do not sense right and wrong. Honor-shame cultures do have morality, but their basis for defining right and wrong happens to be communal and relational (not legal or philosophical). For them, what is best for relationships and honors people is morally right; what shames is morally wrong.

Not only does the process of arriving at guilt and shame differ, but the procedure for alleviating guilt and shame also contrasts starkly. Guilt is removed when a person confesses wrongdoing and makes restitution. Taking ownership of transgressions and apologizing is rewarded. For example, an American politician accused of marital unfaithfulness can generally repair the situation by publicly acknowledging wrongdoing. Since the problem is a wrong action, the solution is a right action performed by the violator. Justice is served through community service, paying a fine or jail time. These interrelated concepts of guilt, introspective conscience, confession, restitution, innocence, forgiveness and justice guide behavior in Western societies, but rarely surface when shame is at play.

Guilt says, "I *made* a mistake, so I should confess," but shame says, "I *am* a mistake, so I should hide." With shame the problem is the actual person, so the group banishes the individual. To avoid such rejection and isolation, people mask their shame from others. Managing shame is essential because a shamed person (unlike a guilty person) can do very little to repair the social damage. Removing shame requires more than forgiveness. The pardon of wrongdoing addresses something external to the person; it doesn't actually change a person's public standing or address the root cause for shame. Overcoming shame requires a remaking or transformation of the self. One's identity must change, and this happens only as their relationship to the group changes. That usually means a person of a higher status must publicly restore honor to the shamed, like the father graciously did for the prodigal son in Luke 15. Table 2.1 summarizes the preceding paragraphs to compare the behavior and "moral logic" of people in guilt-based versus shame-based contexts.

Table 2.1. Comparing moral systems

	Guilt-Based Cultural Behavior	Shame-Based Cultural Behavior
Cultural Context	individualistic, Western	corporate, Majority World
Definition of Normal	rules and laws	expectations and ideals
Guide for Behavior	introspective conscience	public community
Result of Violations	guilt	shame
Core Problem	"I *made* a mistake" (action)	"I *am* a mistake" (being)
Affected Party	the transgressor	the group
Violator's Response	justify, confess or apologize	hide, flee or cover
Society's Response	punish to serve justice	exclude to remove shame
Means of Resolution	forgiveness	restoration

WHO, NOT WHAT

Another way to explain the cultural differences is this: shame cultures focus on *who* you are; guilt cultures emphasize *what* you do.

One day a roadside policeman in Central Asia flagged me (Jayson) to stop for making an "illegal" right turn. Sensing he was trapping people to extort money, I got upset before I even stopped the car. Without even greeting the policeman, I demanded he show his badge with proper identification and explain why he stopped me, requesting the precise traffic violation in the legal code. Then, as if a trained lawyer, I argued the finer technicalities to demonstrate my innocence as a driver. The cultural values of guilt, justice and innocence guided my behavior, though I hardly knew it. I focused entirely on my actions—*what* I did. Realizing that arguing my innocence was going nowhere, I paid the fine (but not without warning the officer that justice would be served when God would judge him for wrongdoing!). My entire approach was about proving my actions were not wrong, and that I was not guilty. I failed to recognize how utterly foreign I appeared to him. In hindsight I realize I actually communicated tremendous dishonor and disrespect.

Then one day as I argued with another policeman over a four-dollar fine, I noticed something bizarre—some drivers would just tell the police their name and be immediately excused. Family name mattered more than the laws; *who* you are is more important than *what* you do. So I began to contextualize my approach toward policemen. When pulled over I would greet the officer in his native language (not the trade language, Russian) with customary questions about his family and health—this acknowledged his status. Instead of arguing my innocence, I would simply hand him my California driver's license. This informed him of my identity—*who* I was. Without fail, my California license prompted a smiley comment about either Hollywood or Arnold Schwarzenegger—both nice conversation pieces to forge a new acquaintance. As we would talk I would invite him to the weight gym our team operated, and even offer him one month free. I treated the policemen like people I wanted to know. Instead of appealing to justice as grounds for dismissal, I appealed to their hospitality: "Please excuse me. I am a foreigner in your country. Please help me out as a guest."

When I changed my strategy from arguing "I am not guilty!" to showing "You are honorable!" the interaction was entirely different. Speaking their cultural language of honor-shame made the encounter friendly and enjoyable for both of us. Addressing who I was (a new friend from California!) instead of what I did (nothing illegal!) made far more sense to them. Our point here is not about avoiding traffic fines, but how the contrasting social systems rooted in justice and honor function so differently.

UNDERSTANDING HONOR

What exactly is honor? Take a moment and try to define the word *honor*.

This question typically stumps people. We all know the words *honor* and *shame*, but find it hard to articulate their meaning since they are such abstract ideas. Another factor is that they are more emotions of the heart than an object of study. People primarily *feel* honor and shame, instead of ponder their meaning. The previous section explored the broader social landscapes in which guilt and shame function. Now we'll examine the specific nature of honor and shame.

Honor is a person's worth in society. Honor is essentially when other people think highly of you and want to be associated with you. Seneca defined honor as the "good opinion of good people."[3] Anthropologist Julian Pitt-Rivers says, "Honour is the value of a person in his own eyes, but also in the eyes of his society."[4] Honor is inherently communal and relational; it comes from harmonious social bonds with other people in your group. Think of honor as a social credit rating measuring one's reputation. A person with a good rating among peers is honored with respect and deference.

Honor includes gravitas and influence in the community. A colloquial word in Central Asia for a man's belly is "authority." If someone has the money to eat that much food, people assume he must be important! The extra weight communicates his social precedence over others—his substance and power. Even the primary Old Testament word for glory (Hebrew *kavod*) also means "weight." Honor is the social weight one throws around to influence and control. Though it took me years to make the connection, this is why the weight gyms in Central Asia turn into a ghost town in the summer months. Men were reticent to exercise on warm days lest they sweat too much and lose their "weight." When the acquisition of honor is a primary concern, it shapes all of life's decisions, even workout schedules.

Honor is intimately connected to the physical person. Parts of the human body symbolically demonstrate honor and shame in many ways: the right hand purveys honor with gestures like touching, waving and shaking; the head embodies a person's honor so is kissed and crowned; face is a metonym for honor; feet are the lowest and dirtiest part of the body and thus symbolize disgrace; private parts signify the shame of vulnerability and desecration; and one's blood transfers honor and is often the price in transactions of honor.[5] Because honor is so abstract, every culture has symbols that display, or embody, a person's status. Cultures ascribe great social meaning to the ways people interact physically—for example, bowing and saluting, or spitting and punching. Because the body showcases a person's honor, the food people eat and the clothing they wear indicate social status as well. For example, the book of Esther opens with King Ahasuerus's displaying the splendor of his majesty though lavish dining and royal attire.

Physical expressions make a person's social ranking tangible and more visual for people to observe. Consider these symbolic actions of honoring and shaming: "Sit at my right hand until I make your enemies your footstool" (Ps 110:1). Or, "Hanun seized David's envoys, shaved off half the beard of each, cut off their garments in the middle at their hips" (2 Sam 10:4).

People utilize gestures, euphemisms, food, clothing and other concrete symbols to claim and defend their honor for themselves and their group. Throughout the book, we explore how these visible aspects of honor and shame are crucial for understanding people, reading the Bible and communicating the gospel.

In November 2014, the British royal heirs Prince William and Duchess Kate attended a Cleveland Cavaliers basketball game. During the pregame photo-op basketball superstar LeBron James broke royal protocol and put his arm around Duchess Kate. Photographers happened to capture her look of surprise and mild embarrassment. The British newspapers quickly cried foul over yet another American's lack of manners, and the incident became a headline. The little incident between two highly honored people touched the nerve of unwritten social decencies on both sides of the Atlantic, and illustrates two types of honor—ascribed and achieved.

Honor you receive by virtue of family or origin is ascribed; it is passively inherited from one's family or group. Royal families exemplify ascribed honor par excellence. Royalty is hereditary. While Prince William and Duchess Kate are surely intelligent and affable people, their royal status has little to do with personal character. Their honor is ascribed. Achieved honor, on the other hand, is earned through one's own activities and accomplishments. It is based on individual performance, as in professional sports— make the game-winning shot and you are immortalized, but miss it and people think much differently of you. For athletes like LeBron James physical ability determines status.

Prince George and LeBron James represent the extremes of both types of honor—one is entirely ascribed, the other entirely achieved. The ascribed honor of British royalty is rooted in ancient castles where bloodline is paramount; the achieved honor of "King James" comes from his spectacular performance on the basketball courts. They each possess an honored status, albeit on different grounds. Though this story comes from Western culture, it helps our eyes see the cultural nuances of honor. This is pertinent for crosscultural workers because status in Majority World societies is ascribed far more than it is achieved. People's identity and status is ascribed based on their ethnicity, place of birth or lineage. Unawareness of this often causes cultural frustration in Westerners who expect people to "pull themselves up by the bootstraps"—a euphemism for achieving personal status.

Defining Shame

Shame means other people think lowly of you and do not want to be with you. After Job lost his physical possessions and became physically sick, he was "filled with disgrace" (Job 10:15) because others thought nothing of him and kept their distance. He lamented, "My family [is] far from me," "serving girls count me as a stranger," "intimate friends abhor me," "even young children despise me" (19:13-19). That is shame—being despised and rejected by the community.

When relationships and social bonds are intact, a person feels peace, security and honor. When relationships and social bonds are damaged or broken, a shamed person senses humiliation, disapproval and loss of status. Shame is connected to exposure and rejection before peers or those in authority. Shame causes someone to "lose face," taking away their identity and value. The Shona (Zimbabwe) word for shaming means "to stomp your feet on my name" or "to wipe your feet on my name."[6]

The national lament in Psalm 44:13-15 illustrates Israel's experience of shame. Feeling rejected by Yahweh and trampled on by the nations, Israel sensed humiliation. Note the multiple synonyms for shame (italicized) denoting Israel's deep sense of worthlessness and devaluation in the eyes of others.

> You have made us the *taunt* of our neighbors,
>> the *derision* and *scorn* of those around us.
> You have made us a *byword* among the nations,
>> a *laughingstock* among the peoples.
> All day long my *disgrace* is before me,
>> and *shame* has covered my face.

Shame enters lives through multiple doors and comes from many sources: transgressions, accidents or stigmas. One source of shame is improper behavior. Innocent mistakes like not flushing the toilet or tripping on stage can cause embarrassment. There is nothing technically wrong or harmful about those actions, but they expose us before other people and make us look for the nearest exit. Shame, however, is not just about embarrassing situations. For instance, consider how indicted criminals shield their faces from press cameras to avoid public exposure. Illegal behavior affects how society perceives a person, so they hide. These actions are variations of *achieved* shame. But the deepest shame is often *ascribed* through the process of "stigmatization."[7]

Groups ascribe shame to people with some "undesirable difference," which is usually present at birth—for example, ethnicity, a physical malady or family association. Society attributes negative characteristics to all members of the stigmatized group purely on the basis of membership in the group. People sense disgrace for being associated with something or someone shameful. An invisible wall begins to separate "us" from "them." The stigmatized lose their status; they are somehow abnormal and defective as humans. In the end, those ascribing shame feel superior and morally justify depriving people of their rights, power and humanity because they are "other." The stigmatized are excluded from full participation in society simply for being a certain person. These unfortunate mechanics of shame keep people from experiencing the life God intends for the human family.

In the New Testament, we see that many recipients of Jesus' grace bore some type of ascribed shame—for example, Gentiles, Samaritans, the bleeding woman, blind, deaf, lame, lepers, demon-possessed. Their shame stemmed from congenital social realities beyond their control. (Though not all whom Jesus freed from shame were in this category, for the prostitutes and tax collectors bore "achieved shame" resulting from their sinful/taboo behavior.) For many people living in honor-shame cultures, their identity depends largely on shame that is ascribed and inherited. But fortunately, God provides a new inheritance and ascribes a new identity through Christ.

Shame hurts; it is a heavy burden to bear. To thrive, humans need to experience liberation from their shame. That does not, however, mean that the act of shaming a person is always inappropriate. Some actions are indeed shameful in God's eyes, and the surrounding community appropriately shames those who commit them. If the people continue in the inappropriate behavior, seemingly unaffected by the shaming, they are called "shameless." Strangely enough, being "shameless" is worse than being "shameful."

As we have described, shaming is a way society minimizes inappropriate behavior. For the sake of all, people should feel shame for inappropriate behavior. The threat of potential shame acts like a cultural stop sign, helping to preserve dignity and avoid offensive actions. Even though the experience of shame will be painful, we can affirm a group's shaming when (1) the action in question is something God would consider shameful, and (2) the intent of the shaming is restoring the person to right living and right relationship with God and others. This "reintegrative" shaming is restorative and temporary.

Tragically much of the shaming in the world today falls short of both these ideals. First, many cultural definitions of what is honorable and what is shameful have been twisted and distorted by sin; many people carry burdens of shame for things that are not truly shameful. Second, the intent, not just the object, of the shaming is also problematic. Many groups and communities use shame to reject, not restore, the shamed person. This disintegrative shame is toxic, debilitating and permanent. Although in chapter eleven we will explore how to practice positive reintegrative shaming, in general when we refer to shame we have the negative, destructive sense in mind.

COLLECTIVISM

In 2013, the Chinese government discovered illicit businessmen selling rat meat as lamb and capturing cooking oil from restaurant drains for resale. In response, the Supreme People's Court (China's highest ruling authority) criminalized the activities because they "seriously affect social harmony and stability, and seriously harm the image of the party and government."[8] Observe how the stated rationale against food crimes was not public health or legal infractions, but a concern for the group's harmony and image. The disgraceful actions of a few businessmen threatened the leaders' reputation and group's cohesiveness.

Honor-shame cultures are naturally "collectivistic." That means their cultural outlook prioritizes the groups' survival and distinction over individual preferences. Members of shame-honor cultures are expected to uphold the status of the group. This is why a father in Afghanistan may feel compelled to kill his own child if she or he marries someone from an inferior family; the community is more important than the individual.

Collectivistic societies define people by their relationship to the group. A person's honor and essential nature is bound to the group they enter at birth (i.e., family, ethnicity and country). The group possesses a collective honor that individual members access and share.[9] People are expected to be true to the group, not true to themselves. So they strive to blend into the group, not stand out from it because "the nail that sticks out gets hammered down."

This collectivism contrasts with the individualism of Western society. Enlightenment philosophy defines people as autonomous individuals—"I think, therefore I am." Western parenting trains children to "think for yourself" and "blaze your own trail," not to blend in or bow down. Western identity comes from individual distinction, not group participation. For example, in America it is somewhat embarrassing if two people wear the same, or even similar, shirts to work. So my wife and I always found it interesting that all the women of one Central Asian community wore the exact same knit sweater. (The fact they always had a large peacock embroidered onto the back made them all the more apparent.)

The social matrix of collectivistic cultures is designed around establishing and expanding a network of relationships. Group-oriented cultures value relational harmony. People strive to maintain interpersonal bonds and avoid offending others. Saving face and keeping peace preserve connections. Gifts and hospitality are always reciprocated to maintain social balance and avoid incurring a "social debt."

People rely on relationships to access the basic necessities of life—food, protection, health, work and information. As an example, getting directions in many countries can be a community-based treasure hunt. Locals would only tell me (Jayson) the general direction of my destination: "It's near the green factory across the river." When I arrived at the green factory, I had to ask another person, then another, until I finally arrived. In collectivistic societies, getting something is often a matter of knowing the right person. The group provides people's core needs, so being a part of the group ensures survival.

In collectivistic societies shame is contagious; the dishonor attached to one person is felt by all. What one person does affects the entire "in-group" to which they belong. Recall the response of the Boston Marathon bombers' uncle mentioned in chapter one: "You put a shame on our *entire family*—the Tsarnaev family. And you put a shame on the *entire Chechen ethnicity*."[10] When Brazil lost 7-1 to Germany in the 2014 World Cup, the team's poor performance affected all 200 million Brazilians. Fans voiced responses like, "Our nation is hurt. We will need to face people making fun of us the rest of our lives," and "I feel ashamed to be Brazilian."[11] In the Bible as well, God's people brought shame on God's name (see Mal 1:6; Rom 2:24). At a young age, children learn they are expected to act as representatives who uphold the group honor.

VARIATIONS OF HONOR-SHAME CULTURES

Though forces of honor and shame drive people in the Majority World, that does not mean all honor-shame cultures are identical. Every society expresses the values of honor and shame uniquely, often in quite contrasting ways. The Central Asian city Jayson lived in for nine years had two rather similar ethnic groups, both Turkic and Muslim. Yet the styles of clothing each group deemed honorable contrasted greatly. One group honored traditional, full-length clothing as badges of loyalty and modesty. The other group esteemed dressy, and even immodest, Western fashion as status symbols reflecting modernity and progress. Every culture expresses honor differently.

Arab and Japanese cultures, both of which are highly honor-shame, respond to conflict in very different ways. Middle Eastern cultures compete for honor. They view conflict as a win-lose game. Confrontations are agonistic, meaning only one person walks away with honor. This explains their use of violence and aggression to repair honor during conflict. Far Eastern cultures like Japan strive for mutual harmony. Conflict is approached as win-win or lose-lose game. Status is intertwined; I lose face if I shame you. So East Asians generally respond to shame by withdrawing, or using an intermediary. The contrasting responses of Arabs and Japanese are calculated to achieve the same purpose—maintain honor and avoid shame.

Another complicating factor is that terminology for honor and shame ranges widely. Languages use different words to hint at honor and shame. The word *glory* is the most common handle for honor in the Bible. In Latino cultures the word *macho* denotes respect and importance. Central Asian Russian uses *prestige* and *reputation* to attribute honor. One common English word for honor is *dignity*, which comes from the Latin word meaning "worthy." Thai people, much like other East Asians, speak about gaining, saving and losing "face."[12] In many languages "name" is a euphemism for honor, for a person is known by their name. Our point is this—the cultural *values* of honor and shame are far broader and more prevalent than the *terms* "honor" and "shame." We note these linguistic variations across cultures because Christians must carefully observe such linguistic nuances to speak their "heart language."

The many variations of honor around the world prompt some anthropologists to say there is no such thing as a universally shared concept of "Honor," but only indigenous taxonomies of "honors." This view emphasizes how every cultural group has unique ideas about what is honorable, as well as unique terms and customs for expressing honor.[13] This astute observation does summon Christians to study and appreciate each culture's (and subculture's) specific construal of honor on its own terms. Yet at the same time, we as Christians do believe that God is the essence and source of all true honor.

The Creator emanates glory and splendor from his very being. God's honor is neither achieved nor ascribed; it simply *is*. So being made in the image of this glorious God, every person and every nation covets the true honor that was lost in the Garden of Eden. The universal pursuit for face gives rise to thousands of cultural systems by which people attempt to construct a name for themselves. But such honor is a mere shadow of the real honor derived from God.

Honor-shame functions as a lingua franca across the world, but every culture has its unique accent. These differences and distinctions point to the reality that it is one thing to have a general understanding of honor-shame dynamics, but something else to navigate those dynamics in daily life in a particular context. We turn our attention to that reality in the following chapter.

DISCUSSION AND APPLICATION QUESTIONS

1. How would you define *honor* and *shame* in your own words?

2. What are the primary words used in your cultural setting for communicating the ideas of honor and shame?

3. Describe one sphere of your own life influenced by honor and shame.

THE FACE *of* HONOR-SHAME CULTURES

There is no getting away from the fact that this idea [of glory]
is very prominent in the New Testament and in early Christian writings.
Salvation is constantly associated with palms, crowns, white robes, thrones,
and splendor like the sun and stars. All this makes no immediate appeal
to me at all, and in that respect I fancy I am a typical modern.

C. S. LEWIS,
"THE WEIGHT OF GLORY"

One looks in vain for a Westerner who understands and utilizes
the positive elements of shame. . . . The negative definition
and evaluation of shame is also virtually unanimous
among Western theologians and missionaries.

DAVID AUGSBERGER,
PASTORAL COUNSELING ACROSS CULTURES

ONE SPRING I (JAYSON) STARTED a community garden with Nepali refugees. I had heard about Nepalis' amazing gardening skills and witnessed their green thumbs at work. Weeks before planting, they worked the ground diligently. Once plants were in the ground, they meticulously watered and put decomposed leaves around each plant. They focused their energy on cultivating the best possible soil for plants. As skilled gardeners, they knew the soil determines the health of the plants. Come late spring the community garden was in full bloom. Visitors admired the lush vegetable plants but hardly noted the soil beneath them.

This image of a garden helps explain honor-shame cultures. The values of honor and shame are like soil from which unique plants emerge. Westerners often see dynamics above the surface, while remaining unaware of the soil. As the Nepali gardeners knew quite well, plants and soil are inseparable—they must always be understood in relation to one another.

What cultural plants typically emerge from the soil of honor and shame? How do the values of honor and shame affect a culture's view of food, time, money, economics, communication, family or space? Whereas the previous chapter discussed the nature of honor and shame (i.e., the soil), we now explore how cultures codify honor-shame values in daily life (i.e., the plants). The social dynamics of patronage, indirect communication, event orientation, purity, social roles and hospitality all grow directly out of honor-shame cultural values, as illustrated in figure 3.1.

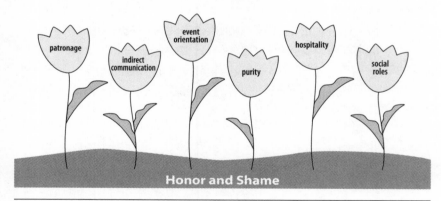

Figure 3.1. Manifestations of honor-shame

Christians engaging people of honor-shame cultures must understand the ways cultures typically express their values in everyday activities. These cultural features represent the level where Christian workers actually encounter honor and shame. An incorrect understanding of these social realities limits our ability to build crosscultural relationships and incarnate the gospel.

We now turn to describe six cultural features that commonly emerge from honor-shame soils; we also explore how ignoring the honor-shame character of these dynamics often leads to incorrect and negative assessments of those cultures (as noted in parentheses).

PATRONAGE (NOT CORRUPTION OR DEPENDENCY)

Alisher possessed the enterprising personality of a Wall Street deal maker. He served as the head administrator of our neighborhood, where he was always networking to ensure the community's needs were met. Whenever we crossed paths on the street our encounters followed a similar pattern. With hardly a pause, Alisher would rattle off my community contributions to the nearest bystander, "When the children have needs, Jayson always meets them! He gives our city office computers. His development center employs dozens of people! His organization pays for the kids' basketball league!" His incessant praise steamrolled my expectations of a personal greeting. I felt rather uncomfortable listening to Alisher publicize my personal contributions. What was he doing?

The social phenomenon of patronage explains Alisher's comments. Patronage refers to a reciprocal relationship between two unequal parties. The superior patron provides material goods to a client, and the client repays with nonmaterial goods such as loyalty, obedience or gratitude.[1] The patron, like a parent, assumes responsibility for the welfare of the people. For example, he covers the hospital expenses, contributes a sheep for the community party or purchases coats for the poorer children in winter. In exchange for financial provision, the client becomes socially obligated to repay the patron with social capital. Along with verbal praise, clients can communicate gratitude with token gifts or acts of service. As a seasoned government official, Alisher seized public opportunities to repay my financial assistance with praise and thanks.

The English word *patronage* can be somewhat misleading. When I paid the taxes for registering a new car in America, the receipt heading stated, "Thank you for your patronage." The English usage of *patronage* hardly resembles the Majority World phenomenon. Patronage in collectivistic societies means the materially rich provide survival and security to clients in exchange for honor and prestige. In developing countries where people acquire goods through relationships, patronage is the de facto economic system. Honor, not money, serves as the primary currency facilitating the transaction of goods and services. Around the globe, leaders at all levels (e.g., the president, a mayor or a family elder) operate according to the precepts of patronage; benevolence ensures respect and allegiance.

Along with the promise of honor, the threat of shame also motivates patronage. Society uses shame to pressure the rich into sharing resources. The failure of a rich person to share resources is a cardinal disgrace in collectivistic cultures. Alisher's words not only served as thanks for past contributions but also obligated me to help in the future, lest I experience shame for not living up to the status he projected of me. The threat of shame also ensures the client's thankful response. Ungrateful clients who do not reciprocate with gratitude are scorned; returning favors is obligatory.

Westerners generally have a rather pessimistic view of patron-client structures. Acquiring goods through relationships instead of official financial transactions seems like *corruption*; we accuse leaders who offer influential positions to relatives of *favoritism* or *nepotism*. Westerners valuing financial independency view the patronage model suspiciously. Relationships based on a commitment to meeting needs rings the sirens of *dependency*. Alisher's effusive thankfulness as a client not only baffled me but also really bothered me. Only after several years did I learn how to respond appropriately. (We will discuss appropriate responses to these honor-shame dynamics in chapter seven, on relationships.)

Indirect Communication (Not Lying or Deception)

Aijana approached me (Jayson) after the Easter church service to borrow money. She wanted to visit her family in the village for spring break, so she needed six dollars for the taxi ride home. As I considered her request, I thought about the several other small loans friends had not yet returned. I wanted to make sure Aijana returned the money. So I asked several questions to confirm her creditworthiness: Existing debts? Repayment history? Income potential? Having worked as a banker at a mortgage company, I treated Aijana as though she had applied for a home loan. She answered every question according to my preferences, and assured me her top priority upon returning after spring back would be repaying the six dollars, just as

I suggested it must be. That was eleven years ago, and I am still out the six dollars.

People in honor-shame cultures communicate indirectly. Words are for the purpose of managing relationships and social identities, not presenting information. Harmony takes priority over ideas. Truth in communication is defined *relationally*, not *logically*. Being truthful means being loyal in your relationships, respecting others and helping preserve face. A person who "cuts to the chase" or "gets to the point" runs the risk of offending others, so it is actually preferable to "beat around the bush" in honor-shame contexts. Western communication is like a download that efficiently transfers information; Majority World communication is more of a dance where you avoid stepping on toes. Indirect communication is a strategic technique for minimizing shame. In her mind, Aijana sought to respect and honor me by agreeing with me. In hindsight, her words were actually very true . . . to the relationship.

Once when my wife and I (Jayson) returned home from a team meeting, we discovered our three-year-old daughter had cut her bathing suit in half because she wanted a two-piece. Our faces displayed our displeasure—not only with the ruined bathing suit but also with the fact that our daughter was unaccompanied with scissors. I immediately asked the babysitter what happened (as if it wasn't obvious!). In a very guilt-innocence fashion, I asked direct questions to get information to determine who was guilty. The baby-sitter giggled, shrugged her shoulders and looked down, saying in the passive voice, "It was cut." Deflecting the confrontation was her strategy for mitigating offense and shame. People downplay conflict and tension to preserve harmony and avoid losing face. In my frustration, I had to ask myself, "What is more important, the bathing suit or relationship?" So instead of "getting to the truth of the matter" at that very moment with a verbal dialogue, we sat down and had lunch together to affirm the relationship.

Indirect communication includes many nonverbal clues. Relationships in such "high-context" cultures require sensitivity to subtle details. Honorific gestures during introductions, such as the correct use of titles or hand-shakes, must be regarded. Western businessmen working in China take classes just on exchanging business cards because the gesture communicates status and respect.[2] Our clothing also confers status. Wearing casual attire to an important occasion downplays importance and could potentially disrespect others. The little details surrounding words reinforce messages of honor and shame.

Unaware of these honor-shame dynamics in communication, a Western person may regard indirect communication as *lying* or *deception*. When absolute honesty is a virtue, indirectness seems immoral and *conniving*. While Aijana sought to avoid offense, my guilt-innocence values took offense with her *sugarcoating*. Looking back, I only imagine her discomfort while fielding all my direct questions and being backed into a relational corner.

Event Focus (Not Tardiness or Laziness)

Weddings in Central Asia usually include several hours between the ceremony and reception for the wedding party to take pictures around the city. On one occasion when I was part of a wedding party, we visited the city's prominent photo spots until 5:00 p.m., when the wedding reception allegedly started. But apparently it was too early to start the reception, so the wedding party waited at my house. From there, the wedding planner called her sister at the banquet hall every fifteen minutes: "Who has arrived?" "Has so-and-so come yet?" "How many people are there?" Finally, near 6:30, the wedding planner determined enough guests had arrived for the newlyweds to enter the banquet hall. How did honor-shame values influence the wedding's start time?

For the wedding planner, the reception did not start at 5:00 p.m., but when everybody arrived. Events are significant in honor-shame cultures because people determine status and identity by who they gather with, not by the tasks they accomplish. So starting an event without some people implicitly uninvites them—an incredibly disrespectful gesture. To start an event on time without certain people suggests exclusion and risks offense. Time is not a schedule to be followed, but a relational opportunity. Time functions as a social tool for conferring honor (or shame). The more important a person is, the later they arrive at gatherings. To show their status, the most important people arrive last.

In Western cultures focused on accomplishing tasks, schedules dictate our gatherings. For example, American wedding planners have notorious reputations for militantly following minute-by-minute schedules. While the Central Asian wedding planner waited out of respect for the latecomers, I worried about upsetting the guests who arrived on time. In English, we speak about "respecting your time," as if someone's time is most important. Without regard to honor and shame values at play in Majority World cultures, the lack of punctuality becomes *tardiness* or *laziness*. Westerners may grow frustrated with repeated lateness, and even interpret it as a moral or spiritual deficiency.

PURITY (NOT LEGALISM OR RITUALISM)

Purity and cleanness are common features of honor-shame cultures. The following story from a Christian in Turkey illustrates how deliverance from a state of defilement is a significant felt need of many people, especially Muslims and Buddhists.

> On one occasion, I was standing outside the church's meeting place to welcome people when a young (unmarried) man arrived late and came up to me. After greeting me, he whispered in my ear that he had just had sexual intercourse, but that he had not washed. Could he go into the meeting, he wondered. He did not think so, and I realized that in his mind the problem was not the illicit sex itself, but the fact that he had not washed to ritually remove the uncleanness before approaching God. I was so bewildered that I ushered him into the meeting room, after hastily telling him it would be good to talk together afterwards.[3]

Purity implies the right thing in the right place. Defilement, or pollution, indicates the wrong thing in the wrong place. For example, we cherish soil in the garden, but promptly sweep away any dirt trudged into the kitchen. Purity codes explain why Muslims never place the Qur'an on the floor, or why Asians typically squat instead of sitting on the ground. Lines of purity define acceptability and cleanness.

Social concerns for purity extend far deeper than physical dirt washed by soap, and includes human purity and social cleanness. My (Jayson's) Iraqi neighbor one day offered us a thirty-six-count box of Pop Tarts. He saw my confusion, so he explained it had gelatin made from pig byproducts. As a Muslim, it would make him unclean. People of honor-shame cultures are deeply concerned about purity.

To illustrate this, imagine if you found a long hair in your dinner at a formal restaurant. Would you just remove the hair and eat the food? Probably not. That is "gross," or "nasty" (the contemporary words for "unclean"). The single hair defiles the entire dish, and you the eater would feel "unclean" for eating that meal. That scenario, granted on a much smaller scale, illustrates the repulsive dynamic of defilement and uncleanness in many cultures.

In Central Asian cultures the cleanliness of your shoes marks a person's social status. A person with clean shoes is viewed as clean. When my shoes were dirty, people would ask me, "Don't you feel dirty?" For this reason, people often carry rags in their pockets to dust off shoes midday, or stop alongside creeks to polish shoes.

Notions of purity are essentially judgments of value. Consequently, purity and defilement are common sources for honor and shame. Purity regulations maintain group boundaries and human identity. Every culture deems certain times, places and actions to be "sacred cows"; doing those things is what it means to be "us." Properly observing such purity codes helps a person remain socially clean. But associating with unclean objects or people pollutes and defiles. Defilement disqualifies a person from the community—the ultimate mark of shame, as we often see in the Gospels with lepers, Gentiles or prostitutes.

In Western thought, codes of pollution and defilement come across as arbitrary distinctions. Science, not social mores, determines what is dirty. Regulations for preserving social purity feel *primitive*. American evangelicalism in particular shuns sacredness in favor of commonness. Moreover, Protestants inherit a theological tradition that views Old Testament ceremonial laws as empty *ritualism* abolished by Jesus, and favors internalized virtues. Observing ceremonial rituals to maintain purity is quickly labeled *legalism* or *Pharisaism*.

SOCIAL ROLES (NOT OPPRESSION OR INEQUALITY)

In my (Mark's) first months in Honduras, my housemates and I befriended Alberto, a neighbor boy. Already poor, his family suffered even more when his father could not work because of an accident. We knew Alberto was hungry. As newly arrived missionaries we were eager to help, and we were intent on doing it "right." We latched on to the idea of the importance of not giving handouts and creating dependency. So we told him he could eat supper at our house any day he wanted, as long as he did the dishes. He agreed, but before he washed the dishes he closed the curtains on all the windows in that part of the house.

In an honor-shame culture, every person has a proper role. People maintain honor by behaving according to that role. Social roles are the tracks society lays down for people to run along. One's social role prescribes the clothes you wear, the spouse you marry and words you speak. Performing one's role and fulfilling expectations demonstrates solidarity with the group. We had asked Albert to go against socially assigned roles—washing dishes was a task done by females. His hunger was great, and the food looked good. For that he was willing to wash dishes, but only if he could avoid the shame of someone seeing him in this inappropriate role.

People generally welcome predefined social roles and behavior. Life is much simpler when the group decides on your behalf. Expectations morph over time as people age into new social roles (e.g., from student to spouse) or status symbols change (e.g., by the time Jayson entered high school, Guess jeans replaced Levi's as cool), but pressures to behave a certain way always exists among honor groups.

Roles and expectations most often crystallize along gender lines. Many cultures expect women to avoid shame through modesty and discretion, and expect men to compete for honor in the public arena. Along with gender and age, social rank determines behavior. Positions of authority come with highly prescribed actions. Hierarchical cultures expect, even require, a high degree of reverence toward authorities. For example, students must always follow teachers' precise instructions and never suggest disrespect by even initiating a question. Failure to play the role dishonors.

When I (Mark) visited Ethiopia as a guest teacher, Ethiopians always picked up my suitcase and box of books. One time I joined in to help unload luggage and supplies from the back of a pickup. I brushed aside my former student's polite statement that others would unload the truck. Operating according to my egalitarian norms, I saw it as a good thing to downplay the status of my social role. I viewed helping to unload the truck as the "right" thing to do. Then my former student pulled me aside and more directly said, "Mark, as professor and guest preacher you are an honored guest. Do not try to help unload the pickup." From that point on I sought to graciously accept the respect and honor given (which actually honored them).

Westerners bristle at social roles. They violate our sacred ideals of autonomy and individual expression; everyone should "be themselves." In an egalitarian culture, gender distinctions reflect antiquated *sexism*. Expectations from others to behave in a prescribed way suggest *oppression*. Western culture assumes all people should have equal access and opportunity, so unique treatment based on someone's rank or age seems like an *injustice*. Separating social roles from their collectivistic contexts leads to these negative evaluations.

Hospitality (Not Obligation or Ostentation)

Jargul was of the age to get married. Since his family did not have the financial means to secure a bride and host a wedding, he emigrated to Russia to earn money. In Moscow he worked seventy-hour weeks and lived in a room with ten other migrant laborers to save every dollar he could. After two years Jargul returned home with enough money. Within a few weeks he found a bride and got married. The extravagant wedding cost thousands of dollars, and consumed all of his savings. So to provide for his new family, he returned to Russia by himself to work. The status associated with hosting one magnificent feast was worth years of migrant labor for Jargul.

Hospitality and feasting provide opportunities to accumulate honor by publicly sharing food. Large banquets with endless provisions merit tremendous status in many cultures. George Lamsa says of traditional Middle Eastern culture, "In the East, a man's fame is spread by means of his table and lavish hospitality rather than by his possessions. Strangers and neighbors alike discuss tables where they have been guests. Such tales spread from one town to another and are handed down from one generation to another."[4] Failure to offer the best belittles the guests and shames the host. The materially dispossessed often sense tremendous shame for being unable to set a generous table for a guest, so sadly avoid hosting altogether. When the World Bank asked the poor themselves what it means to be poor, many people noted the shame of not providing food to guests.[5]

Hospitality functions as a common tool of honor. It transforms an outside stranger into an inside friend. Food honors the guest. Eating together means sharing life together. Breaking bread symbolizes community and acceptance.

The table indicates acceptance, togetherness and incorporation. For this reason, the thought of eating alone in a car or in a cubicle is incomprehensible to non-Westerners—it's better go hungry than to eat alone.

Again, only with a proper regard for honor and shame can we rightly understand the dynamics of hospitality. Without considering the social dynamics of honor and shame, the extravagant feasts are mere *ostentation*, and hospitality becomes an *obligation* upheld by the threat of gossip. For Westerners accustomed to vending machines and fast food, hospitality and meals lasting all evening feel onerous. But for many returning missionaries and immigrants to America, a defining feature of American culture is the absence of this hospitality.

The Cultural Clash

These aspects of honor-shame cultures are curious and unique when first encountered, but over time a cultural clash takes place. The reason is because Westerners interpret those very dynamics of honor-shame cultures through the lenses of their guilt-innocence cultures. So when they see something happening in the culture, they attribute a different meaning to the cultural event. The same plants of the honor-shame garden from a Western perspective look more like weeds than flowers, as illustrated in figure 3.2.

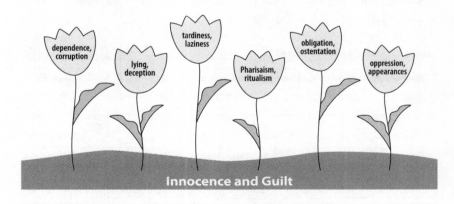

Figure 3.2. Western interpretation of honor-shame cultures

There are consequences to Westerners' negative misunderstanding of honor-shame cultures. First, Christian discipleship simply becomes transplanting Western cultural values. Since corruption, lying, tardiness, ritualism, obligation and inequality (all the ways we misinterpret social dynamics rooted in honor-shame) are "immoral" and "wrong," Western missionaries feel obligated to confront these cultural "sins."

So then Western missionaries implicitly communicate that maturing as a Christian means learning to be financially independent (e.g., we teach Bible studies about saving money), forthright (e.g., we confront Christians for speaking indirectly), on time (e.g., we buy our disciples day planners), scientifically rational (e.g., we replace traditional medical remedies with prescription medicine) and egalitarian (e.g., we urge people to disregard any social hierarchy). This approach categorically rejects honor-shame values, and the fruit of the Spirit begins to look strangely Western. Majority World Christians are not taught to live skillfully within their honor-shame context, but to reject all these aspects of their culture.

Second, Western Christians must realize that their own cultural values (i.e., independence, direct speech, efficiency, scientific rationalism, convenience and egalitarianism) are equally strange in the eyes of non-Westerns. As table 3.1 summarizes, the values of guilt-innocence cultures are rather immoral when interpreted through the lens of honor-shame cultures. Stinginess, inconsideration, arrogance, uncleanness, neglect and disrespect are hardly Christian virtues!

Table 3.1. Crosscultural assessments

Arena of Life	Honor-Shame Cultures	G-I Assessment of H-S Cultures	Guilt-Innocence Cultures	H-S Assessment of G-I Cultures
money	patronage	corrupt, dependent	independence, capitalism	stingy, ungenerous
communication	indirectness	lying, deceptive	direct, explicit	inconsiderate, crass
time	event	lazy, tardy	task, efficiency	arrogant, unkind
hygiene	purity	ritualistic, pharisaical	science, secularism	defiled, unclean
food	hospitality	obligatory, ostentatious	convenience, functionality	isolated, neglectful
behavior	social roles	unequal, oppressive	egalitarian, equality	disrespectful, presumptuous

EVALUATING HONOR-SHAME CULTURES

The above descriptions of honor-shame cultures may have provoked an emotional response in you. Perhaps they triggered some past experiences, along with the emotions and evaluative responses you had. Humans base their perceptions of other cultures more on emotional responses than cognitive reflection. For this reason we will take a moment to discuss the affective dimensions of Christian ministry in honor-shame cultures. One's heart evaluation of those cultures generally proceeds through five phases: unknown (?), positive (+), negative, (-), critical (-/-) and balanced (+/-), as figure 3.3 indicates. We explain each of these phases, along with how they impact our view of one honor-shame dimension: hospitality.

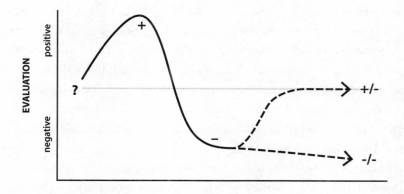

Figure 3.3. Evaluative phases

Phase one—unknown (?). Before any crosscultural encounter, people remain unaware of cultural differences. They hear interesting stories of other cultures, but hardly assess the legitimacy of those cultural dynamics. The fact is, you don't know what you don't know. But then you encounter another culture and begin observing differences.

Phase two—positive (+). Lucy visited Central Asia for two weeks to teach an English summer camp. As part of her trip, we arranged for the team to eat dinner with a local family. The host's boundless generosity left an indelible impression on Lucy. Even several years after that evening, she recounted the lavish mounds of fresh bread, local fruit and homemade pilaf. "They were so welcoming, and kept feeding us! Even though they live so modestly, they fed us so generously!" Initial encounters with honor-shame cultures prompt positive evaluations. The hospitality, generosity, laid-back attitude and family orientation merit admiration. Newcomers rarely perceive the values of honor and shame undergirding those cultural features, but sincerely appreciate the resulting emphasis on relationships.

Phase three—negative (-). As relationships deepen with time, disturbing realities emerge: an abused girl buries her shame, your Christian friend insists on avenging a family insult, neighbors commonly gossip. The damaging role of shame becomes increasingly apparent, and unattractive. The honeymoon phase ends as we begin to see the whole picture.

Westerners understandably develop a negative view of shaming in society as they become aware of it, but many Western missionaries disapprove of honor dynamics as well. Toward the end of my first year in Central Asia, I (Jayson) was teaching American literature at the local university. I enjoyed the course discussions with students, but internally resented their attempts to honor me as a teacher. As an egalitarian American, I bristled when students stood upon my entrance into the classroom, answered every question positively or addressed me with honorific titles. Out of frustration, I challenged and confronted those cultural features rooted in honor. I came to resent honor as much as shame.

The charm of hospitality fades away when an unannounced visitor knocks on your door. You know they will stay and just chat for hours, seemingly oblivious to the time and your other plans for the day. That story of a missionary to Africa who posted visiting hours on their front door begins to resonate! But knowing how "shameful" it would be to not welcome the unplanned guest, you open the door, but not your heart. Hospitality, once an amazing blessing, becomes a burdensome aspect of the local culture.

Phase four—critical (-/-). Negative sentiments of honor-shame dynamics lead to critical evolutions. One critiques not just the actions but also the underlying cultural systems and the people themselves. People educated in Western contexts inherit a long intellectual tradition that uniformly views shame-based cultures negatively.[6] Psychology has long viewed shame as a childish emotion to be replaced by guilt as people develop. In Western thought, honor-shame cultures are inferior and immoral, reflecting outdated or undesirable social mores. "The civilizations of the West have striven

hard and consciously for two thousand years and more to liberate themselves from the thrall of honour and shame. . . . We accepted in their place
a moral system where guilt and forgiveness are supposed to replace honour
and shame."[7] Christians easily adopt this critical assessment of honor and
shame from Western culture.

Through the years of mentoring Othman in his business and ministry, I
(Jayson) had become close friends with him. When Othman's father died
prematurely, he assumed family leadership as the oldest of four children. As
funeral arrangements progressed, the village expectations of hospitality
weighed heavier than the emotional pain of death. Othman and his mom
felt bound, by the threat of shame, to feed relatives and neighbors for days.
Custom also dictated they provide extra food and gifts to all the guests who
came to pay their respects. The expectations of hospitality forced Othman's
family into great financial debt. In those moments I concluded hospitality
was an oppressive evil that destroys people financially and emotionally by
holding the gun of shame to people's head. I reacted by defining all expressions of hospitality as irredeemably bad, so Christians should reject such
family obligations.

If your view of honor-shame cultures is entirely critical, what would your
relationships and ministry in the Majority World look like? How much
would you enjoy living in that culture? If you reject the honor-shame value
system outright, you eventually disrespect the people who live by that
system. If you dis honor, you dishonor. Critical sentiments of honor-shame
contexts can ensnarl Westerners, but that is not the biblical approach.

Phase five—balanced *(+/-).* The ideal posture is one of balance, noting
the positive *and* the negative aspects of honor-shame cultures. Think of patronage, indirect communication, event-focus, purity, social roles and hospitality as neutral tools. The tools can be used for honoring *and* shaming.
Without neglecting the warped facets of honor-shame cultures, we advocate
a missiological approach that biblically and wisely utilizes these cultural
manifestations as channels to bless and honor people, as well as glorify and
honor God. The rest of the book develops this biblical missiology for honor-
shame cultures.

Abigail is one example in the Bible of someone who utilized the cultural
nuances of hospitality for God's purposes (1 Sam 25). Her husband Nabal

acted foolishly and offended David's men. When they recounted Nabal's insulting words to David, he gathered all his men to violently avenge the disrespect. Abigail, upon hearing of the incident, quickly gathered mounds of food and rushed out to meet David. Abigail's feast spared Nabal's house from bloodshed.

Jesus repeatedly used food and hospitality to bless and honor people. Yet observing Jesus underlines the importance of the slash in the balanced +/- approach. Jesus utilized manifestations of honor *and* also confronted many aspects of the honor-shame system of his day. Honor and face are not universally sinful (they originally came from God), but do need to be redeemed in light of God's true honor.

Returning to the metaphor of soil and plants from the beginning of the chapter: the missionary's goal is not simply to identify all the plants growing out of the honor-shame soil in a given context and live in harmony with them all. Nor are we called to uproot all the plants and replace them with imported varieties. Rather the missionary is called to work with others to discern what native plants are appropriate, what new varieties are called for and even how the soil can be amended with the gospel.

The Bible itself provides significant help in this challenging task of living out God's kingdom in honor-shame cultures. The following two chapters will explore honor and shame in God's mission, as revealed in the Bible.

DISCUSSION AND APPLICATION QUESTIONS

1. Recount an instance when you encountered one of the above dynamics of honor-shame cultures. What was your response to that situation?

2. What was your response to table 3.1, which describes how the guilt-innocence and honor-shame cultures negatively interpret one another?

3. When is honor a good thing? Is it always sinful for Christians to seek honor?

PART TWO

BIBLICAL
THEOLOGY

4

OLD TESTAMENT

I will change their shame into praise
and renown in all the earth.

ZEPHANIAH 3:19

My salvation and my honor depend on God;
he is my mighty rock, my refuge.

PSALM 62:7 NIV

*P*EOPLE LONG FOR HONOR, and God acts to honor all peoples. As much as humans obsess about honor, God cares even more about human honor. A key feature of God's mission in the world is to restore status to the human family. From Genesis to Revelation, God honors his people. To only view the concept of honor-shame as an exegetical tool for reading biblical texts misses the forest for the trees. Honor and shame are foundational realities in God's mission and salvation that flow through the entire Bible. By honoring his people, God himself reaps glory as the source of true honor. Ultimately the story of the Bible is about God's honor and God's face, not just ours.[1]

Biblical theology consistently addresses honor and shame because the cultures of the biblical world revolved around those values. The dynamics of honor and shame saturate the biblical texts and shape the narrative of salvation history.[2] The grand drama of Scripture reveals the very heartbeat of God for humanity to become his family and bear his honor.

Only by understanding God's mission can we rightly join in God's mission to bless people in honor-shame cultures. These two chapters are not merely theology, but outline the divine mission and global project that God calls Christians to participate in. In chapters two and three we examined how human cultures cover shame and project honor; the next two chapters examine how God covers shame and restores honor in the biblical narrative. Along the way, we'll examine several Christian doctrines (e.g., sin, judgment, Christ, salvation) to suggest a potential systematic theology for honor-shame cultures.

Then in chapters six through eleven we build on this biblical foundation to explore concrete ways to mediate God's honor in our ministry as Christians. Our goal is to help the church extend the good news of the kingdom of God to people in honor-shame contexts.

For now, we begin in the beginning, when shame entered the world.

The Face of Shame (the Fall and Sin)

Shame began in the Garden of Eden. After eating the fruit Adam and Eve sewed together fig leaves to cover themselves. They did not want to be seen. Their disobedience to God's commands created shame. They felt unworthy and embarrassed. They sought to cover their nakedness.[3] When God walked about the garden, they hid. Adam and Eve bore a dreadful sense of unacceptability before their Creator. So they withdrew from communion into isolation, hoping God would not see them. Dietrich Bonhoeffer explains the tragedy this way: "Man perceives himself in his disunion with God and men. He perceives that he is naked. . . . Hence there arises shame. . . . Man is ashamed of the loss of his unity with God and with other men. . . . Shame is more original than remorse."[4] The sin of Adam and Eve makes them not only guilty for transgressing God's command but also shameful for being disloyal to God.

For Adam and Eve, shame was an entirely new emotion. Immediately prior to the temptation, Genesis 2:25 says, "The man and his wife were both naked, and were not ashamed." A primary characteristic of sinless paradise was the absence of shame. Adam and Eve stood naked before each other and their Creator without any sense of defectiveness or inferiority because God created them complete with honor.

While studying Genesis 1–3 together with my Central Asian friend Kairbek, I asked, "What kind of person was Adam?" I anticipated a more philosophical answer like "a rational being comprising soul, spirit and body," but Kairbek replied, "A person of great honor!" Being from an honor-shame culture, he intuitively understood the great honor God ascribed Adam at creation—blessing, land, food, naming privileges and a wife. Adam was like a royal prince endowed with the King's prestige and status. Most significantly, Adam and Eve were created in "the image of God," which denotes precedence and glory.[5] According to Psalm 8:5, God "crowned them with honor and glory." For these reasons Adam and Eve felt no shame, even though they were naked. (Perhaps they preferred to be naked, so their honor could be seen!) But then, shame entered paradise.

The shame Adam and Eve felt was not just a private emotion but also a public social reality. They not only felt ashamed, they were actually shameful before God. Western theology emphasizes guilt over shame, often with the false idea that "guilt is before God, and shame is before people." This falsely suggests that guilt is the real theological problem faced by people apart from Christ, and shame is just a social anxiety fixed by psychology. But biblically shame has both objective *and* subjective dimensions, much like guilt.[6] Shame is a theological problem, not just a psychological abnormality. In the Bible, shame is an integral aspect of humans' broken relationships with God.

In Genesis 3, Adam and Eve lost face and status before all creation. As disloyal children they lost honor. They were cursed with pain, grueling labor, weakness and dirtiness—indicators of low status. Death is the ultimate shame; humans return back to the lowly dust they came from. Ultimately Adam and Eve were banished from God's community, exiled from the presence of God. The human family lost its face. We lack honor before God. "To us, O LORD, belongs open shame, to our kings, to our princes, and to our fathers, because we have sinned against you" (Dan 9:8 ESV). We bear shame in the eyes of people *and* God. People are internally ashamed and externally disgraced.

Old Testament prophets often used the imagery of a prostitute (or adulterous wife) to explain Israel's shamefulness for sinning. Consider Ezekiel's rebuke of Israel.

> How sick is your heart, says the Lord GOD, that you did all these things, the
> deeds of a brazen whore. . . . Adulterous wife, who receives strangers instead
> of her husband! . . .
>
>   So be ashamed, you also, and bear your disgrace. (Ezek 16:30, 32, 52)

Sexual miscreants are deep symbols of shame. Their unfaithfulness and pro-
miscuity threaten group purity and solidarity. To call someone a prostitute,
or the son of a prostitute, is an insult of utmost disrespect. Like a prostitute,
Israel's unfaithfulness and impurity brought shame on themselves and their
spouse (God). Upon seeing the shameful sin of their harlotry, Israel says,
"Let us lie down in our shame, and let our dishonor cover us; for we have
sinned against the LORD our God" (Jer 3:25). Sin leaves people in shame
before God.

> The more they multiplied, the more they sinned against Me;
> I will change their glory into shame. (Hos 4:7 NASB)

Collectively marred with shame, humanity faces exposure, judgment, alienation, degradation and pollution before the Creator. But the issue of human
shame is only half of the problem.

   Our sin also shames and dishonors God. Sin devalues God and disrespects
him. God is not properly valued; his glory is not respected. Sin besmirches
God's name. John Piper similarly explains sin in terms of dishonor: "What
is the nature of sin?—The profaning of God's name. In other words, they
have not lived as though God's values were supremely important to God,
and to themselves. They belittle and diminish God."[7]

   Western theology typically limits sin to an individual transgression of a
particular rule or law. But biblical writers also view sin in a relational context
(e.g., parenting, marriage, covenant). Sin breaks relationships (not just laws).
Simon Chan notes,

> Within the family context, sin is not just the wrong an individual does against
> some objective law. It is an affront to God's honor (Anselm) and an act that
> dishonors the family name. . . . The idea of sin as shame implies that sin is not
> against an impersonal law but against a community of which the sinner is a
> member. It breaks the harmony of the community.[8]

   When these communal dynamics are applied to the divine-human relationship, the essence of sin is dishonoring God. Sin is disloyalty to a

relationship, not merely violating a rule. Israel's problem was that "their hearts were not loyal to him [God], they were not faithful to his covenant" (Ps 78:37 NIV), and this brought dishonor on God. "A son honors his father, and servants their master. If then I am a father, where is the honor due me? And if I am a master, where is the respect due me? says the LORD of hosts to you, O priests, who despise my name" (Mal 1:6; cf. 2:2-3). Israel failed to glorify God. Their sin was exchanging glory for shame (see Ps 106:20; Jer 2:11; Rom 1:21-23).

When the prophet Nathan confronts David, he explains the king's affair with Bathsheba in terms of shame. The typical Western reading of David's adultery interprets it as a violation of the law; David broke God's rules.[9] However, the prophet Nathan never mentions the Ten Commandments (though David obviously broke several of them), but frames David's behavior as fundamentally shameful. First, Nathan identifies David in one of the most shameful images possible—an inhospitable rich person who refuses to share with a guest. But worse, David's behavior shamed God. Three times in the story Nathan, speaking on behalf of God, says David "despised" and "utterly scorned" God (2 Sam 12:9-10, 14). David's sin was foremost against God and his honor. David despised God's name by dismissing God's promises (see 2 Sam 7:7-14). This dishonored God and brought further shame on David (see 2 Sam 12:11-14; 16:22). This view of sin as objective shame is also present in the New Testament, as the next chapter will examine.

The story of Genesis 3 shows how sin causes shame, at multiple levels. Then Genesis 4 illustrates the converse—shame causes sin. When Cain and Abel bring offerings to God, he "had regard for Abel and his offering, but for Cain and his offering he had no regard" (Gen 4:4-5). Consequently Cain lowered his face. He was looked over and disregarded. God offered the possibility of recognition and acceptance by asking, "Will there not be a lifting up of your face?" (Gen 4:7).[10] But Cain felt no hope for his shame. His status envy causes him to kill his brother in an effort to regain respect. Cain kills Abel out of a sense of inferiority and unacceptability. His shame led to sin.

Cain's descendants also responded to dishonor with violent retaliation. Cain's genealogy (Gen 4:17-24) ends with Lamech boasting to his wives,

I have killed a man for wounding me,
a young man for striking me. (Gen 4:23)

This is honor-shame speak for, "Nobody gets away with disrespecting me!" Sin shames (Gen 3), and shame sins (Gen 4)—it is a spiral of death. This reality has shadowed humans ever since.

King Saul had the honor of being Israel's first king. But when young David began garnering more praise, Saul's heart filled with jealously and envy. In 1 Samuel 18 Israel's soldiers return home from defeating Goliath and the Philistines. The women of Israel came out to celebrate the victory, singing,

Saul has killed his thousands,
and David his ten thousands.

The higher status they gave to David angered Saul. As a result of feeling dishonored, Saul looked on David with jealousy and envy. He coveted the honor and praise of another person. This status anxiety drove him to seek David's life. Saul's shame produced sin.

In 2003, an al-Qaeda operative drove a truck bomb into the United Nations headquarters in Baghdad, destroying the building and claiming twenty-two lives. Afterward, an al-Qaeda spokesperson explained the rationale of the suicide attack in terms of shame. "When the Americans came, they stepped on our heads with their shoes, so what do you expect us to do? Death is more honorable than life."[11] For this young Iraqi, intense feelings of disgrace drove him to destroy and murder. The violent sin of suicide bombing was a response to shame. James Gilligan, former director of mental health for the Massachusetts prison system and author of *Violence*, observes,

> I have yet to see a serious act of violence that was not provoked by the expe-
> rience of feeling shamed and humiliated, disrespected and ridiculed, and that
> did not represent the attempt to prevent or undo this "loss of face." . . . The
> purpose of violence is to diminish the intensity of shame and replace it as far
> as possible with its opposite, pride, thus preventing the individual from being
> overwhelmed by the feeling of shame.[12]

When someone sins out of shame, that sin often takes the form of shaming others. The destructive actions of terrorism, ethnocentrism, exclusivism, gang behavior, exploitation, abuse, violence and gossip are all attempts to make ourselves, or our group, appear higher by lowering others. When honor is derived by comparison, superiority means another person is demeaned. We fabricate a relative honor by dishonoring others; we transfer our shame. In this way, shame is a pernicious threat to shalom and community.

Shame also causes people to sinfully turn against themselves. The noted shame researcher Brené Brown comments that shame

> now permeates our personal and public lives in destructive and insidious ways. Shame was once largely misunderstood and discounted by social scientists, but now a growing number of researchers and practitioners are examining shame and its role in a wide range of mental and public health issues, including depression, anxiety disorders, addiction, eating disorders, bullying, suicide, sexual assault and all types of violence.[13]

Though Brown's research is limited to Western contexts, it confirms the correlation between various manifestations of sin and shame.

Shame undermines God's design for the human family on so many fronts. As God's ambassadors of shalom and restoration, Christians must understand the devastation shame wreaks on the human family theologically, spiritually, socially and personally.

- Sin dishonors God.
- Sin makes us objectively shameful before God.
- Sin leaves us feeling ashamed.
- Shame induces sin.

Sin and shame intersect and overlap in an inseparable fashion. This is not to say sin and shame are synonymous; sin involves more than shame. But any Christian theology of sin devoid of the theme of shame is clearly sub-biblical. A shame-less view of sin fails to see how shameful sin truly is. A biblical view of the problem is essential, lest we miss the solution of honor emerging from God's covenants with Abraham, Moses and David.

PROMISES OF HONOR (COVENANTS AND SALVATION)

Israel's bondage in Egypt was a low point for the nation. As subjugated slaves, Egypt humiliated them with impossible workloads and by murdering their male children. The prophet Ezekiel described Israel as a lowly orphaned nation, rejected and despised.

> As for your birth, on the day you were born your navel cord was not cut, nor
> were you washed with water to cleanse you, nor rubbed with salt, nor wrapped
> in cloths. No eye pitied you, to do any of these things for you out of com-
> passion for you; but you were thrown out in the open field, for you were ab-
> horred on the day you were born. (Ezek 16:4-5)

Israel was destined to disgrace. But God drew near to save her from shame
and grant a new honor. Note the various metaphors and images of social
prominence that God uses to explain Israel's election and exodus from Egypt
in this passage.

> I pledged myself to you and entered into a covenant with you, says the Lord
> GOD, and you became mine. Then I bathed you with water and washed off the
> blood from you, and anointed you with oil. I clothed you with embroidered
> cloth and with sandals of fine leather; I bound you in fine linen and covered
> you with rich fabric. I adorned you with ornaments: I put bracelets on your
> arms, a chain on your neck, a ring on your nose, earrings in your ears, and a
> beautiful crown upon your head. You were adorned with gold and silver,
> while your clothing was of fine linen, rich fabric, and embroidered cloth. You
> had choice flour and honey and oil for food. You grew exceedingly beautiful,
> fit to be a queen. Your fame spread among the nations on account of your
> beauty, for it was perfect because of my splendor that I had bestowed on you,
> says the Lord GOD. (Ezek 16:8-14)

The relationship God initiated with Israel overcame shame and restored
honor. Only a relationship with the one true Creator confers true honor to
people. Recall that honor comes from knowing the right people and being
in the right group. Election brings us into relationship with the Right Person
and into the Right Group.

In the Bible, covenants form the basis of such relationships. In ancient
Near Eastern cultures, covenants were contractual arrangements for establishing a family-like relationship. The two parties became "kinship-in-laws"[14]
bound by honor—both sides pledged to honor the other, and shame was the
consequence for failing to do so. The public reputations of both groups were
intertwined.[15] In his covenants with Abraham, Moses and David, God
promised to protect and exalt his people in exchange for their loyalty and
praise. God would be the patron, and Israel would be the client. God bestows
his own splendor and glory among people through covenants. Covenants

are the primary framework by which God mediates salvation, and honor and shame are prominent features of biblical covenants, as we will examine.

Through the exodus event, God formed a special relationship with Israel. He elected them to be his special nation and blessed them above all peoples. "For you are a people holy to the LORD your God; the LORD your God has chosen you out of all the peoples on earth to be his people, his treasured possession" (Deut 7:6). God promised to set his treasured possession "in praise and in fame and in honor high above all nations that he has made" (Deut 26:19 ESV). Israel is the new Adam called to bear God's glory to all creation.[16] The special relationship Yahweh formed with Israel at Sinai made her an honored nation, characterized by divine blessing, abundant descendants, fertile land, strong government, divine presence, economic abundance and military peace (Lev 26:3-13; Deut 6:1–7:26).

God's plan to restore honor to the human family after the fall actually began with Israel's patriarch Abraham. To remedy the problem of shame, God calls Abraham to a life of divinely granted honor. In Genesis 3–11, the human family faces a tragic descent into shame. Humans were striving to reverse the Adamic shame by lifting themselves to the heavens and making a name for themselves (Gen 11:4). But God descended from the heavens to honor Abraham's family with a great name and universal prominence.

> Now the LORD said to Abram, "Go from your country and your kindred and your father's house to the land that I will show you. And I will make of you a great nation, and I will bless you and make your name great, so that you will be a blessing. I will bless those who bless you, and him who dishonors you I will curse, and in you all the families of the earth shall be blessed." (Gen 12:1-3 ESV)

The Abrahamic covenant is saturated with promises of honor: land, a great nation, divine blessing, a great name, abundant offspring, royal descendants and being the source of universal blessing.[17] God's covenant with Abraham was an invitation to a life of honor. Abraham's family would be global mediators of God's blessing to all people. God, as a loyal patron, even covenanted to vindicate Abraham's descendants if other nations dishonored them—"him who dishonors you I will curse." God's covenantal promise of honor is the answer to the shameful plight of humankind. God's promise to

Abraham underscores all of Israel's history, and climaxes with God's unique relationship with David.

When the young boy David was shepherding flocks in the pastures, forgotten by his own family (1 Sam 17), God chose him to rescue and lead Israel. Once David became king, God covenanted to honor David and his royal dynasty with an everlasting throne. Note the language of status and honor in 2 Samuel 7:8-14 (cf. 1 Chron 17; Ps 89; 110; 132).

> Thus says the LORD of hosts: I took you from the pasture, from following the sheep to be prince over my people Israel; and I have been with you wherever you went, and have cut off all your enemies from before you; and I will make for you a great name, like the name of the great ones of the earth. And I will appoint a place for my people Israel and will plant them, so that they may live in their own place. . . . I will raise up your offspring after you, who shall come forth from your body, and I will establish his kingdom. He shall build a house for my name, and I will establish the throne of his kingdom forever. I will be a father to him, and he shall be a son to me.

God bestowed splendor and majesty on the king, making his glory great (Ps 21:5). God promised the Davidic king would be honored as God's firstborn and the highest of the kings of the earth (Ps 89:27), as well as receive a global inheritance and authoritative rule over other nations (Ps 2; 110). Through the reign of David's family, Israel as a whole would experience the promises of honor God made to Abraham and Moses, and all nations would receive the blessings of Israel's glorious God.

The honor of God's people is grounded on these divine promises to bless and exalt. God's covenants with Abraham, Moses and David define the nature of God's salvation, as seen in the lives of many Israelites, such as Ruth.

RETURNING HOME (REDEMPTION AS STATUS REVERSAL)

Redemption is a common term for salvation in the Bible. But what does God redeem from? The book of Ruth uses the word *redeem/er* more than any other book in the Bible. Thus it can help answer the question. As we retell the story of Ruth highlighting its sociocultural aspects, it will emerge that "redemption" is largely the reversal of status from shame to honor (cf. Is 49:7; 54:4-5).

At the outset of the story, Naomi seems set in life. She has a husband and two sons. When her sons take Moabite wives, the daughters-in-law will live in Naomi's house and assume most of her domestic duties. As a woman, she enjoys a respectable position.

But then calamity strikes; Naomi's husband and sons die (Ruth 1:5), leaving her with no heir and no caretaker. Not only will the family name die off with no legacy (a great shame in itself), but Naomi also seems destined for the shame of widowhood in her final years. She has no land and no roof in Moab. There were no welfare services or employment options in Moab for Naomi to fall back on.

In collectivistic societies, people depend on family for meeting their essential needs. Without a family, Naomi is a homeless, foodless, foreign widow facing social isolation. The Moab community would have disregarded her. Isaiah refers to the disgrace of widowhood to foretell how dire God's judgment of Judah would be.

Seven women shall take hold of one man in that day, saying,

> "We will eat our own bread and wear our own clothes;
> just let us be called by your name;
> take away our disgrace." (Is 4:1)

The shame of widowhood in ancient cultures was profoundly deep.

Naomi doubts her status will ever change. She is too old to remarry and produce a son for her daughters-in-law to marry (Ruth 1:12). Naomi despairs, "The LORD has dealt harshly with me." When Naomi decides to return to Bethlehem, her widowed, Moabite daughter-in-law Ruth accompanies her.

Through his sovereign grace, God orchestrates the reversal of Naomi and Ruth's shameful status. He uses Boaz, a prominent rich man from the family of Naomi's in-laws, to restore their standing. The text says Boaz was *hil*—this Hebrew word for "prominent" or "worthy" (ESV) is a key term denoting honor throughout book of Ruth.

Ruth shows up in Boaz's fields to gather leftover grain, the ancient equivalent of dumpster diving. When seeing Ruth, Boaz offers protection and provision, thus functioning as a patron for the vulnerable widow. This act of grace prompts Ruth to fall prostrate, face to the ground, and say, "Why have

I found favor in your sight, that you should take notice of me, when I am a foreigner?" (Ruth 2:10). Ruth knew her standing as a foreign widow merited little attention from a respected person like Boaz, so she responds with the effusive thanks of a provisioned client. After the workday, Boaz invites Ruth to dine with everyone at the table, another sign of gracious acceptance.

In the next scene, Naomi schemes to remarry Ruth (Ruth 3:1-4). Finding a husband for a previously married foreigner would have been challenging, but crucial for Naomi. The grandchild(ren) resulting from Ruth's marriage would be Naomi's heir and caretaker, ensuring her family's legacy and status for generations to come. A grandson ensured Naomi's survival and honor (the latter being a greater concern).

According to Naomi's plan, Ruth sneaks into Boaz's resting place at night and suggests an intimate relationship (Ruth 3:6-10). According to Israel's custom of levirate marriage, Boaz has the right to redeem Ruth out of widowhood, and was probably expected to do so. Boaz responses to Ruth, "May you be blessed by the LORD, my daughter; this last instance of your loyalty is better than the first; you have not gone after young men, whether poor or rich. And now, my daughter, do not be afraid, I will do for you all that you ask, for all the assembly of my people know that you are a worthy [hil] woman" (Ruth 3:10-11). Because Ruth is honorable, by virtue of her repeated loyalty and outstanding reputation in the Bethlehem community, Boaz pledges to "redeem" her.

Before all the elders at the city gates, Boaz publicly declares his intention to acquire Naomi's land and marry Ruth. As a prominent rich man in the community, Boaz would have been eager (and expected) to exercise his wealth for the benefit of relatives. The purpose of Boaz's public declaration was not to increase his landholdings or take a young bride, but the preservation of his brother's name (4:11). Boaz committed to produce an heir and ensured that heir would have land to raise his own family, thus preserving the family name of Naomi and Elimelech's family. The elders publicly bless Boaz: "May the LORD make [Ruth] like Rachel and Leah. . . . May you have standing [hil] in Ephrathah and be famous in Bethlehem" (Ruth 4:11-12 NIV). The elders recognize Boaz's commitment to restore honor to Naomi's family, so they ask God to bless Boaz with the honor of a renowned family and prominent name. (Notice the repeated exchange of honor between the characters throughout the story.)

God's hand in exalting Naomi and Ruth becomes most evident in the final scene of Ruth. "When [Boaz and Ruth] came together, the LORD made her conceive, and she bore a son" (Ruth 4:13). The perpetuation of Naomi's family name and honor was secure. The birth of their child was a public event, celebrated by the entire community. "Then the women said to Naomi, 'Blessed be the LORD, who has not left you this day without next-of-kin; and may his name be renowned in Israel!'" (Ruth 4:14). God has given Naomi a kinsman redeemer (the newly born grandson), whose name would become renowned through the entire nation of Israel. Being a collectivistic society, the famous grandson would bring honor on Naomi as the grandmother.

Then Naomi's peers in the community testify how God has provided for Naomi as an elder widow. "He shall be to you a restorer of life and a nourisher of your old age; for your daughter-in-law who loves you, who is more to you than seven sons, has borne him" (Ruth 4:15). This pronouncement of a foreign, widowed daughter-in-law being more loving than seven sons indicates the complete reversal of Ruth's status.

Since the entire community of Bethlehem stands to benefit from the renown of this one child (see Mt 2:5-6), the "women of the neighborhood gave him a name." They said, "A son has been born to Naomi." Though this may come across as a typographical mistake to Western readers who assume a child belongs to the birth parents, the ancient Israelite community recognized the child as the entire family's since reputations were intertwined multigenerationally.

The concluding genealogy connecting the newborn child to King David is the climax of the book of Ruth—"They named him Obed; he became the father of Jesse, the father of David" (Ruth 4:17). There is no person more renowned in Israel than David, who descended from Naomi and Ruth. God redeems Ruth and Naomi from being homeless widows in Moab to the royal matriarchs in Israel, from shame unto honor.

The prophet Isaiah interweaves the same themes of deliverance from shame, marriage and redemption to speak of God's salvation toward his people in exile.

Do not fear, for you will not be ashamed;
do not be discouraged, for you will not suffer disgrace;

for you will forget the shame of your youth,
    and the disgrace of your widowhood you will remember no more.
For your Maker is your husband,
    the Lord of hosts is his name;
the Holy One of Israel is your Redeemer,
    the God of the whole earth he is called. (Is 54:4-5)

Getting the Story Straight

The book of Ruth illustrates a common pattern of biblical salvation—God reverses the status of his people. Naomi and Ruth are rescued from shame and lifted to a position of honor. Old Testament scholar Timothy Laniak notes two patterns of salvation in Old Testament stories.[18] Understanding these two narrative structures shines a light on biblical literature.

The first narrative pattern of "guilt → innocence" begins with an innocent person transgressing a rule or law (see figure 4.1). To remove the guilt of their offense, they must make reparation. Once punishment is endured and/ or they repent for their wrongdoing, forgiveness is granted and normalcy returns. The goal of this narrative structure is to return transgressors to the original state of innocence.

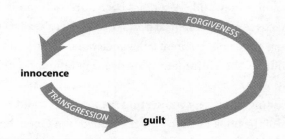

Figure 4.1. Guilt-innocence narrative paradigm

This "guilt → innocence" narrative structure is helpful for some biblical stories, such as Judges, but a problem occurs when we read all biblical stories according to this narrative framework. For example, some suggest Naomi's family committed a sin by leaving Israel, despite no mention of such in the story. When readers assume a story is primarily about forgiveness of transgressions, they misread biblical stories and fail to see how God redeems people from shame.

The second narrative pattern of "shame → honor" begins with the characters in a respectable state (see figure 4.2). But as the story develops, their status is threatened and shame appears imminent. Their status may be jeopardized by personal sin, or by external factors like a skin disease or military invasion. After the Israelite cries to the divine Patron for deliverance, God eliminates the threat of shame and vindicates their honor. God reverses their social position. Such stories conclude with an increase of honor for the main character(s), not simply a return to the original state.

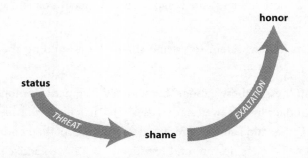

Figure 4.2. Shame-honor narrative paradigm

Consider how this "shame → honor" paradigm structures the plot of Ruth. Enjoying a respectable status in Moab, Naomi is quickly threatened with shame when her husband and sons die. Then through Boaz, God exalts Naomi and Ruth from shame to honor. While Naomi and Ruth were certainly sinful people in need of God's forgiveness, the central point of the book is their divine exaltation from shame, and the revelation of a God who honors his people. This "shame → honor" framework interprets God's salvation in the lives of many Old Testament figures (see appendix 2).[19]

- Adam was raised from dirt and given God's image to be God's vice regent (Gen 1–2).

- Abraham was a sojourner blessed with a great name and family (Gen 12–25).

- Leah, the unloved wife, bore Israel's first four sons (Gen 29).

- Joseph was raised from a pit of death to the throne of Egypt (Gen 37–41).

- Moses was a speechless shepherd who overcame Pharaoh and led God's people (Ex 2–4).

- Hannah, a barren woman, gave birth the Israel's leader Samuel (1 Sam 2).

- David, the youngest son chasing sheep, became a great king (1 Sam 17–2 Sam 7).

- Mephibosheth, a handicapped enemy, dined at David's table (2 Sam 9).

- Esther and Mordecai, indicted as usurpers, become royal officials in Persia.

- Job was a sick reject, then restored to wholeness and community.

- Shadrach, Meshach and Abednego survived executions and were promoted (Dan 1–6).

- Nehemiah led Jerusalem to escape shame by rebuilding the walls of Jerusalem (Neh 1–8).

The faithfulness of these national heroes amid disgrace summons readers to wait on God for his renewed status (Ps 62:7). Particularly during the exile, figures like Esther and Daniel represented the fortunes of their entire people. They embodied Israel's destiny, and revealed how Yahweh actively worked in history to exalt his people. The "shame → honor" motif also structures the worldview narrative of Israel as a nation. The covenantal soteriology of "God saves his people from shame to honor" continues into the New Testament. So what emerges from Scripture is a unified story of the human family being saved from shame to honor by the gracious hand of God. The "shame → honor" narrative pattern diagramed above ultimately structures the entire drama of salvation history. God is working to exalt humanity from shame (Gen 3) to honor (Rev 21–22).

The stories of Genesis 3–4, Ruth and Mephibosheth (below) hardly mention the words *shame* or *honor*. Yet they are essential themes for properly interpreting the purpose and theology of each narrative. Because the Bible emerges from collectivistic social contexts, honor and shame are inherently embedded throughout its story. Honor-shame values serve as the default grammar of biblical cultures. Grammar in language is hardly visible in conversations at the surface level, but actively works behind the scenes to structure meaning and purpose. Honor and shame function similarly in the Bible. They are not merely external lenses modern interpreters apply to read the Bible, but are the core foundations of the biblical testimony. We explicitly highlight those realities in the narratives to help Christians develop a more robust, biblical view of Christian theology and God's mission, for the purpose of joining God's mission of blessing the shamed with honor.

GRACED WITH HONOR (MEPHIBOSHETH, FEASTING AND SALVATION)

One fundamental rule of shame-based cultures is that people cannot lift themselves from the pit of shame. Rather, shame is alleviated only when another person of higher status initiates and restores. I once asked a Central Asian, "How could a divorced women alleviate her shame and be considered acceptable for remarriage?" The reply was, "She can do nothing herself. Another man must choose to accept and take her." An outcast cannot invite themselves to the party; they must be invited. The story of David and Mephibosheth (2 Sam 9) shows an example of grace removing shame, and reflects the nature of God's grace.

Upon establishing his reign over all Israel, David seeks an opportunity to bless Saul's family. "Is there still anyone left of the house of Saul to whom I may show kindness for Jonathan's sake?" (2 Sam 9:1). Most likely, David sought an opportunity to display his newfound prominence by aiding the family of a loyal friend (i.e., patronage). David learns of Jonathon's son Mephibosheth. He was not, however, someone who was expecting help or honor from David—quite the opposite. He bore the shame, and risk, of being Saul's grandson. In ancient honor-shame cultures, family loyalty was assumed and political power inherited. So to avoid rival claims to the throne, kings vanquished relatives of the disposed king. As a descendant of Saul, Mephibosheth expects David to execute him, and thus cement David's royal glory throughout Israel.

For Mephibosheth, however, being grandson of the defeated king was not his greatest shame in his ancient community. Mephibosheth was also severely handicapped. The first mention of him is not by name, but as "a son of Jonathan; he is crippled in his feet" (2 Sam 9:3). His physical handicap defined him. Society viewed him as deformed and defective. His crippled feet were also a social stigma and basis of exclusion in ancient Israel. Anyone with a physical blemish, including a disfigured or broken limb, was excluded from making sacrifices and participating in festivals in the temple.

On the other hand, David's social status is at peak levels; he is respected and feared by all at this point in the narrative. David has restored God's presence to Jerusalem (2 Sam 6), established an eternal covenant with Yahweh (2 Sam 7), enjoyed great military success (2 Sam 8) and established his government throughout Israel. At this pinnacle of royal grandeur, the great king invites the handicap grandson of his archrival into his palace.

Upon entering David's presence, Mephibosheth prostrates himself and pleads, "What is your servant, that you should look upon a dead dog such as I?" (2 Sam 9:8). The self-declared label of "dead dog" reveals Mephibosheth is keenly aware of his lowly status; he cannot erase the shame. But from that point, David's actions drastically reverse Mephibosheth's status.

David acts graciously to restore Mephibosheth to a notable place in Jerusalem. The first step is to transfer all of Saul's possessions to Mephibosheth. This is a surprising move; people would have expected David to seize those assets for his own family. Then David establishes a system to provide for Mephibosheth's long-term sustenance. David instructs Ziba (Saul's head servant) and his fifteen sons and twenty servants to cultivate the land so that Mephibosheth may have food to eat. With Saul's possessions and servants, Mephibosheth would lead a dignified life.

But most significantly, David says, "Mephibosheth shall always eat at my table" (2 Sam 9:10). Eating with the king, even if only one time as a guest, would have conferred great honor on any Israelite. But to eat regularly at the king's table implies Mephibosheth is "like one of the king's sons" (2 Sam 9:11). From a dead dog to a royal son at the king's table! Such a reversal of status perhaps eclipses David's own exaltation from young shepherd boy to king of Israel.

David's gracious acceptance alleviates Mephibosheth's shame and transposes his status. The honored one acts on behalf of the shamed. David's grace toward Mephibosheth mirrors the nature of God's grace toward his people. Before God we are shamed. Consequently our only hope for removing shame and restoring honor comes from God—the one seated on high who comes down to us. Our God is the one royal King who lifts us from shame and provides a new identity—this is the good news! Psalm 113:5-9 praises the exalted God who raises the shamed.

Who is like the LORD our God,
   who is seated on high,
who looks far down
   on the heavens and the earth?
He raises the poor from the dust,
   and lifts the needy from the ash heap,
to make them sit with princes,
   with the princes of his people.
He gives the barren woman a home,
   making her the joyous mother of children.

As David knew so well, the cultural mediums of food and hospitality confer honor (perhaps even more than words). For this reason Scripture often uses the imagery of food and hospitality to communicate our spiritual status as guests welcomed by God. The language of feasting and hosting conveys an imputation of honor throughout Scripture.

- In Psalm 23 God is our host (not only shepherd):[20]

   You prepare a table before me
      in the presence of my enemies;
   you anoint my head with oil;
      my cup overflows. . . .
   I shall dwell in the house of the LORD
      my whole life long. (Ps 23:5-6)

- Isaiah envisions a future day when

   On this mountain the LORD of hosts will make for all peoples
   a feast of rich food, a feast of well-aged wines,
      of rich food filled with marrow, of well-aged wines strained clear. (Is 25:6)

- In the parable of the prodigal son, the father welcomes home the prodigal son by telling his servants, "Get the fatted calf and kill it, and let us eat and celebrate" (Lk 15:23).

- Jesus said, "Many will come from east and west and will eat with Abraham and Isaac and Jacob in the kingdom of heaven" (Mt 8:11).

- Revelation 19:9 refers to bride of Christ, the church, as "those who are invited to the marriage supper of the Lamb."

Roland Muller, a Western missionary to Arabs, recounts a story of his friend Mohammed, a young Jordanian man who was discovering the Bible. Mohammed threw the Bible down on the table when he read 1 Samuel 2:8.

> He raises up the poor from the dust;
>> he lifts the needy from the ash heap,
> to make them sit with princes
>> and inherit a seat of honor.

"No," Mohammed said emphatically. "This cannot be true. A beggar is a beggar, a prince is a prince. This is garbage." The emphatic protest of Mohammed, an Arab who naturally intuited honor-shame realities, captures the scandalous nature of God's grace for the shamed.[21] The amazing reversal of status from shame to honor may be unfathomable to people, but is commonplace in God's kingdom. But sadly Israel did not always experience that honor.

CAPTIVE TO SHAME (EXILE AND JUDGMENT)

In 586 BC the Babylonian king Nebuchadnezzar captured Jerusalem, demolished the temple, eliminated the Davidic dynasty and led Israel into exile. This national tragedy created a theological crisis for the people of Israel—God was not being God. Why did God seem absent? Israel was humiliated and disgraced. Despite God's promises to bless and exalt them, God's people were captive to shame. The poet of Psalm 89 describes the foreign conquest as God "spurning," "defiling," "scorning," "humiliating" and "shaming" David's royal dynasty and nation of Israel.

The shame of exile deeply troubled Israel's prophets. The destruction of Jerusalem and the temple caused Jeremiah to lament,

> Remember, O LORD, what has befallen us;
> look, and see our disgrace! (Lam 5:1)

He bemoaned the shame of God's judgment.

> How the Lord in his anger
>> has humiliated daughter Zion!
> He has thrown down from heaven to earth
>> the splendor of Israel. . . .
> He has brought down to the ground in dishonor
>> the kingdom and its rulers. (Lam 2:1-2; cf. 1:1, 6, 8; 3:30, 45; 5:14-16)

For Jews in exile, shame was the defining element of the captivity, not just physical hardship. While in Babylon, Daniel confesses that Israel's sinful unfaithfulness left them covered in shame. "Lord, you are righteous, but this day *we are covered with shame. . . . We and our kings, our princes and our ancestors are covered with shame,* LORD, because we have sinned against you" (Dan 9:7-8 NIV).

The destruction of Jerusalem compounded Israel's shame. When relatives from Jerusalem visit Nehemiah in Persia, he inquired how the remnant in Jerusalem was doing. The Jerusalemites reported, "The survivors there in the province who escaped captivity are in great trouble and shame" (Neh 1:3). With Artaxerxes's blessing, Nehemiah returns to Jerusalem to help his people. After assessing the situation, Nehemiah rallies Israel to work: "Come, let us rebuild the wall of Jerusalem, so that we may no longer suffer disgrace" (Neh 2:17). When Jerusalem lay in rubble, her people felt national humiliation.

Israel's encounter with shame during the exile highlights a sobering reality—the hand of God brings both honor *and* shame.

No one from the east or the west
    or from the desert can exalt themselves.
It is God who judges:
    He brings one down, he exalts another. (Ps 75:6-7 NIV)

God's covenantal relationships were intended to promote Israel's honor (as a means of magnifying God's renown among the nations). But she often failed to properly honor God, and so faced the shameful consequence of foreign captivity.

Israel's exile illustrates the nature of God's judgment—when people fail to properly honor God, they face divine shame. In 1 Samuel 2 God confronts Eli's sons for honoring themselves more than God. (They were eating the choicest part of each sacrifice, instead of burning them unto God.) God outlines the fate of those who demean his worth—"Those who honor me I will honor, and those who despise me shall be treated with contempt" (1 Sam 2:30). In Peter's words, "God opposes the proud, but gives grace to the humble" (1 Pet 5:5; cf. Prov 3:34-35). The judgment of God involves both honoring and shaming, as Israel experienced.

The shaming judgments of God were not limited to historical Israel. Old Testament prophets foresaw an eschatological shame for those outside of God's family. Those who reject God will face eternal shame.

> Many of those who sleep in the dust of the earth shall awake, some to everlasting life, and some to shame and everlasting contempt. (Dan 12:2)

> They will be greatly shamed,
>> for they will not succeed.
> Their eternal dishonor
>> will never be forgotten. (Jer 20:11)

Fill their faces with shame,
> so that they may seek your name, O Lord.
> Let them be put to shame and dismayed forever;
> let them perish in disgrace. (Ps 83:16-17)

> All the makers of idols will be put to shame and disgraced;
>> they will go off into disgrace together.
> But Israel will be saved by the Lord
>> with an everlasting salvation;
> you will never be put to shame or disgraced,
>> to ages everlasting. (Is 45:16-17 niv; cf. Is 23:9; 42:17)

Those who chose to live apart from the Creator will live in isolation forever. Their earthly glory will be stripped away, and they will endure the painful awareness of shame for eternity. In the final day the trivial status symbols once used to cover our nakedness and create a façade of honor will be cast aside. Our true identity will be exposed for all eternity. C. S. Lewis explains the final judgment in these terms: "In the end that Face which is the delight or terror of the universe must be turned upon each of us either with one expression or with the other, either conferring glory inexpressible or inflicting shame that can never be cured or disguised."[22]

In the book of Revelation, God subjects all those who showed greater concern for the demands of the culture than the honor of God to eternal shame. The lie is exposed; the honor challenge is answered. Babylon, along with all those who praised her benefaction, will be "thrown down, never to be found again" (Rev 18:21 NIV). Those united against God's Messiah are reduced to slain corpses unworthy of human burial. Wild birds gorge themselves on their rotting flesh (Rev 19:17-18, 21), a symbol of utter desecration and disgrace. People who oppose God's purposes are debased, as Pharaoh and his armies were in the original exodus (Rev 18:8).

God's judgment is not the lashing out of an angry abuser, but the restoration of honor. The New Testament word *orgē* (commonly translated "wrath" or "anger") indicated revenge for dishonoring slights. David deSilva explains, "God's wrath in Revelation is the anger of a slighted benefactor, whose favor met not with gratitude but with rejection and affront in the form of idolatrous worship or in the form of violence against God's loyal clients."[23] God-imposed shame is not an end but a means of vindicating God's renown and glory (Rev 15:1-4) and creating a new heaven marked by honor and glory (Rev 5:13; 19:7-8; 21:23-27).

THE HOPE OF HONOR

The prophet Isaiah wrote to exiled people daily facing the realities of shame as subjugated servants. To comfort his people, God spoke of the future day when his people would be saved from shame to enjoy eschatological honor. These promises of future, eternal honor in God's kingdom sustained God's people through seasons of disgrace.

> Do not fear, for you will not be ashamed;
>> do not be discouraged, for you will not suffer disgrace;
> for you will forget the shame of your youth,
>> and the disgrace of your widowhood you will remember no more.
>> (Is 54:4)

> But you shall be called priests of the LORD,
>> you shall be named ministers of our God;
> you shall enjoy the wealth of the nations,
>> and in their riches you shall glory. (Is 61:6)

> The nations shall see your vindication,
>> and all the kings your glory;
> and you shall be called by a new name
>> that the mouth of the LORD will give. (Is 62:2)

God's promises of future shame removal and honor restoration would come through the Suffering Servant of God (Is 50:6-8; 53:3; 52:13), whose sufferings would bring eschatological honor to the shamed in all nations.

Discussion and Application Questions

1. How would you define the nature of Israel's covenantal relationships with Yahweh? Where do you see that sort of relationship playing out in the Old Testament?

2. What is the relationship between sin and shame/dishonor in the Bible? How might you explain to an unbeliever their spiritual shame before God?

5

JESUS

*When you are invited by someone
to a wedding banquet, do not sit down
at the place of honor. . . . For all who exalt
themselves will be humbled, and those who
humble themselves will be exalted.*

LUKE 14:8, 11

*For the sake of the joy
that was set before him [Jesus]
endured the cross, disregarding its shame,
and has taken his seat at the right hand
of the throne of God.*

HEBREWS 12:2

*I*N SEVERAL WAYS JESUS LIVED AN ignominious life. He was born in a manger to an unmarried couple from a backwater town. As an adult he was rejected by his family; he wandered homelessly and died in thorough humiliation on a cross. Yet the four Gospels also highlight Jesus' honorable status in many ways: he was God's unique and beloved Son, he healed with God's power, he rebuffed opponents' honor challenges, he received worship from others, and he now sits at God's right hand. Jesus was shamed, yet honored by God. This tension, as well as the trajectory of his mission, was prefigured at Jesus' birth. His honorable status was underscored by a chorus of angels glorifying the newborn Messiah. Yet to whom do they sing? To people on the margins—shepherds.

As the honor*able* one, Jesus was also the honor*ing* one who opened new vistas of honor for humanity. His words revealed God's code of honor, and his deeds restored the dignity of the shamed. Jesus spent his years of ministry reincorporating the socially disenfranchised into the new people of God by removing their disgrace and granting a new honorable identity. Jesus conducted a ministry of status reversal. His life, death and resurrection finally solved the problem of shame and restored honor, as God promised to do through Israel.

In the Old Testament, Israel's king was expected to broker God's benefaction. God honored the king so that the king might honor others. When the king reigned justly, oppressors and enemies bowed down while the afflicted and dispossessed were vindicated (see Ps 72). God's king fixed the problem of misplaced value, declaring people's true value by upholding the honor of the marginalized. So when the Messiah—the Son of David anointed by God's Spirit—inaugurates God's kingdom we should anticipate that his life and ministry will restore human honor according to God's original design.

The dynamics of honor and shame abound throughout Jesus' life and ministry. For example, the biblical language referring to the preexistent and resurrected Christ is rich in honor vocabulary.[1] Developing a Christology through the lens of honor and shame is an essential task for mission in honor-shame contexts, as his ministry is the pattern for Christian mission. In this chapter we take steps in that direction through reflecting on two of his famous teachings, two ministry encounters and then his death and resurrection.

By examining the central place of honor and shame in select texts, we hope to give readers eyes to see similar things throughout Jesus' life and ministry. The chapter is not just to increase knowledge of the New Testament, but to understand the Messiah's mission of honoring the shamed and thus to shape missiological practices in honor-shame contexts today.

REDEFINING HONOR (SERMON ON THE MOUNT)

The Sermon on the Mount is Jesus' longest and most famous teaching. Honor-shame dynamics are latent throughout the passage. For example, the Greek word *makarioi* in the Beatitudes (Mt 5:3-12) is often translated "blessed" in English Bibles, but scholars indicate "honored" would be a more culturally accurate translation.[2] The Beatitudes were not pithy sayings for ensuring our happiness or moral rules for entering heaven, but subversive declarations of honor and worth.

Every culture has a code of honor—a set of social rules determining how people should behave to gain a positive standing in the community. The code of honor defines what behavior and which people deserve respect and honor. In first-century Judaism, the regulations of Torah and subsequent rabbinical interpretations defined who and what deserved esteem in the community.

In the first century, Pharisees, Sadducees, Essences and zealots squabbled to define their own group as rightful heirs of Abraham's promises and God's true people. This intra-Jewish competition resulted in competing codes of honor. As is the human tendency, each group positioned its teachings as the right way to be faithful to God's covenant, and hence receive honor from God. In this factional context, Jesus outlines an alternative code of honor. The Sermon on the Mount is a countercultural "code of honor"—divine in origin and eternal in scope.

Jesus taught what God considers worthy of eternal honor. The Sermon on the Mount does more than outline ethical behavior; it transforms our notions of identity, worth and value at the heart level. To capture Jesus' subversive intentions, we paraphrase the opening portion of the Sermon on the Mount (Mt 5:3-20). The words in italics are not in the original text, but make explicit the implied meaning Jesus' audience would have heard because of their shared cultural context.[3]

> Honored *by God* are *those who are shamed for being socially* dispossessed *and underprivileged*, because *(believe it or not!)* all the honorable blessings of God actually belong to them.
>
> Honored *by God* are *those who are shamed because* they mourn *the complete loss of social standing and identity from losing their family for following*

Christ, because *(believe it or not!)* they will be comforted *as they become a part of God's own family.*

Honored *by God* are the meek *who are shamed because they disengage from false honor games by not avenging insults*, because *(believe or not!)* they *are the ones who* receive everything *in the end, though it seems like they are letting other people take everything from them and appear weak.*

Honored *by God* are those who hunger and thirst for justice *in this world, where the seemingly godless get all the glorious rewards*, because *(believe or not!)* they *are the ones who* will be satisfied *and vindicated when the proud are humbled.*

Honored *by God* are the merciful ones *who are shamed since they foreswear cultural expectations of demanding honor from others*, because *(believe or not!)* they *are the ones who* will receive *eschatological* mercy *in God's kingdom.*

Honored *by God* are the *truly* pure *whose hearts have not been defiled before God by the human traditions that falsely promise purity and honor*, because *(believe or not!)* they *are the ones who will be clean enough to enter into God's very presence and* see *the face of* God, *despite being labeled "impure" and excluded from entering the temple.*

Honored *by God* are the peacemakers *who forfeit any claim to honor when challenged and sacrificially love their enemies during conflict*, because *(believe it or not!)* they *are the ones whose honorable status will be completely restored when they* are called sons of God.

Honored *by God* are those who are *shamed when* persecuted for the sake of *remaining faithful to me in the face of cultural pressures*, since *(believe it or not!)* God's own *glorious* kingdom belongs to such people.

Honored *by God* are you when people revile you, *banish you from community*, persecute you and *slander your name by* falsely uttering all kinds of evil, all on account of me. *Amid this temporary shame*, rejoice and be glad since the heavenly reward *that vindicates your true worth* is great. The prophets before you were humiliated and ridiculed, *but we all know their honorable destiny.*

So, you, *who follow me and not the social prescriptions for honor*, are the *true* salt of the earth. But once salt has lost its flavor, do you think its saltiness can actually be restored? No! Since it is no longer of value, it is thrown out and trampled *as worthless and rejected. Take heed, Israel was chosen by God, but they now live under the thumb of Roman rule. Even the sons of the kingdom can be thrown into outer darkness.*

You *who follow me and not other groups* are the light of the world. Now you know that a city on a hill does not hide. Nor does anyone hide their light under a bushel, but they put it on a stand so it lights up the whole room. *In that way,* let your own light shine is such a radical way that people will immediately see and acknowledge the great glory of your heavenly Father. *Make your family's name known to all people.*

I am interpreting Torah so you can understand how to be truly faithful to God and truly honored by God. *There are a lot of false ideas about honor, but I came to set things straight for you.* The law is going to be around until its purpose *of establishing God's glory among all peoples* is accomplished. *Regardless of what people are teaching,* anyone who thwarts God's code *of honor,* and then leads others away from being faithful to God, this one is going to be the lowest, *most shamed* person in God's kingdom. But whoever follows my new code *of honor* and teaches it to others, God will exalt *and honor* this one in his kingdom. I tell you honestly, you can and must follow my teaching to be faithful to God *and reckoned honorable in God's kingdom.* Doing what the Pharisees do will not make you a part of God's family. That excludes you from the kingdom of heaven. *If you want to be a part of the new group honored by God, you must follow me and my teachings, however counterintuitive they may seem.*

Jesus' subsequent teaching in the Sermon on the Mount illustrates how this new code of honor played out in everyday aspects of life: anger, lust, divorce, oaths, persecution, alms, prayer, fasting and anxiety. Having received honor from God and assurance of their inclusion in the divine community, Jesus' followers are now free to disengage from cultural mechanisms of status acquisition in order to bless others with honor.

Throughout his teaching, Jesus subverted the two main channels of honor of his day—reputable conduct and purity regulations. First, Jesus taught that honorable behavior in God's eyes comes from things most often associated with cultural disgrace: the loss of wealth, family and reputation due to loyalty to Jesus, bearing one's cross, enslavement, humility and debasement to last place (Mt 10:38; 18:4; 19:30; 20:27; Lk 6:20-22). Enduring shame confirms one's trust in God as the sole arbiter of worth, and merits honor in God's kingdom. The last shall be first; the shamed shall be honored.

Second, Jesus' teaching also redefined notions of purity—what makes a person clean and acceptable. Judaism had certain badges of cleanness and inclusion. They practiced the ethnic distinctives of circumcision, food laws and sabbath to distinguish themselves from unclean Gentiles. In that setting, Jesus' teaching functions as a new Torah marking out God's faithful and pure (Mt 5:17-20; 6:1-18; 11:28-30; 23:1-36).[4] This overturned Jewish purity maps. Purity now results from association with Jesus, not from proper observance of the Torah. Jesus refashioned around himself Jewish conceptions of sacred time (Mt 12:1-8; Jn 5:1-15), holy places (Mt 12:10; 21:12-13; 27:51; 1 Cor 3:16-17) and clean food (Mk 7:14-23; Acts 10:9-16; Rom 14:14).[5] Purity and divine acceptance now come from Jesus, not the temple or Torah. Those who trust in him are holy and sanctified.

Jesus' teaching restructured the basis of membership into God's people, and revealed the path to the eschatological honor God promised. Obeying Jesus' words reckons a person faithful to God and part of true Israel. In this way Jesus overturned prevailing notions of honor and offered liberation to those burdened with shame.

TOUCHING SHAME (THE LEPER AND JESUS' HEALINGS)

The *Africa Mercy* is the world's largest civilian hospital ship at 499 feet long. When the medical ministry visits ports in underdeveloped countries around Africa, thousands of people line up for medical treatment and care. The ship's chief surgeon, Gary Parker, described the social shame of patients with physical abnormalities in the *60 Minutes* episode "Floating Hospital of Hope."[6] "These are people who go out at night and forage for food. They can't go to the market; they certainly can't go to school. They are isolated." When asked what the patients feel as they come up the gangway for treatment, he said, "I've seen it happen over and over and over again. When they are greeted on the ship or when they are greeted at the screening, and someone comes and shakes their hand, it's like, 'someone recognizes that I am inside of here.'" The physicians on *Africa Mercy* observed a profound reality—as they treated peoples' facial deformities and sicknesses, they were healing people of their social shame, not just physical illness. In much of the world, people with physical abnormalities bear great shame and live on the margins of society, as was also the case in the first-century world of Jesus' day.

In Mark 1:40, a leper with an unsightly skin condition came to Jesus. The religious priests long ago pronounced the man "unclean." To symbolize his apparent defectiveness and defilement to other people, he was required to wear torn clothes, keep his hair disheveled and cover half his face. And to avoid defiling others in the community, he lived alone outside of the city. Whenever approaching public crowds, he announced "Unclean! Unclean!" (Lev 13:43-46). Every facet of his life broadcasted the shame of his leprosy. His disease defined and devalued him in the community. He was excluded from the temple and from people's homes.

Having lived in isolation and disgrace for so long, he came begging Jesus for healing. Kneeling, he said, "If you choose, you can make me clean." The leper would have hardly expected Jesus to touch him though. Like the purity customs of many cultures in today's world, ancient Israelites believed impurity and uncleanness were contagious. If a clean person touched an unclean person, even unintentionally, they were defiled before others and God (Lev 5:2-3). People steered away from lepers to avoid social pollution. However, Jesus disregarded the prevailing norms of his day. Instead of disassociating from the shamed, he approached the leper.

Jesus stretched out his hand and touched the leper.

Immediately the leper was made clean. His leprosy miraculously dissipated. Rather than Jesus receiving the leper's defilement as expected, the leper received Jesus' purity.[7] As the Source of purity and holiness, Jesus repelled the shame of unclean leprosy. With the extension of a single finger, Jesus rewrote the entire social matrix of cleanness and acceptability. Jesus' touch was both the *means* and *essence* of the healing—Jesus declared the leper was touchable.

The physical healing had profoundly social consequences. The leper became a new person. To make the leper's new status public, Jesus instructed him to visit the temple and make the appropriate sacrifices. This action was not required to simply fulfill the legal requirements of Torah and become morally cleansed, but was a public ratification of his status restoration. At the temple the priests would pronounce him "clean" and worthy to join other Israelites in worshiping God at the temple. The priest's pronouncement officially granted the leper a new reputation in the community.

For the blind, deaf, lepers, demon-possessed, lame, crippled, bleeding and even dead, Jesus' miraculous healings removed alienating social stigma and integrated people back into society. According to N. T. Wright,

For a first-century Jew, most if not all of the works of healing, which form the bulk of Jesus' mighty works, could be seen as the restoration to membership in Israel of those who, through sickness or whatever, had been excluded as ritually unclean. . . . The effect of these cures, therefore, was not merely to bring physical healing; not merely to give humans, within a far less individualistic society than our modern western one, a renewed sense of community membership.[8]

In the Mediterranean world, where bodily purity, honor and group inclusion were interdependent constructs (Lev 11–15), Jesus' miracles restored the social dignity, not just physical health, of the maimed and marginalized. As the Holy One of Israel, Jesus was renowned for his authority to cleanse and restore.

Washed with Honor (Simon the Pharisee and the Sinful Woman)

During the midday break of a seminar in Nekemte, Ethiopia, a local family invited me (Mark) for a meal.[9] A few regional church leaders accompanied me. One of them knocked on the host's gate. A family member opened the gate, warmly shook hands and invited us in. Not having running water, one of the sons brought a pitcher of water, soap, towel and a basin to wash before we ate. He handed me the soap and poured water over my hands, catching it in the basin held below with his other hand.

The next day, before reading the text for my sermon, Luke 7:36-50, I asked the congregation how they would feel if they had been invited to a meal, but when they knocked on the gate the host did not offer words of greeting or extend his hand, and then seated them for the meal without providing water to wash their hands. The Ethiopians' shocked faces communicated how disturbing they found this scenario. They said words like *angry*, *disrespected*, *insulted* and *confused*. This is precisely what happened to Jesus at the house of Simon the Pharisee. He too was invited to a meal, but was not shown the proper regard expected from a host. We will reflect separately on the story's three main figures: the woman, Simon the Pharisee and Jesus.

We know from the biblical text that the woman had a bad reputation; she was publicly known as a sinner (Lk 7:37, 39, 47). She apparently came to Simon's house with the intention of anointing Jesus with ointment. She did not come prepared to wash his feet. We can deduce other things with reasonable confidence. She probably was a prostitute who had been marginalized and shamed in her village—especially by the highly religious like the Pharisees.[10] Jesus speaks of her having her sins forgiven before this event (Lk 7:41-43, 47), implying she had already had a significant encounter with Jesus. We can imagine that Jesus showered her with love and acceptance and that like a thirsty plant she soaked it up. Apparently in the midst of that encounter they spoke of her sins and Jesus pronounced forgiveness. This experience contrasted radically with the shame and exclusion she experienced from others. Jesus' forgiveness so moved her that she desired to express her gratitude to Jesus. Hearing that Simon the Pharisee was hosting a dinner and Jesus was an invited guest, she went to the house, prepared to honor Jesus with ointment. She arrived either before or simultaneously with Jesus (Lk 7:45). What did she see? Simon insulted and disrespected the person she had come to honor when he did not offer Jesus customary gestures of hospitality. Shocked, and probably with a mix of anger and sadness, the woman took steps to show Jesus the honor and hospitality that Simon had not offered. Jesus explained to Simon, "Do you see this woman? I entered your house; you gave me no water for my feet, but she has bathed my feet with her tears and dried them with her hair. You gave me no kiss, but from the time I came in she has not stopped kissing my feet. You did not anoint my head with oil, but she has anointed my feet with ointment" (Lk 7:44-46).

We do not know why Simon invited Jesus to this meal. Was it, from the beginning, a plan to insult Jesus for his own social gain in the community? (On other occasions the religious leaders attempted to challenge Jesus' growing fame.) Or had the invitation been sincere but Simon had a change of perspective when Jesus actually arrived? What was his motivation? As a Pharisee Simon not only carefully complied with the law and the traditions of the Jews but also worked to motivate others to do the same. As we observe in his actions toward both Jesus and the woman, Simon sought to honor those who complied and to shame those who did not. He threatened exclusion to pressure people to live according to the Pharisees' definition of piety.

In that time and culture it was acceptable for people who were not invited guests to gather around the edges of the room and observe the event. Hosts desired this. They accrued honor through others' participating in this way. More people meant more honor.[11] So it was not unusual that an uninvited guest would enter the house. But for a woman known as a sinner to enter his house was certainly unusual. Her presence itself would likely have been cause for gossiping the next day, but it is her actions that especially would have caught people's attention. She made a scene not only by weeping and washing Jesus' feet with her tears, but in particular by loosening her hair to dry Jesus feet—an intimate act only done in the presence of one's husband. Everyone present, not just Simon, would have been surprised that Jesus let this sinful woman continue these scandalous actions.

Simon demonstrated an attitude of superiority, and used threats of shame and exclusion as tools for motivating behavioral conformity and religious compliance. Jesus practiced the opposite—a strategy of inclusion, love and forgiveness. This is obvious in the case of the woman, but also apparent in relation to Simon. Rather than dishonoring Simon by refusing the invitation, Jesus went to his house. And when Simon dishonored him, Jesus did not immediately move into a competitive stance, such as exiting the house or exposing Simon's mistreatment of him.

Jesus' conversation with Simon redefined the meaning of true honor on multiple fronts. We could identify Jesus' interaction with Simon as a public game of challenge and riposte—a common occurrence in an honor-shame context. But Jesus did more than tussle with Simon over a limited quantity of honor. First, Jesus' challenge is motivated by love—love for the woman, but also love for Simon. Until Simon steps away from his life of exclusionary line-drawing, he will not truly be living in authentic communion with God or others in his community. In a twist of irony, his social rules actually isolate and distance him from other people, and God. Moreover, Jesus' public actions forced the spectators to consider the question, who does God consider shameful and exclude? The entire incident challenged the distorted honor system of the day.

Most prominently, Jesus confronts Simon in order to defend the women from further shaming. When the woman began her surprising and then scandalous actions, Jesus had various options. If he was most concerned about his own reputation and honor, he could have rejected her actions—kicking her away and insulting her. Or he could have apologized for her actions. Kenneth Bailey suggests that to save face Jesus could have said something like this:

> Gentlemen, I am embarrassed by all of this. Yes, on occasion I do eat with sinners, but we always keep the numbers down and we try to clean them up a bit before our meals, which are always in private. This is not at all the kind of scene with which I am comfortable, and so do not be upset. I grant that no easy acceptance of such types is possible. Standards must be maintained! These "people of the land" must learn how to behave.[12]

These actions would have protected Jesus' honor, but at the expense of the woman. Such insincerity from Jesus would have confirmed her shame and disgrace. But Jesus did not act to save his own honor. At cost to his own reputation he accepted *and* defended her. Jesus' public declaration demonstrated concern not just for her individual experience of pardon and acceptance but also her restoration in the community. Jesus' forgiveness removed the barrier of sin that excluded her from the community. Divine forgiveness releases people from the social bondage of shame and carries profound social overtones.[13]

He counters the shame she had experienced by honoring her and giving her a new identity. With his final words he honors her publicly, placing the emphasis on her faith, not on his actions: "Your faith has saved you; go in peace." The peace, or shalom, Jesus commissioned her toward was not just the internal serenity of a guiltless conscience, but public restoration to community and wholeness. She was freed to live in harmony with others.

Before Jesus spoke up in her defense, all the eyes in the room would have been glued on the woman—shaming eyes of accusation. When Jesus began to speak he became the scandal, and the eyes of accusation would have shifted to him. He takes on the shame in her place. Because of Jesus' surprising defense, the woman would have left feeling even more loved, more accepted and more graced than before. Jesus' actions were a "costly demonstration of unexpected love."[14] Jesus loved her so much he was willing to suffer shame to save her from being shamed. This story is a precursor of the costly demonstration of unexpected love at the cross.

This incident marks a common pattern in Jesus' ministry of honoring the shamed via public association. Whereas his miraculous healings honored those with "ascribed shame," Jesus' public relationships honored those with "achieved shame." Tax collectors, prostitutes, adulterers and sinners were all shamed for violating cultural norms. They were moral lepers outside of the covenant community. By talking and eating with them, Jesus erased their social taboo and presented a live portrait of participation in the new messianic community. Jesus' "radically inclusive and non-hierarchical table fellowship was a central strategy in his announcement and redefinition of the inbreaking rule of God. In so doing, Jesus challenged the inherent exclusivism and status consciousness of accepted social and religious custom and presented a living parable of a renewed Israel."[15] Jesus was God's Messiah bringing God's honor to God's people, in both word and deed. We will explore one more such occurrence before reflecting on the cross itself.

Jesus, the Shamed and the Shamers (the Prodigal Family)

Jesus, at the beginning of Luke 15, is once again communicating acceptance and honor—to the excluded and shamed. He even goes so far as eating with sinners and tax collectors. And once again, scribes and Pharisees display a posture of accusation—shaming both Jesus and those gathered around him by grumbling about his actions. Imagine how the shamed gathered around Jesus felt when they heard those words: "He even eats with them!" Jesus responds to the complaints by telling those gathered, both the religious insiders and outsiders, three parables: the lost sheep, the lost coin and the lost sons.

In the parable of the two lost sons, Jesus did not have to explain to them the meaning or significance of ancient customs like inheritance, a man running down the street or celebratory dinners. Westerners, however, are from a different time and culture, so many of these details are lost. Rather than turning Jesus' parable into a catalog of various cultural insights that we have gleaned from our own crosscultural experience and Kenneth Bailey's work,[16] we will retell the parable of the lost sons from the perspective of a neighbor living in the village. This expanded version of the story makes more explicit the scandalous shame and radically gracious honor of Jesus' original story.

> Amazing things have been happening in one family in our village! The younger son asked the father for his inheritance. Can you imagine? Have you

ever heard of such a thing? What nerve! What disrespect! He might as well as said, "Father, I wish you would die."

Of course we all expected the father to scorn the son, perhaps disown or stone him, like it says in Deuteronomy 21. Instead, he gave the inheritance! It also amazed us that the older son didn't intervene, or at least protest that he didn't want to have anything to do with this.

As news spread around town, a lot of people were pretty upset. I think the younger son started feeling uncomfortable. So what do you think he did? No, he didn't try to give the land back to his father. He sold it. Can you imagine, selling ancestral land, the very land God gave our forefathers! What will his father have to live off of when he grows older? And where would he raise his family? What would his children inherit? Not only is it disrespectful and in-considerate, it's against our Jewish law to sell the land before his father died.

Well, trying to sell it made things worse. Each person he'd try to sell it to just got angry and insulted him. The son certainly couldn't have felt very welcome here after having done such shameful things. So he took the money and left town.

He went to a Gentile land and squandered all his money. At about the same time a famine hit that area, and being a foreigner he was one of the first to feel the effect of the shortage. So, there he finds himself—in a foreign land, hungry and feeding pigs for a living. He was so hungry he wanted to eat the pigs' food! Obviously he'd lost all regard for being a good Jew, and dignity as a human being.

He was starving, but he knew if he returned home he would face the scorn of the village. After all, if we had shamed him when he left, how would we re-spond now in the condition he was in? He knew he had further complicated his situation by blowing all his inheritance in a Gentile land. Not only did he worry about his father's anger, he knew about our custom to banish anyone who lost or sold family inheritance among Gentiles—called the *kezazah*. We'd break a large pot of roasted nuts and declare, "You are rejected from this community!"

In his desperation he hoped that perhaps his father would give him a job as a worker so that he could pay back the inheritance and escape the ban. But would his father even talk to him? He decided to first apologize, with the hope that his father would listen to his request. As he walked home he carefully crafted his speech, deciding he would say:

"Father, I have sinned against heaven and before you; I am no longer worthy to be called your son; treat me like one of your hired hands." He thought he couldn't be a son again.

He was probably wishing there was a back way into town, but there is not. Our homes are all together with our farmland spread out all around the village.

I was one of the first to see him, and he was a sight—dirty, thin, barefoot, old patched up clothes, rags really. He walked with his head low hoping we would not recognize him. Honestly I was glad to see how bad he looked. I didn't want my sons running off and doing the same thing. As you could guess we started yelling at him, insulting him, "You worthless pig!" and "Leave our village, you foreigner!" A crowd gathered and people began the *kezazah* ceremony to ban him from the village.

But all of a sudden we heard a shout from the other direction. His father was running, yes running, down the street! We were shocked. In our culture, old men do not run. Not because of physical inability, but because of social decorum. Old men wait for others to approach them. Running is for school-children, not elders. It was a thing of shame to do so. Just imagine what might be exposed with robes flying up in the air!

Then the father hugged and kissed his filthy son. The son stood there in shock, never having imagined such a response. That shut us all up. We could not really insult or disown the son if his own father did not. In fact his father risked humiliating himself to stop us from shaming his son.

I think the son was as surprised as the rest of us by his father's action. I think it changed his whole perspective on the situation. Maybe he was so impressed by his father's love and acceptance, and so grateful that his father had saved him from our scorn, that he decided he'd be better off to rely on his father's mercy than to try to earn some kind of reconciliation. Or maybe he realized he couldn't bring about reconciliation or buy back the relationship. He had done more than waste money; he hurt his father, so all he could do was ask for mercy.

The father left no doubt he was accepting the son back. He told his servants to put sandals on his feet, a ring on his finger and a fine robe on his back. Without saying a word, the father covered his filth and restored him as a true son. He also told the servants to set up a feast and kill the fatted calf—not a lamb or a chicken! He was going to invite the whole village. I was glad to hear that! I would get to go! The father was not only accepting him back, he was honoring him and celebrating his return with the entire village. But that's only half the story.

Everybody was arriving at his house for the evening celebration. I got to the house just about the time the older son got back from the fields. I paused to let him enter and take his role as greeter, something older sons do at parties hosted by their families. But instead he stopped and asked a servant what was going on. The servant explained what had happened and said, "Your father is celebrating and welcoming back your brother." The older son started complaining and turned away from the house, saying, "I'm not joining in this. I deserve a party, not him." He rejected an invitation to eat. In our village, you can *never* say no to food, but the older son did . . . to his own father! He made a huge scene with all these guests around, yelling and shouting right there in front of everyone. This was just as shameful to the father as the younger son asking for an inheritance and selling off family land.

Just then I saw his father look out the door toward the commotion, waiting for the son to come in. I expected the father to be furious and put his older son back in place for insulting him like this. Instead, the father came out and pleaded with the son to join in the celebration. For the second time that day, the father went out to restore a dishonoring son.

But the older son continued to insult his father. He spoke with no respect, not even using a title. He yelled into his father's face, "Listen! For all these years I have been working like a slave for you, and I have never disobeyed your command; yet you have never given me even a young goat so that I might celebrate with my friends. But when this son of yours came back, who devoured your property with prostitutes, you killed the fatted calf for him!"

But the father kept going out of his way to try and bring the older son into the family celebration. Once again he was willing to experience shame himself for the sake of his son. He responded with the words, "Son, you are always with me, and all that is mine is yours. But we had to celebrate and rejoice, because this brother of yours was dead and has come to life; he was lost and has been found."

With those words the parable ends abruptly. Jesus leaves the listeners wondering: Did the older son go in and join the celebratory meal, or leave in disgust? Is the family ultimately restored? To understand why Jesus stopped here without concluding the story, we need to think about the two groups of people listening to this parable in Luke 15:1-2.

On one hand, there are sinners and tax collectors, those outside of the acceptable boundaries of society. Then there are the Pharisees and scribes, those respected and admired. To the tax collectors and sinners, Jesus' words communicate that God welcomes them, and is willing to demonstrate his love, even at the expense of his own reputation.

What is Jesus communicating to the Pharisees and teachers of the law? They are the reason he does not finish the story. They need to finish it. Jesus is functionally saying, "I'm offering love and forgiveness to these people. Will you, the 'older son,' come in and join the welcome-home party?" Jesus ends the story midscene, because the listeners' real-life response to this invitation *is* the conclusion of the parable.

But isn't Jesus communicating something else to the Pharisees? Anyone in that culture would have seen that the older son, although keeping the letter of the law, also had done things that were shameful and damaged relationships. Jesus is saying to the scribes and Pharisees, "Yes, you too are sinners!" But like the father in the parable, who comes out of the house to invite the older soon to come into the celebration, Jesus does not scorn or reject the Pharisees. He invites them to join him in welcoming the excluded people. Jesus is communicating God's gracious welcome to the Pharisees and scribes as well.

Jesus' story questioned the flawed identities of both groups—the falsely shamed *and* the falsely honored. The parable is an invitation to abandon their old identity as either a despicable rule breaker or respectable rule keeper, and embrace the new status the Father offers. Jesus summons the Pharisees to adopt his radical, shame-bearing love and join his mission of honoring the shamed through table fellowship.

Although we commonly call this the parable of the prodigal son, the central figure in the parable is the father. The father reaches out in love to both sons—the one lost in a foreign land, the other son lost at home. By inviting his sons to come together and eat at one table again as a family, the father pursues restoration and harmony. The father willingly suffered shame to communicate love and forgiveness in order to restore relationships with each son personally and together as a family.

The parable reveals the loving and honoring nature of God at the theological level, but also interprets the meaning and significance of Jesus' ministry among the shamed. As God incarnate, Jesus lived out the parable of the lost sons and the pursuing father through his table fellowship. It is important to repeat the question we asked above: If Jesus had focused on saving his reputation and honor, what would he have done when the Pharisees and scribes grumbled about his eating with sinners? To save face Jesus could have turned his back on the tax collectors and sinners and walked off with the religious leaders. But what did he do? Considering the interests and status of others a higher priority than his own, Jesus stood in solidarity with the excluded and told the three parables in Luke 15. As the father in the parable did, Jesus stepped out on their behalf to restore identity, community and honor. It was a costly demonstration of unexpected love, something Jesus did in a much greater way at the cross.

BEARING SHAME AND BARING HONOR (JESUS' CRUCIFIXION AND RESURRECTION)

We now turn to look through the lens of honor and shame at how the cross and resurrection provide salvation. In theological terms this section focuses on atonement. Just as in the previous chapter in the section on sin we did not claim to present the one and only biblical understanding of sin, so too in this section. To articulate the atonement in honor-shame terms does not imply that other articulations are wrong. We maintain this approach is most appropriate for honor-shame contexts; other contexts will naturally consider other explanations of the cross more appropriate. The meaning and significance of the cross cannot be captured in any one image or explanation. As Kevin Vanhoozer states, "Like the five thousand, we discover that after our centuries-long banquet of atonement theology, there are still more fragments of the cross left over."[17] This is evident in the New Testament itself, where in different contexts biblical authors emphasize and proclaim different aspects of the saving significance of the cross.[18]

Two other clarifying comments are important. First, not only is an honor-shame perspective only one of a variety of ways of understanding the meaning of the cross, but there is diversity also within an honor-shame perspective. It is not a singular stream alongside others; rather there are various tributaries to this stream. Second, in these few pages we name some of these tributaries, walk along them a bit, but do not explore them in depth. There are, however, other works to turn to for those who are interested in fuller explorations of honor-shame and the atonement.[19]

A key element in understanding the atonement is to recognize the centrality of shame to crucifixion itself. Depictions of the cross in Western contexts have emphasized the physical pain and suffering of the cross. Crucifixion indeed was savage and heinous, but for reasons beyond the physical pain involved. In the honor-shame culture of Greco-Roman antiquity, physical pain was not the worst sort of injury. To be crucified was a great ignominy. Rome purposefully opted for crucifixion as the preferred deterrent to seditious crimes against the empire on account of its public, humiliating quality.[20] The shame of crucifixion is evident in these words of Cicero defending a Roman senator: "The very word 'cross' should be far removed not only from the person of a Roman citizen but from his thoughts, his eyes and his ears. For it is not only the actual occurrence of these things or the endurance of them, but liability to them, the expectation, indeed the very mention of them, that is unworthy of a Roman citizen and a free man."[21] Death on a cross was associated with such shame that it was hardly a topic for polite company. It is no wonder, then, that Paul states that proclamation about the crucified Christ was received as foolishness by many (1 Cor 1; cf. Heb 12:2)—the notion of "crucified Lord" was an oxymoron in the first-century Roman world.[22]

The Gospel writers recognize and highlight the shame factor of Jesus' death by listing the many affronts dishonoring Jesus in the crucifixion process: spitting on him, striking him in the face and head, stripping him, ridiculing him, insulting him and derisively mocking him. Then worst of all, they hung Jesus' mangled, naked body near the city gates on the busy Passover weekend for all to behold. Jesus even suffered the humiliation of his closest friends' abandoning him.[23] Set within Roman conventions, Jesus' crucifixion is a tale of shame and humiliation, the ultimate form of labeling a person as an outcast. The early Christians saw in Jesus' experience the fulfillment of Isaiah's vision of a servant of God who would bear tremendous shame (see Is 49:7; 50:6-8; 53:2-3).

Clearly then the actual concrete shame of the cross is central to its saving significance. Equally important is to not divorce the cross and resurrection from the life and ministry of Jesus. His words and actions in life led to his death. As we have observed, he challenged the honor system of the day and it retaliated with the ultimate shaming move—crucifixion. Jesus was so committed to the shamed and excluded that he loved them in unexpected and costly ways. He did not turn from that commitment even under the threat of death. We begin our reflection on the saving significance of the cross at this point.

One way the cross liberates from shame is by displaying Jesus' deep affirmation of and commitment to the new identity he offered to people with shame. Jesus was so committed to their inclusion that he was willing to die rather than accept the false cultural norms of social exclusion. Through the resurrection God validates Jesus and his actions of loving acceptance. Thus the cross reveals that God is a God who willingly gives up status and honor, to the point of death, in order to include the excluded and honor the shamed. For someone shamed and excluded by a society's twisted concept of status, it can be life-transforming to comprehend and experience that God does not stand with the shamers. In fact God stands with the excluded (see Heb 2:9-10).

Although what the cross reveals about God is significant and has saving import, the cross and resurrection do more. They also address what is often referred to as the objective issues of sin and shame. In the paragraphs that follow we will explore this dimension in Paul's writings. We begin by examining the nature of the sin from which Christ saves us.[24]

In Romans Paul describes sin in line with what we observed in the Old Testament in chapter four—sin dishonors God and shames people (including oneself). In Romans 1 Paul portrays sin as a strategy of covering up shame through seeking to usurp the honorable position of God. Evil actions flow from this deception.[25] Paul explicitly uses language of honor and shame: "They did not honor him as God or give thanks to him . . . and exchanged the glory of the immortal God for images. . . . For this reason God gave them up to dishonorable passions" (Rom 1:21-26 ESV).

Paul's exposition on sin climaxes in Romans 3:23, "All have sinned and fall short of the glory of God." The phrase "fall short of the glory of God" carries a double meaning—people fail to properly glorify God *and* lack the glorified existence God intended. Romans 3:23 refers to the Jewish theological tradition of Adam being deprived of the glory of God at the fall.[26] The glory and honor bestowed on the primal pair at creation is now absent in all peoples.

In Paul's letter to the Romans, humanity's error is not "lawbreaking" per se, but the "untruthful distortions of social systems."[27] Because sin opposes God's established code of honor, human sinfulness results in a perverse redefinition of what deserves honor. In other words, humans justify their sin by constructing a false alternative status. Such social engineering rejects the honor God gives and upstages God as arbiter of honor (Rom 1:20-32; 2:29). Made in the image of the glorious God, humans strive for honor. But in a world pervaded by sin, we forsake the honor God offers for an alternate means of status and identity. Essentially, then, sin is an illegitimate claim to honor that dishonors God and shames ourselves.

As we have emphasized in this book, honor and shame are not just internal emotions; they are concretely expressed in actions that affect others. What happens when humans grasp for honor that is rightly God's? Paul gives a long list of the self-degrading and communally destructive actions that are the fruit of that sinful grasping (Rom 1:29-32; Gal 5:19-21, 26). Paul also describes sin as a power that enslaves. In the vulnerable state of having turned away from honoring God, humans became enslaved to the power of sin that leads to dishonorable conduct and ultimately death (Rom 5:21; 6:16-22). The collusion of the power of sin with human shame-based grasping was expressed at its worst at the cross. It was the ultimate dishonoring of God—shamefully killing God incarnate. The crucifixion was the ultimate expression of a culture's honor gone awry—killing a truly honorable human who had lived faithfully according to God's ways.

The crucifixion is the representative culmination of human rejection of God. Whenever we dishonor God and shame others created in God's image in an effort to grasp status for ourselves, we carry out a small act of crucifixion. Even the shamed and excluded are themselves shamers and "crucifiers."[28] The cross reveals the depth of human sin and need for salvation. All humans need the multifaceted saving work of the cross and resurrection.

How do the cross and resurrection provide salvation? The cross itself was not a series of separate, mechanical steps, but more like a gathering of threads woven together in God's saving action through Jesus' death and resurrection. Though the threads are interrelated, we isolate and follow a number of them to explain the atonement for those not accustomed to thinking about the cross in terms of honor and shame.

There are consequences to the way of sin described above—namely, shame and death (Rom 1:18-32; 6:23). Paul proclaims that Jesus has borne them in our place (Rom 6:10, 13; Gal 3:13). The cross and resurrection provide the possibility of escape from death and the ultimate consequences of a system of honor-grasping out of control. Adam lost his original glory, but Paul explains that Jesus as second Adam restores that glory (Rom 5:1-21; 1 Cor 15:57). This glory in Christ is one aspect of being brought into walking in "newness of life" (Rom 6:4).

Jesus did not only bear the consequences of sin in our place but also honored God in our place. Jesus did not fall short of God's glory. He embodied the opposite of the human sinful ways described above. He faithfully obeyed God; he kept covenant in a way Israel had not; he was obedient to the point of death. Unlike other humans, Jesus lived in a way that was, from God's perspective, truly honorable. Jesus never brought shame on God's name. He thus honored God as humans had not. Although in the Roman context Jesus' death on the cross was the epitome of shame, from God's perspective this ultimate act of faithful obedience was the epitome of honor (Phil 2:6-11). Jesus did what no other human could ever do—live honorably and completely honor God. Jesus brought honor to God on our behalf.

Paul proclaims that believers in Christ Jesus are reconciled and justified in and through him (Rom 5:11, 17; Gal 2:16). The previous sentence is intelligible and has great significance for those who live in a guilt-based culture. Reading Paul through the lens of honor and shame does not require that we deny that significance. Rather it recognizes that being united with Christ has saving implications that go beyond the narrower guilt-oriented interpretation—implications evident in Paul's writing. In places the honor-shame language is explicit, such as when Paul states, "so that we may also be glorified with him" (Rom 8:17).[29] Paul's language about the cross and resurrection relates to liberation from shame and restoration of honor. For shamed people to leave their place of disgrace and exclusion, they need a new identity and they need to receive honor and acceptance from others. Since shame is a relational issue, the solution must be relational. To become adopted children in God's family offers the needed new identity. And as children we are heirs—underlining our honored status (Rom 8:15-18;

Gal 3:26-29). Imagine the power of this declaration for someone excluded and disgraced: "You have received a spirit of adoption. When we cry, 'Abba! Father!' it is that very Spirit bearing witness with our spirit that we are children of God, and if children, then heirs, heirs of God and joint heirs with Christ—if, in fact, we suffer with him so that we may also be glorified with him" (Rom 8:15-17).

These obviously relational notions of adoption, new identity, reconciliation and status communicate the saving works of the cross in an honor-shame context. But even the term *justification* in the honor-shame setting of the first-century Mediterranean world was a relational word that communicated more than just a rectifying of legal standing. All the more so if we consider the Old Testament covenantal meaning that Paul would likely have in mind when he used the word. To be "made right with God," or as some prefer to interpret the term, to be "brought into right covenantal standing," speaks of new honorable status with corporate and relational implications. To be justified is to be placed in proper relationship to God, to be made a full participant in the community of God's people. Justification is not simply being declared not guilty, but God's declaration that we belong within his community.[30]

God works through the cross and resurrection not only to restore humans' honor but also to display his glory. Jesus' death demonstrates God is honorable. In contemporary honor-shame terminology we might say the cross is a "face-saving" action, or "honor death"—something done to mitigate potential shame and reserve status. The cross saves God's face by demonstrating his ultimate loyalty and faithfulness to do what he promised. God does not renege on his promises (see Rom 3:3-7).[31] Despite humanity's complete lack of faithfulness and loyalty (Rom 3:9-20), God has persistently maintained his covenantal promises. The Messiah's disgraceful death revealed God's covenant loyalty in an unexpected way. The work of Jesus demonstrates God's justice (Rom 3:25) and proves that he himself is just (Rom 3:26).[32]

God deserves praise because Jesus fulfills the obligations God long ago placed on himself to provide salvation (Rom 1:2; 3:21; 16:26)—"Christ has become a servant of the circumcised on behalf of the truth of God in order that he might confirm the promises given to the patriarchs" (Rom 15:8). God is not all bark and no bite; he can deliver on what he says. The cross preserves God's good name. He *can* bring about salvation to his creation and exalt his people. God is a patron worthy of our loyalty and praise because he does act on our behalf, as proven on the cross.

God acts to demonstrate he is honorable, and does so in a way that coheres with the countercultural code of honor Jesus taught in the Sermon on the Mount. Worldly honor codes demand that attacks against one's honor require a response. Vengeance to vindicate honor leads to ongoing cycles of violence. In contrast Jesus called for loving enemies and not retaliating. He summons disciples to disengage from false honor games by not avenging insults (Mt 5:38-48). Jesus not only taught this but also proved it with his very life. On the cross Jesus asks the Father not to avenge those who condemned and shamed him through crucifixion. Jesus said, "Father, forgive them" (Lk 23:34; cf. 1 Pet 2:21-24). Paul acknowledges that from the perspective of the honor systems of the day the cross was foolishness—a sign of weakness. Yet God works through this apparent foolishness to bring salvation (1 Cor 1:18-25). Honor, wisdom and power are all redefined at the cross. The false honor systems, including requiring revenge, that killed Jesus were exposed and triumphed over (Col 2:15). The cycle of violence and revenge was broken. An aspect of the saving significance of the cross and resurrection is the possibility of living in freedom from that cycle and living according to God's code of honor.[33]

Whereas the cross is an event of shame, the resurrection overflows with honor and glory. But as Philippians 2 communicates so poetically, it is the crucified one who is honored. The resurrection is God's triumph and death's dishonorable demise—"Death has been swallowed up in victory" (1 Cor 15:54). The resurrection is God's seal of approval and affirmation that the way Jesus lived and his faithful obedience to the point of death was the truly honorable way. The resurrection enables Paul to quote Isaiah 28:16 and assure the Romans that "no one who believes in him will be put to shame" (Rom 10:11); they will be "raised in glory" (1 Cor 15:43). The resurrection opens a new path to glory for the human family.

Paul clearly talks of future glory for believers, but the resurrection has concrete implications for today. Jesus was killed by religious and political forces, principalities and powers, seeking to shame him in an ultimate and final way. On the cross people saw a failure not worthy of association, certainly not glory and honor. But Paul proclaims the surprising reversal: "He disarmed the rulers and authorities and made a public example of them, triumphing over them in it" (Col 2:15). The shamers where shamed. Their lies and distorted honor systems were exposed. The cross and resurrection thus expose improper shame and break its power to instill fear. Jesus' death and resurrection invite and enable us to live in freedom from this dehumanizing shame that he disregarded on the cross (2 Cor 3:18; Heb. 12:2; 1 Pet 2:6). The power of shame to exclude is destroyed.

INTO THE WORLD

We have observed that Jesus lived in an honor-shame-saturated world. He reached out to the shamed. He critiqued honor systems that inappropriately shamed people and confronted people who stepped on others as they grasped for honor for themselves. Honor and shame were major themes in the cross and resurrection—both in leading to his crucifixion and in the liberating salvation provided through his death and resurrection.

In the Gospels Jesus not only engaged the honor-shame dynamics of his day but also called his followers to live as he had lived. At times he exhorted them to live in ways counter to what culture defined as honorable. This set his followers on a collision course with the honor system of the day and created a significant challenge for early Christians, and for the apostles as they started and shepherded the first churches. For this reason the New Testament helps Christians live out the gospel in honor-shame settings. We will reflect on a number of these texts in the chapters ahead as we turn to the practice of mission in honor-shame contexts.

DISCUSSION AND APPLICATION QUESTIONS

1. How does Jesus advance God's mission to honor the shamed?

2. What specific stories or teachings from the Gospels most profoundly speak about God's salvation from shame?

3. How might you explain the saving significance of Jesus' death (i.e., the atonement) in honor-shame terms?

PART THREE

PRACTICAL
MINISTRY

6

SPIRITUALITY

Shame may be the hidden key to understanding
our civilization, in the sense that shame
or its anticipation is virtually ubiquitous,
yet, at the same time, usually invisible.

THOMAS SCHEFF,
"SHAME AS THE MASTER EMOTION
IN MODERN SOCIETIES"

Look to him and be radiant;
so your faces shall never be ashamed.

PSALM 34:5

BEFORE PROCLAIMING THE GOSPEL OF GOD'S HONOR, we as Christians must receive and embody it ourselves. Being precedes doing in the Christian life. A key element of Christian spirituality is living with a biblical view of honor and shame. Only then can we minister God's honor to other people. Up to this point, we have examined the social and communal aspects of honor and shame. But in this chapter we will explore their personal and spiritual dynamics, particularly in the Christian life. The aim is to help readers along the spiritual journey of releasing cultural shame and appropriating divine honor. We give biblical examples and share our own stories to cultivate a healthy spirituality of God's grace for shame. But first we examine the nature of shame in Western culture—our context and, we assume, the context of many readers.

WESTERN SHAME

It is often said that Western cultures are guilt-based, and Eastern cultures are shame-based, but that is not entirely accurate. Shame is not an Asian or Arab issue; shame is an Adam and Eve issue, present in all humans ever since the Garden of Eden. Shame is a global problem, inherent in all cultures. When we teach on honor-shame dynamics to North Americans, people often comment, "We talk about other cultures being shame-based, but I sense shame is a big issue here in America." True, shame is a ubiquitous scourge in Western culture. For this reason we discuss the dynamics of shame in Western contexts in this section, and how all followers of Christ can dispel shame with the light of God's glorious grace.

Shame rears its head in many pockets of Western society. Various subcultures use public praise or scorn to regulate people's behavior. Consider these subcultures in North America that employ the carrot of honor and stick of shame: teenagers talk and dress a certain way to be "cool" and accepted, gangs abide by a street code to ensure "respect," the military uses public honors and rewards to commend group commitment, sports teams give high-fives and trophies to outstanding performers (especially if they play through a personal injury for the team's sake), and rural communities where everybody knows everybody spread gossip quickly. Honor and shame are universally present; these are just some of social groups through which Westerners may have experienced shame.

Another shaming community, unfortunately, is the church. Many people raised in Christian circles encounter rules, often implied, about how they should behave. Though it is ironic considering the term, legalism typically uses shame more than guilt to induce certain behaviors; people follow the rules to be accepted by the group. Christians struggle with the false shame of "not being good enough," and work hard to hide those apparent shortcomings from other Christians—the result is isolation and more shame.[1]

One can hardly live in Western culture without encountering corporate promises of false honor. Television commercials, website advertisements and roadside billboards all bombard us with the hope of status, if only we buy the right thing or look as good as the people in the ads. Failing to "keep up with the Joneses" threatens us with social inferiority.

People commonly note that Western culture is becoming increasingly shame driven. Even the anthropologist who pioneered the "West is guilt-based, East is shame-based" cultural dichotomy already observed in 1946, "But shame is an increasingly heavy burden in the United States and guilt is less extremely felt than in earlier generations."[2] Andy Crouch in *Christianity Today* notes how North America's new media-amplified shame culture "is starting to look something like a postmodern *fame*-shame culture" (wherein fame comes from a broad audience only loosely connected to the acclaimed).[3]

The advent of social media reveals the Western craving for face. Observe the language of *Face*book—"friends," "like," "status." It hijacks the language of community to project social value onto digital activities. When your audience becomes unknown "friends," then "you are out to entertain and seek their approval and the danger lies then in constructing an artificial identity that's not really you at all."[4] To influence opinions people project images of their idealized life, as if their entire life is as glamorous as that one really cool selfie suggests. Social media can turn individuals into brands, carefully groomed to obtain "followers" and "friends." Crouch observes, "As our social network chimes, blinks, and buzzes with intermittent approval, we are constantly updated on our success in gaining public affirmation. But having attracted us with the promise of approval and belonging, the personal screen can just as easily herald exclusion and hostility."[5] Hiding safely behind the digital wall of anonymity, digital bullies degrade with a snide comment or exposing image, producing shame. As social media integrates into our daily lives, it becomes the new playing field for social games of honor and shame, and an increasingly stronger influence on our constructions of human worth and value.

Shame in Western cultures takes a different form than in Majority World cultures. Western shame is more *private* and *personal*, centered on the individual and his or her internal feelings. Eastern shame is *public* and *communal*, resulting from *others'* negative evaluation and community reputation. Brené Brown's helpful definition of shame illustrates that Western shame is a private feeling: "Shame is the intensely painful feeling or experience of believing we are flawed and therefore unworthy of acceptance and belonging."[6] The antonym of shame in Western societies tends to be *self-esteem*—"I think highly about myself." The opposite of Eastern shame is *honor*—"others respect me." Shame in Western cultures is less contagious, so an individual's actions do not significantly affect their family's reputation. American shame often stems from social anonymity and lack of relationships. But the seedbed of Eastern shame is a strong communal culture, where the prying eyes of gossipy neighbors constantly cast judgment on every behavior.

One significant source of shame is the failure to meet expectations. Because we cannot live up to expectations or be who we are supposed to be, we feel inadequate. The constant barrage of social expectations misleads us to believe that being imperfect is synonymous with being inadequate.[7] Men and women both hear unique messages of who and what we should be. The expectations of gender roles create feelings of deficiency and make us hide so our shame is not exposed.

Women, generally speaking, are supposed to be everything all at the same time. One should have a Hillary Clinton career, a Martha Stewart house and a June Cleaver family. So advertisements enforce the message that women are to have perfect kids *and* the appearance of somebody without kids. Men, on the other hand, have one primary expectation—maintain power and control. This means bringing home the bacon and never falling off your white horse. The workplace is the new battlefield where people measure prowess and strength. Be tough, be dominant and never show a chink in the armor. These social expectations are ludicrously unattainable, but shout at our souls like blaring megaphones. If you cannot do and be all these things, we hear "shame on you!" We feel like a failure and want to hide it. This was Jayson's experience while learning language.

Speechless and Ashamed

Our family moved to Central Asia in 2005. We committed our first year to learning the Russian language. We moved in with a local family, found language tutors and hit the books right away. I was determined to learn Russian. After just a few weeks in country I made a startling discovery—I could not talk, and that would not change soon! This created a crisis for my soul. How could I control what other people thought about me without knowing the language! For the first time since infancy, I could not use words to manipulate other people's perception of me. I worried that people might see me for who I really was—an adult who spoke like an infant. That unnerving prospect made me feel defenseless and naked.

According to Jeremiah 9:23 humans base their status on three things—their minds, their bodies or their possessions. God warns, "Do not let the wise boast in their wisdom, do not let the mighty boast in their might, do not let the wealthy boast in their wealth." My flesh succumbs to the first of these three. My heart boasts in being smarter than the average bear, or at least appearing to be so. In high school I enjoyed opportunities to argue with classmates and sought to prove teachers wrong.

As a young adult, I began realizing my argumentative words were destructive to other people, especially to my new bride. The word picture of Proverbs 12:18 explained my relationships: "Rash words are like sword thrusts, but the tongue of the wise brings healing." My acerbic tongue produced a battle scene filled with wounds and carnage. My speech was not a field hospital for healing and restoration. Behind this piercing tongue was a desire for face. Though I had confessed my sin and received God's forgiveness as a Christian, shame captured my imagination and behavior, and I was hardly aware of it.

During a season of reflection, God revealed a vivid image that has shaped my spirituality ever since. I saw a chisel fly into a rock and chip off a segment. Then another chisel came and carved off another chip, then another and another until the square stone became a perfectly sculpted bust of an attractive person. The chisels were my own words I used to craft a perfect image of myself for other people to see—insightful, witty, joyful, confident, circumspect and so on. I feared that people who knew me would begin to see inadequacies. So I covered them up with words. My technique in conversations was to carefully craft an image of an alternative Jayson that people would admire and respect. Considering the tremendous energy and time I invested in shaping this alternative Jayson, it was a functional idol. Because of the shame in my own heart, I worshiped the admiration of people more than the glory of God. But without knowing Russian, I was unable to serve this long-standing idol.

My language-learning scenario quickly snowballed out of control. Just three weeks in country, I was filled with anxiety. My heart would race and my palms sweat as I lay awake at night. The pressure to learn Russian became so great that it distracted me during my language lessons. I quickly lost hope of learning Russian, and dreaded an even worse reality—returning home to friends and churches in America as a failure, as a missionary too dumb to learn any Russian words. During the sleepless nights, I began scheming ways to return to America without ever having to see people; I would never show my face again. Though my thoughts were obviously irrational, the emotion of shame and its physiological consequences were painfully real. The sirens of shame drowned out common sense.

Fortunately my team leader sat me down and reminded me of two basic truths—learning any language takes time, and my language ability never changes my identity or worth. That year of full-time language learning proved to be one of the most spiritually fruitful seasons of my life. I learned to surrender my identity to God. Living without the language required me to hope only in God for honor, identity and acceptance. After God warns us to not boast in our wisdom, might or strength, he tells us what we should boast in. "But let those who boast boast in this, that they understand and know me, that I am the LORD" (Jer 9:24). Our relationship with God is the only basis for boasting, the only basis for claiming honor. Knowing God banishes shame, especially for people in ministry.

OVERCOMING "MINISTRY SHAME"

People in full-time Christian ministry encounter a unique type of shame. This "ministry shame" is not the result of any particular sin, but comes from unrealistic ministry expectations. People presume Christian leaders should be dynamically involved in evangelism, discipleship, prayer, study and counseling, all the while fostering a thriving family and spiritual vitality. American churches place missionaries on pedestals for being exceptionally spiritual since they go to minster in a foreign country.

But we each know our true self. We see in our own hearts the weaknesses, the doubts, the selfishness, the spiritual apathy. We are not nearly the person we are expected to be (and never will be!). In that very gap between expectations and reality, we develop a sense of shame for not being adequate. We feel deficient for "not being good enough." Regardless of what we know to be true, a gnawing sense of inadequacy controls our minds. We feel like we should be cut from God's team because there is something wrong with us. We feel spiritually defective because we lack a particular spiritual gift, do not pray enough or see only limited fruit in our lives. Moses also faced these sentiments of ministry shame.

In Exodus 3 God reveals his plans to Moses with great splendor and glory. God appears in the middle of the wilderness through a burning bush, reveals his divine name and promises to liberate Israel from Pharaoh with signs and wonders. After four hundred years of torturous slavery, the glory of God was about to be revealed in spectacular fashion. Moses, having suffered with his people, would surely celebrate the epic news of Yahweh's grand revelation in history.

But instead, Moses' response focuses on his own inadequacy. "But God, they might not believe me or listen to me." He fears his own people might reject and mock him because of his criminal record, so he seeks to avoid potential exposure and shame before his people. To assure Moses, God provides three signs to counter future doubts—turning the staff into a snake, healing his leprous hand and turning Nile water into blood (Ex 4:2-10). And how does Moses respond to these three assurances of God's power and presence? He again backpedals from God because of shame. "I have never been eloquent, neither in the past nor even now that you have spoken to your servant; but I am slow of speech and slow of tongue" (Ex 4:10). In other words—I am not adequate; I am not perfect; I am not worthy; others will not accept me. Moses' shame belittles God's power and demeans God's glory. God reminds Moses that he, as the Creator, gives mortals their speech. But yet for a third time, Moses dismisses the honor God is revealing and responds out of shame. He does not fabricate any excuses this time, but directly requests, "O my Lord, please send someone else" (Ex 4:13). Moses avoided God's calling to make his glory known in Egypt because he felt inadequate for the task. Shame silenced and sidelined Moses. This type of ministry shame made Moses reluctant to fulfill God's calling, and continues to do so today.

However common "ministry shame" may be, it is entirely false. The unrealistically high views and expectations of "professional" Christians are demoralizing. We are baited with pride of success, then trapped by the shame of failure. The invisible expectations of who we should be corrode our connection with God and his mission. John Piper, in "From Misplaced Shame to Mission Flame," exhorts,

> Shame tries to cancel your missions commitment in two ways. You can feel that you're not good enough for missions. Or we can feel that missions is not good enough for you. Shame for sin can keep you away, and shame for God can scare you away. You can feel crushed beneath the shame of sin, or you can feel comfortable above the shame of the cross. In either case shame wins and you lose.[8]

Shame is often Satan's scheme to deactivate God's people from mission by getting them to feel unqualified and unworthy of the calling.

A Healthy Sense of Shame

As destructive as shame can be, there are occasions when shame is helpful. One aspect of healthy Christian spirituality is discerning which instances of shame are appropriate. Christians should feel broken before God, humble toward others and ashamed of sin. We examine each of these.

An awareness of God's infinite glory rightly creates a sense of creaturely inadequacy and finiteness. When David gazed into the heavens filled with stars created by God's hand, he was amazed such a God would ever acknowledge specks of mortal dust like human beings, let alone crown us with glory and honor (Ps 8:3-5). He felt incredibly small, in a good way. Isaiah likewise immediately felt woeful and unclean when his eyes beheld God's full glory in the temple (Is 6:1-5). Unworthiness, or a desperate acknowledgement of our brokenness, before God is good and right. Prostrating before God's throne in worship will fill our future days in his presence.

Humility toward other people is another way Christians should think lowly of themselves. Jesus calls his followers to be servants of all (Lk 14:7-11). To honor and serve others inevitably requires humbling and lowering oneself. Paul tells the Philippians, "Do nothing from selfish ambition or conceit, but in humility regard others as better than yourselves. Let each of you look not to your own interests, but to the interests of others" (Phil 2:3-4). In this regard, Jesus is the ultimate example—he was the very form of God equal with the Father, yet became a slave who humbled himself to the point of death on a cross (Phil 2:5-8). Kingdom ethics call us to voluntarily un-dignify ourselves out of love toward others. This heart of service and edification grows out of humility.

The difference between humility and shame is rather subtle, so it is often blurred in human hearts. Humility is the righteous counterpart to shame. Humility flows from a heart filled with divine honor, whereas shame is the absence of any honor. In one sense humility involves purposely taking on unearned shame for a righteous purpose or willingly setting aside one's honor for a greater good, such as Jesus did in his incarnation, life and crucifixion. Shame, on the other hand, perverts humility, as it hardly leads to serving or exalting others.

Distinguishing between pride and honor can further align our hearts with God's values. Pride is the deep feeling of pleasure derived from one's own achievements, typically leading to an inflated hubris. Honor is recognition or esteem from others, based on how a person embodies moral ideals. Pride is self-declared; honor is granted.

The world equates humility with shame and pride with honor. But God inverts this social matrix. Pride ultimately produces shame, and humility is the counterintuitive path to genuine honor. "Before a downfall the heart is haughty, but humility comes before honor" (Prov 18:12 NIV).[9] Table 6.1 below compares cultural perspectives of humility and pride with kingdom values.

Table 6.1. Comparing perspectives of pride and humility

Human Culture		God's Kingdom	
Humility ——————⟶	Shame	Humility ⟶	Shame
Pride ——————⟶	Honor	Pride ⟶	Honor

Third, God's people should also sense shame for their sin. On several occasions, Paul tells the Corinthians, "I say this to your shame" (1 Cor 6:5; 15:34). It was right for the Corinthians to feel shame because their actions and beliefs dishonored God. In Ezekiel 43:10 God wants Israel to be "ashamed of their iniquities." John Piper says about these verses, "Well-placed shame (the kind you ought to have) is the shame we feel when there is good reason to feel it. Biblically that means we feel ashamed of something because our involvement in it was dishonoring to God. We ought to feel shame when we have a hand in bringing dishonor upon God by our attitudes or actions."[10] This sort of well-placed shame, much like guilt, can be used positively by God's Spirit to convict and correct us after sinning. Recall how God critiqued Israel for having no sense of shame for their sin.

> They acted shamefully, they committed abomination;
> yet they were not at all ashamed,
> they did not know how to blush. (Jer 6:15; 8:12)

Their conscience was numb to any sensation of shame, and that was a bad thing. To rectify this dysfunction in their heart, God said he would atone for their sins and restore the covenant *so that* Israel would remember her ways and be ashamed (Ezek 16:59-63). One aspect of God's salvation is a renewed sense of healthy shame.

It is good and right to feel unworthy before God, humble toward others and ashamed when sinning; to not sense shame in these instances would be truly "shameless." But sadly our primary experience of shame is entirely different. We instead feel inferior for wearing the wrong clothes to a Christmas party, possessing a unique body type or coming from "that" family. This is false, misplaced shame. We should not feel shame for these reasons, for none of them dishonor God's name. But in reality these instances of embarrassment or derision produce a false shame that influences our values and emotions far more than healthy shame. Therefore we need God's truth to recalibrate our view of shame.

A SPIRITUALITY FOR SHAME

The promises and love of God obliterate misplaced shame. Christians access God's grace for shame through his Word. We explore two biblical texts—Hebrews 12:2 and 2 Corinthians 2:14—for the devotional purpose of combating false shame with God's truth.

> Jesus . . . for the joy that was set before him endured the cross, despising the shame, and is seated at the right hand of the throne of God. (Heb 12:2 ESV)

Shame lurks about, waiting to debilitate and bury people. Like a terrorist, shame strikes fear by threatening to expose our vulnerabilities and remind us of our weaknesses. When shame terrorizes and taunts, our hearts fear what shame might do. Shame controls and defines us only when we live in fear of it. But the reality is that shame has no actual power over believers. It can only bluff as though it has the upper hand, but it has no legitimate right. A key strategy of overcoming shame is exposing and despising it. Despising shame means ignoring its threats. We shame shame as a despicable outsider with no place in our life. According to Hebrews 12:2, Jesus shamed shame. He had the boldness to disregard shame because it was ultimately inconsequential in God's plans.

Martin Luther King Jr. recounts an instructive story of how blacks exposed the Ku Klux Klan. This story exemplifies how people can despise shame by exposing its fecklessness and calling its bluff.

> Ordinarily, threats of Klan action were a signal to the Negroes to go into the houses, close the doors, pull the shades, or turn off the lights. Fearing death, they played dead. But this time they had prepared a surprise. When the Klan arrived—according to the newspapers "about forty carloads of robed and hooded members"—porch lights were on and doors open. As the Klan drove by, the Negroes behaved as though they were watching a circus parade. Concealing the effort it cost them, many walked about as usual; some simply watched from their steps; a few waved at the passing cars. After a few blocks, the Klan, nonplussed, turned off into a side street and disappeared into the night.[11]

Rooted in the identity and power of Christ, we ignore the taunts of shame and watch it disappear into the night, nonplussed.

Paul's words in 2 Corinthians 2 also redefine shame.

> But thanks be to God, who in Christ always leads us in triumphal procession, and through us spreads in every place the fragrance that comes from knowing him. (2 Cor 2:14)

God not only removes our shame but also transforms our shame into glory. His sovereign grace brings together our broken shards to form a beautiful mosaic. Shame and disgrace are tools for God's purposes. This message echoes throughout 2 Corinthians. When the apostle Paul forsook his honored status as a Pharisee to follow the crucified Messiah (2 Cor 11:22;

Phil 3:4-8), his life became a catalog of shame: poverty, imprisonments, beatings, hunger, homelessness, weaknesses, rejection, slander, shipwrecks and affliction (2 Cor 4:8-11; 6:8-10; 11:23-33). These trials degraded his status as God's messenger in the Corinthians' eyes. The Corinthians, in line with the ancient Greco-Roman honor code, further dismissed Paul and his message because of his unpolished oratory and disreputable vocation (i.e., he labored manually instead of accepting their patronage). Paul corrects their specious beliefs regarding shame on two fronts.

First, shameful circumstances are a reason to claim honor. "If I must boast, I will boast of the things that show my weakness" (2 Cor 11:30; cf. 2 Cor 12:9-10; 13:9). In a world where weakness is synonymous with shame, boasting in weakness magnifies God's grace. Paul praises God for the very afflictions that makes the Corinthians reject him, and even insists they be aware of them (2 Cor 1:3-8). This "shame-is-honorable" reasoning shines through 2 Corinthians 2:14—"But thanks be to God, who in Christ always leads us in triumphal procession, and through us spreads in every place the fragrance that comes from knowing him." The Greek verb *thriambeuō* ("to lead in triumph/triumphal procession") is a technical term that refers to the Roman tradition of triumphal procession.[12] The processions were lavish parades hosted in Rome to celebrate military victories. Spoils of war were paraded through the city, as the citizens cheered and Roman generals basked in the glory of victory. The defeated prisoners were dragged in chains before the conqueror's chariot to signal their utter humiliation, on their way to be offered as sacrifices of gratitude to the gods. Shockingly, Paul views himself as the defeated person being led in triumph, not the triumphant victor. In Paul's metaphor, he is a willing slave being shamefully led to death (2 Cor 1:9; 4:10; 6:9) and bringing glory to his master. In God's economy, shame is honorable. Christians boast in weakness.

Even more profoundly, shame is an instrument in God's mission. Disgrace was not a side element of Paul's ministry, but the very channel through which divine glory was manifested. The imagery of fragrance and aroma (2 Cor 2:15-16) reimages ministry in a world of power and glamour. Suffering and rejection are the redolent means by which people encounter the pleasing sacrifice of Christ crucified. The cross of Christ is not only the content of the gospel but also the christological pattern for Christian mission. As an extension of the cross, Paul understood his lifestyle of constant social disgrace as the very medium of God's salvific work.[13] Dying daily, both physically and socially, proclaims God's resurrection life in this age. The shameful afflictions of daily carrying the death of Jesus manifest the life of Jesus (2 Cor 4:10-12). The messenger's shame reveals the message's glory (2 Cor 3:1-11). This perspective on shame and suffering naturally derives from the humiliating crucifixion of Jesus. What is true of the Messiah becomes true of his people—they are raised from death to display the glorious power of God (2 Cor 1:5, 9). So Paul proclaims the redemptive benefits of ignominious afflictions, hoping the Corinthians' encounter with God's disgraceful apostles provides a whiff of the aroma of Christ—the divine image whose face radiates the very glory of God (2 Cor 4:4-5). Our shame proclaims God's glory.

Second Corinthians was not simply Paul's attempt to secure approval and acceptance as a leader. The letter defends God's very gospel, which the Corinthians are at risk of rejecting. If they dismiss Paul as shameful, that would demonstrate that the eyes of their heart were incapable of perceiving the glorious truth of Christ crucified. Our view of shame reflects the gospel we believe. God's transformation of shame into glory is an undismissible linchpin of Christian spirituality and mission.

ALIENATION BLOCKS COMMUNITY

As we begin to see the dynamic of shame and honor in God's salvation, it begins to bear fruit in various aspects of our lives. God's grace makes us different people, literally.

In 1992 I (Mark) transitioned from ministry in Honduras to doctoral studies at Duke University. To enter the world of a doctoral program at a major university is, like in many jobs and professions, to enter into a situation where one feels constant pressure to improve one's status among the scholars of the field. Those who have already achieved their degrees seek status by giving papers at conferences and publishing books and articles. Other scholars measure them not only by how much they have published but also by which publishers and journals publish their work. Not yet at that level, graduate students hope that impressing a renowned professor with a great paper will help them move off the bottom rungs as they begin to climb the academic ladder to success. On a day-to-day basis they feel the pressure to impress others by comments they make in seminars.[14]

In my first days in graduate school I was not so much reaching for a higher rung on the ladder as trying to figure out how to demonstrate to others that I was even on the ladder. In a variety of ways I perceived myself as being at the bottom of the group of first-year students. I longed to show that I could speak intelligently about theology, but I lived in fear of saying something that would confirm what I already felt—I was not really in the same league as the other students. Usually the fear of shame won out and I sat quietly in seminars.

One particular moment portrays well the way I felt and acted my first semester. It was midsemester and I had not said anything in one particular seminar. The professor mentioned something that reminded me of a certain theologian. Part of me wanted to seize this opportunity and demonstrate I was "well-read," but my shame-driven habit of silence seemed to push a mute button. I said the name in a whisper, but the professor, perhaps reading my lips, repeated the name and affirmed the connection.

In contrast to the seminar room the atmosphere at lunchtime in the student lounge was of course more relaxed. I talked with other students, but still there was a sense that I was hiding. At times I said some things as a way of covering up and at other times did not say things for fear of what they would think of me.

Then one day in a seminar the guest speaker said something that so disturbed me that I spoke out before the image-protecting part of me could hit the mute button. It was not a statement that was calculated to impress anyone; I simply reacted. Everyone remained silent after I spoke. I immediately assumed that what I had said was so dumb that people did not even know how to respond. To make matters worse all the theology professors attended this seminar. I wanted to crawl under the table. In a moment someone made another comment and the discussion went off in another direction.

After the seminar I went, not to the student lounge, but out into the parking lot—fleeing my shame. But I started praying. I thought about the cross and the extreme shame Jesus experienced. I continued praying with the confidence that God understood what I was feeling, and I sought to rest in God's love for me. That allowed me to be compassionate to myself, but also to reflect honestly about my drive to impress others and hide my perceived weaknesses. Why was I feeling ashamed? Was my academic reputation a false idol?

Those moments of prayer did not give me a permanent freedom from the pressures I felt. I was still reserved in most seminars, and I prayed similar prayers many times in the remaining three and a half years in graduate school, but one thing did change. Sensing God's love overcoming my shame, I felt enough security to begin speaking honestly with other students. As I told them how I felt, I was surprised to find that they experienced similar doubts and fears. In moments of vulnerability the suffering and scared part of me connected with the suffering and scared part of others, forming community and friendships of deep solidarity.

The contrasting image is a person who, in the words of Frederick Herzog, "seeks security in external things . . . [and] has built a wall between his true self and the pseudoself he displays."[15] Wearing masks and presenting a pseudoself means one is not in open relationship with others. It is a counterfeit community of one pseudoself talking to another pseudoself.

The context of my story, a graduate studies program in a renowned university, may be foreign to many readers of this book, but I am sure my experience of shame, the act of wearing masks and presenting a pseudoself is not foreign to most readers. It is certainly not unique to doctoral students.

Christian spirituality entails much more than a couple graduate students standing in the hall sharing their fears about seminars. But my experience demonstrates the link between a person experiencing peace with God, dropping his mask, and having richer relationships and more authentic community. As we come into God's family, we possess an honorable identity that leads to peace and reconciliation with other people. I have taped a quotation by church historian Roberta Bondi to my wall. She makes a clear connection between a person's resting in God's love and expressing love to others.

> Peace is a deep disposition of the heart. It is humility, an ability to let go of the need to be right in our own eyes or the eyes of others, an ability based on the knowledge that our rightness or wrongness in any issue is totally irrelevant to God's love for us or for our neighbor. The peace that comes with claiming our

self in God is the foundation of our ability to carry God's reconciling love to others in the most humble places and humble everyday ways.[16]

The flip side of Bondi's words is that if people are not secure in God's love then their alienation from God will lead them to live in ways that hurt others. Some people are so alienated from God and others that they respond to people around them with violence and abuse, or exploitation and manipulation to transfer their shame. Alienation leads other people to be very "good" and perform tremendous acts of charity and service to neighbors. But if these good deeds flow from a person's insecurity as a way to be noticed or gain approval, then the action itself will be tainted. Neither morality nor religion can cover up shame. The helper's need to be needed will get in the way of offering the help her neighbor needs most deeply. Paul would tell her she has gained nothing (1 Cor 13:3). He writes this not to communicate that her good actions fail to qualify her for merit points with God, but that they add nothing in relation to establishing honoring and loving relationships in an authentic community.

As we each experience God's saving love, we are honorably included in the people of God. In the security of this relationship we have the freedom to drop our masks and live as the vulnerable, finite humans that we are. That in turn provides freedom for a community of people to relate honestly and sincerely with each other. As we personally grow in God's shame-removing and honor-restoring love, God's honor extends into the lives of others through our relationships.

REFLECTION AND APPLICATION QUESTIONS

Eliminating shame is not a one-time task like changing a light bulb. Spiritual transformation is a lifelong process of molding our being into Christ and daily appropriating the honor he secured for us. To help readers along the journey into the shame-conquering honor of God, we invite you to take time to reflect on the role shame (and honor) play in your own heart.[17]

1. In what areas do you sense feelings of inadequacy, worthlessness, isolation or shame?

2. What about yourself do you hide from other people?

3. How did you feel while reading the various stories and ideas in this chapter?

4. When have you been deeply shamed by others' words or actions toward you?

5. Have you been abused or victimized? What feelings of shame are attached to those memories?

6. What aspects of your self-identity are based on comparison to other people?

7. How is your view of yourself influenced by false understandings of shame and honor?

8. What role does shame play in areas related to your sexuality (gender, marriage, body, sex, etc.)?

9. When you experience shame, how does your heart react?

10. What biblical stories or truths from chapters four and five affected you personally? How so?

11. How might grace, from both God and people, reshape your view of shame and yourself?

12. To live free of shame, what is a biblical truth (or verse) you could remember daily?

13. How might recognizing you are a beloved child of God reshape your relationships and actions?

7

RELATIONSHIPS

It takes effort to learn how to honor the dignity of others,
which significantly enhances the experience
of being in a relationship.

DONNA HICKS

Honor everyone.

1 PETER 2:17

*R*ELATIONSHIPS ARE CENTRAL TO MINISTRY. Yet as we recounted in chapters one through three, by operating according to the logic and values of our default culture we have often unknowingly sown hurt and alienation in honor-shame contexts. We interpreted our actions as positive, yet we inadvertently shamed people. Logical actions from one frame of reference can create barriers to relationships when interpreted from a different frame of reference. For example, not giving to avoid dependency or paternalism (the Western logic) can be interpreted as "no gift means no relationship" (the honor-shame logic). In this chapter we share some guidelines for relationships in honor-shame contexts. Recall how honor and shame function as the grammar of most cultures; this is how we "speak their language" relationally.

Learning to address problems and resolve conflict while maintaining relational harmony is crucial for living in honor-shame contexts, lest we irreparably burn bridges. The first three suggestions in this chapter—find a cover, reconcile symbolically and become a client—will aid in resolving conflict honorably. The final five suggestions—give gifts, be pure, guest well, be a patron and give face—will help to secure and strengthen relationships. Taken together these form our "Eight Commandments" of relationships in honor-shame societies.

It has become commonplace for leaders in business endeavors or military operations to be briefed on aspects of honor and shame. But Christians should not approach the topic simply as tips for gaining a hearing or influencing people. Such a utilitarian approach belittles people and their culture.[1] Without genuine love and humility our actions devolve into degrading self-interest and half-baked exploitation. This chapter does not present cultural gimmicks to manipulate circumstances or bend people to our will, but culturally meaningful avenues to form relationships that embody the gospel. Of course, in part what distinguishes this chapter from a crosscultural business book is that the ultimate goal is much different. God instructs his people to honor others. So we not only explore ways honor can be used to enhance relationships but also ask how we can honor others through our relationships.

Considering the dual realities that God is on mission to honor people, and that honor always comes through relationships, mediating God's honor relationally is a vital component of Christian witness. The reality is that people encounter the honor and glory of God through relationships with believers. Honoring relationships are at the heart of the gospel. Here we present relational ways to tangibly incarnate God's love and honor into cultures operating by honor and shame.

USE A COVER

David Augsburger recounts an incident involving a European physician working at an Indian hospital. The physician urgently needed lab results for an essential surgery, but the Indian technician in charge of the hospital laboratory was sick. So the European physician sent a servant to the lab technician's house to get the lab keys, but the lab technician refused to give the keys to a subordinate. So in anger, the physician walked to the technician's house, demanded the keys and ran the lab tests himself. He finished the surgery and forgot the whole incident until he noticed that his relationship with the lab tech was strained.[2] The Western physician had unknowingly dishonored the technician—twice. First by disregarding his work status by sending the servant for the keys and second by directly demanding the keys.

The physician may have been more successful, medically and relationally, by finding a cover. A cover is an indirect way of making a request so as to minimize conflict and avoid exposing others to potential shame. Instead of directly addressing the issue at hand, a cover reframes the problem to the person *while* addressing the issue. How could the doctor have received the keys *and* honored the lab technician at the same time?

One option would have been for the doctor to personally visit the sick technician at home, perhaps bringing a meal of some kind, and broach the issue like this: "Sir, I know you have many responsibilities at the lab and everybody depends on your work. We want to help you so you can rest and fully recover. If we could have the keys, maybe we could help you by doing some of the lab studies on your behalf. That way you could return without being behind in your work." An angry demand for the keys exposes short-comings, whereas a cover requests the keys while maintaining a relationship of honor. When people sense their shame is being exposed, they naturally become resistant and defensive. Exposure spoils the relationship and accomplishes little, but using a cover can avoid conflict altogether.

The objective is not merely to obtain the lab keys but also to leverage the situation to honor others. A cover regards the relational impact of our approach. The Western focus on efficiency and truth neglects relationships and people in times of conflict. "Speaking the truth in love" (Eph 4:15) is not merely confronting somebody in a polite voice, but appropriately honoring them in all our interactions.

There are many ways to resolve an issue without exposing the person to shame. Instead of asking someone, "Why are you late?" with an accusing tone of voice, simply ask, "Are you okay?" They are probably aware of the time, so mentioning their tardiness serves little purpose. Or when you must decline an invitation, consider using a "relational yes." Instead of directly saying no to their invite, you can choose to affirm the relationship with a polite euphemism for no, such as a simple "Oh, thank you!" These are basic ways to address issues without exposing people, an essential element of building relationships of trust in many cultures. Most importantly, pay attention to and learn from how non-Western people tactfully navigate thorny issues. Their social diplomacy is often quite admirable!

Some readers may feel discomfort employing such indirect communication. Using a cover to resolve a conflict may appear to lack integrity and honesty. Remember, the purpose of a cover is not to avoid the problem but to avoid unnecessarily shaming people and to preserve relationships while addressing the issue. Using a cover is hardly deceptive in Majority World cultures; everybody fully understands, and respects, the intention of your indirect request. If someone knows what you mean when communicating indirectly, it would hardly be deception or lying.

Our communication must keep one eye on the issue and one on the relationship. We must consider the relational impact of our communication. Paul instructs, "So far as it depends on you, live peaceably with all" (Rom 12:18). If you expose someone to shame, you will likely sever the relationship. And regardless of our intentions or convictions, we are responsible for the relational impact of our words on other people. Hebrews exhorts us to "make every effort to live in peace with everyone" (Heb 12:14 NIV). When our speech offends other people, our first response should be assessing *our* role in the conflict. Living peaceably with all depends on me, not them. If we prioritize relationships, we will accept other forms of communication to honor and value other people.

RECONCILE SYMBOLICALLY

After the above incident between the European physician and the Indian lab technician, their strained relationship became more and more obvious. Seeking reconciliation, the physician privately spoke with the technician. Desiring to make amends the doctor asked, "Is there a problem?" Even though the lab technician denied any problem, the relationship was never the same. Though the doctor had the right intentions and desires, his attempt to reconcile had limited effect because of how he tried to make amends.

To restore the relationship, the doctor could have sought ways to remove the technician's shame and repair lost face. People can reconcile damaged relationships with symbolic gestures that confer honor. For example, publicly praising the technician at the next staff meeting or inviting him to lunch would contribute to restoring the relationship more than verbally apologizing. Without mentioning the incident, these gestures address the problem of dishonor and symbolize a reconciled relationship.

Isfara's conversion from Islam to Jesus brought shame to her family. When her brother was at the mosque during Ramadan, certain men, burning with religious zeal, began discussing those who left Islam. Isfara's name came up, and the men told her brother that he must kill her, or they would kill him and his family. They insisted that the killing must be public as a warning to others; they suggested dragging her behind a horse through the village. So Isfara's brother called her with an ultimatum: convert back to Islam and marry a man they choose for her, or face a humiliating death. Her brother threatened to find her in the city and take her back to the village. A few months later Isfara's siblings called to invite her home for a meal. She feared it was a trap, but trusted her family anyhow. Her brothers and sisters hosted her to an elaborate dinner. They said nothing about Jesus or the death threats and had a good time dining together. Isfara understood the meal was their "olive branch" and reacceptance of her. The food symbolized reconciliation.

In the parable of the prodigal son, the father reconciles without verbalizing a word to his returned son, but through symbolic clothing and food. "The father said to his slaves, 'Quickly, bring out a robe—the best one—and put it on him; put a ring on his finger and sandals on his feet. And get the fatted calf and kill it, and let us eat and celebrate" (Lk 15:22-23). The entire village knew the father fully restored the son's family status with the robe, ring, sandals and feast.

In Central Asia, offended parties sometimes reconcile by purchasing and giving an article of clothing. In situations of reconciliation, symbolic actions often speak louder than words, so are often the best route for restoring a relationship.

Be a Client

Recall Alisher (chapter three), the neighborhood deputy who always announced to others my financial contributions to the neighborhood. Throughout his lifetime of public service, Alisher developed a wide network of influence and relationships that could rectify many problems. Over time, I learned how to position myself as a client under his patronage. Once he finished introducing me to others with grandiose words, I would declare all the ways he used his influence to help our team. Rather than deflect my praise, Alisher held his head up high and let me speak. This made me a grateful client who could count on his future help/patronage. So when it was time to sell our ministry building, I asked Alisher to help find a buyer. Before showing the building to each prospect he introduced me to, I purposefully recounted all the ways Alisher had helped the community. He was eager to help and live up to his role as a benefactor in the community. Of the dozen interested buyers, Alisher introduced us to all of them except two, and was glad for the opportunity to do so. Praising and thanking Alisher cultivated a "friendship" of mutual benefaction, thus inviting him to help us solve a problem.

Becoming a client may be another culturally relevant way to resolve a situation. This means creating a patron-client relationship, wherein you are the client requesting help from a patron. You deliberately put yourself under another person without whose help you would lose face. Becoming a client utilizes the social network and capital of your acquaintances to address a dilemma. Patrons are expected to help clients with their problems. In his book *Cross-Cultural Conflict* Duane Elmer explains how this works. "Generally, if one holds the power to keep another person from being shamed, that person is morally obligated to do something to keep shame from coming to the other. However if the person does not act to save another's honor, she or he is in danger of losing face and being shamed."[3]

Though it may seem counterintuitive for a "privileged Westerner" to function as a client in a "developing country," this works because notions of hospitality include assisting foreigners in their country. People relish the opportunity to help solve problems (especially with a foreign guest), for they acquire honor for themselves through the process; having a client brings honor to the patron. A patron relationship can be cultivated through thanks (as per the above story), or with a gift or direct appeal (as below).

Steve worked as a Christian aviator in a Latin American country where the government regulated the fuel supply. His station ran out of gas, and there was none available on the open market to purchase. Steve had a previously scheduled meeting with the official responsible for managing fuel in his region. During that meeting, he brought with him the largest cabbage from his personal garden at home. Steve respectfully presented the cabbage to the official, then in the course of the conversation mentioned his need for more gasoline. Steve's unique gift communicated respect and thanks for future patronage. A gift can position you as a client politely requesting assistance.

We (Jayson's family) wanted to put wall-to-wall carpet in our bedroom, but it was only sold in the capital city. Transporting a roll of carpet on the small plane to our city was an issue. When we arrived at the airport with our twenty-feet-long roll of carpet, the check-in attendants immediately balked. They stated that the excess cargo would prevent the plane from lifting off. The attendant, in a tone of fabricated concern, suggested fifty dollars might lighten the plane's load just enough to lift off. My mom was visiting at the time, so happened to be flying with us. I pointed her out in line, then leaned in quietly and said, "Please help me. My mom is visiting our country for the first time. She bought this carpet as a gift for us, and I will be embarrassed if we can't get it home. I am afraid she will be upset or think badly of our country. Can you help me?" Sensing the potential embarrassment, he agreed. A verbal appeal positioned me as a client in need of his benefaction (and spared me from explaining the airport's enigmatic policies to my mom). Asking for help to avoid embarrassment or shame invokes a patron-like obligation. Gifts, thanks and appeals can cultivate a client-patron relationship that can be beneficial for solving problems.

Obtaining services through relational channels does feel ethically questionable at times. Is it right to curry special relationships to gain special access? Certainly not in all instances. Human sin can turn systems of patronage into outright corruption. But patronage is not always negative. We suggest a balanced view of patronage-client exchanges. As I (Jayson) reflected on my experiences, I realized my initial objections to the structures of patronage often came more from my own pride and ethnocentrism—I assumed my cultural system for exchanging goods and services was superior, and that their system of patronage must be reformed.

Over time I realized patronage simply uses honor as a form of payment instead of cash. Is it wrong to use a different currency to buy something (assuming, of course, justice is not perverted and no one is harmed)? Usually not. Having come to appreciate the nuances of patron-client systems, I now feel rather callous during many economic exchanges in America—I give the cashier money and take the items without any sort of relationship. That may be legal, but not nearly as honoring. Rules and laws ensure equality and predictability, but can dehumanize and minimize interaction. In contrast, patron-client systems foster relationships and community—you have to know people to get things. Becoming a client requires setting aside Western ideals of self-sufficiency and humbly depending on other people for help.

Yes, patron-client systems can be time-consuming, frustrating and even outright corrupt—we know from years of personal experiences. Yet we believe there is a missional upside to a balanced view of the system. Becoming a client can be a way to communicate honor and form relationships in many cultures of the world.

EXCURSUS: ADHERE TO CULTURE OR TRANSFORM CULTURE?

Some aspects of honor-shame cultures fail to represent God's ideals. Because of this, navigating relationships and situations in those fallen areas is stressful and challenging, especially for cultural outsiders. How should Christians engage the honor-shame elements of culture?

For example, reciprocity is a key concept in honor-shame contexts. Reciprocity is a type of social debt—if I give you something, then you must repay to avoid shame. For instance, reciprocity is expected when hospitality is offered. That is one reason hospitality generally flows between people of similar status. A person of high status and means would not invite a poor person of low status to a meal, not only because the presence of a low-status person at the table would reflect poorly on the host, but also to avoid shaming the person. The invitation would put the low-status person in the awkward position of being obligated to reciprocate but being unable to do so. Yet Jesus advocated practicing hospitality without a focus on reciprocity.

> When you give a luncheon or a dinner, do not invite your friends or your brothers or your relatives or rich neighbors, in case they may invite you in return, and you would be repaid. But when you give a banquet, invite the poor,

the crippled, the lame, and the blind. And you will be blessed, because they cannot repay you, for you will be repaid at the resurrection of the righteous. (Lk 14:12-14)

When does a missionary in an honor-shame context disregard, follow or transform the norms of the culture? This is an important question to reflect on in relation to the guidelines of this chapter. We will take a brief step aside from describing the guidelines to share our perspective.

There are three general approaches to engaging culture in regard to the sort of issues addressed in this chapter.

1. Ignore the host culture (defaults to ethnocentrism).

2. Learn the host culture to facilitate communication and relationships.

3. Learn the host culture to transform it and engage people redemptively.

The negative examples in this chapter, and other places in the book, reflect the first position. Whether out of ignorance or knowing rejection, the person in the first category lives according to Western values and practices. The second approach leverages the patterns built into honor-shame societies to foster relationships. Knowing how to function in relationships on their terms is foundational, but is not the complete picture.

Approach three recognizes that God calls Christians at times to go beyond the calculus of the cultural systems in order to honor people as God intends. Christians must not only know how to navigate relationships honorably but also be someone who is generous in honor and respect in all circumstances. Jesus calls us to model a type of honor that extends beyond the cultural system. The kingdom of God rooted in God's radical grace transforms the cultural systems of honor and shame.

Approach three does not reject the honor-shame paradigm; it works within it to transform aspects of it. Therefore, you cannot skip from approach one to approach three. You have to learn the culture (approach two) before you know when to go beyond the culture (approach three). We must underscore that it is not just breaking the rules as an uninformed person would (approach one). We still operate within the realm of honor and shame in order to communicate a greater honor rooted in an ethic of the kingdom.

Jesus' example of table fellowship illustrates approach three. In chapter five we noted Jesus' table ethic with the sinful women (Lk 7) and the sinners

(Lk 15). Jesus did not categorically reject the cultural systems of hospitality and table fellowship by boycotting all meals (approach one) just because of how the Pharisees abused the structure to falsely honor themselves and inappropriately shame others. Rather, Jesus honored the Pharisees by eating with them (approach two), then went beyond the cultural games to reveal the kingdom by welcoming those who were not invited (approach three).

If you choose to purposefully break the social rules to bear witness to kingdom values (approach three), it is important to explain your actions. If you purposefully do something "countercultural" to communicate kingdom values but do not verbally explain the action, then people will think you are a clueless foreigner (at best) or a disrespectful and shameful person. Westerners assume that a countercultural action alone will automatically convict people of their false honor systems and attract them to Jesus. But it rarely works that way; actions intended to be "countercultural" get interpreted by the default honor code as "wrong" or "shameful." One must seek the opportunity to explain, "We do this because Jesus . . ." This pattern of "action-plus-explanation" follows Jesus' example when he associated with the sinful woman (Lk 7) and the sinners and tax collectors (Lk 15). This verbal explanation is one of the main things that separates approach one from approach three (at least in the eyes of nationals perceiving our actions) and further bears witness to God's true kingdom honor and challenges people to rethink their honor code.

Learning to engage culture with approach two is not merely a stepping-stone to approach three. Approach two is itself a part of kingdom relationships in many positive ways, so should not be left behind. The examples of this chapter focus mostly on the second approach, but we will occasionally bring in some examples of the third approach as they relate to other aspects of relationships in honor-shame cultures. (Chapter eleven will explore the third approach in more depth.)

Guest Well

One Sunday morning at a church service in the United States an Anglo-American pastor was teaching about humility from Philippians 2:1-5. To illustrate how we must "look to the interest of others, and not just ourselves," he recounted a personal story of visiting a house fellowship of Japanese

American Christians. As he was an older pastor, the group of Japanese Americans invited him for encouragement and teaching. Upon arrival, he entered the house and removed his shoes. But in the entryway only one pair of slippers remained, and they were pink ladies' slippers. When a younger, Japanese American host saw the problem, he offered his own slippers to the guest. But the pastor humbly refused to accept the host's slippers and wore the pink slippers the entire evening, believing this action "looked to the interests of others."

When he finished the sermon illustration, my (Jayson's) wife turned to me with wide eyes saying, "Oh, no! He did the exact opposite of what he intended." The Japanese American hosts likely felt embarrassment and shame anxiety that evening as their older, honored guest was wearing pink slippers. The pastor undoubtedly had the right intentions, but actually disgraced others by not allowing them to be good hosts. One of the greatest sources of shame people face is not hosting well.

It may seem counterintuitive, but receiving honor as a guest is an important way to honor people. Westerners have strong reservations about receiving special treatment. Insisting on Western expressions of humility—not taking anything or showing any need—prevents hosts from fulfilling their obligations. When hosts are unable to provide for guests, they sense shame. Not receiving hospitality indicates the host has nothing of value to offer you and suggests they are socially inferior. A great way to honor others is to receive their honor. For that indicates they possess an honor to grant, which makes them feel secure and equal in the relationship.

Receiving honor is only half of guesting well; the other half involves reciprocating appropriate honor to your host. Be incredibly grateful; lavish thanks on them for their generosity and hospitality. Say it many times, until you think you are being annoying! Tell them it was incredible; eat lots. Being a good host does not mean demanding and hoarding honor, but facilitating the flow of honor in all directions. The goal is mutual honor. This involves thankfully receiving the host's honor.

Playing the part of a good guest occurs not just in homes, but in any social context where you are the outsider. If you are an expatriate living in a foreign country, people will generally treat you as a guest even in public interactions. So the strategy of guesting well includes receiving honor in a variety of socially appropriate ways, such as honorific titles. Since the hierarchical aspects of many cultures contradict Western egalitarianism, Westerners often seek to sidestep honorific titles, thinking it will help the relationship— "Oh, just call me Joe! We're buddies!" But rejecting honorifics creates relational confusion and face anxiety, as members of the host culture are unsure what social role is most appropriate for the relationship. When the efforts of Majority World people to communicate honor encounter your firewall, they are socially insecure and unsure how to relate. Being a good guest in all cultural contexts can help grant honor and build relationships.

SHARE GIFTS

Our family owned a Soviet-era apartment in Central Asia. When our American teammates agreed to buy it, I assumed the transaction would be simple. But two weeks before we left the country I learned that I needed to get a document affirming there were no liens against the property before transferring the title. Getting documents from government officials often feels like walking into a den of hungry lions. My standard approach was to play hardball with the clerks, but my confronting, demanding and arguing accomplished little.

With all the packing and farewells to leave the country in two weeks, I lacked the emotional margin for a logistical hassle. So I prayed for wisdom. The next day, a local Christian told me how his organization's administrator navigated bureaucratic channels—before any official meeting, he would simply present a chocolate bar and say, "Here, this is for your tea break." So I hatched a plan.

I went to a local market and purchased a chocolate bar with fancy wrapping, knowing packaging and presentation were significant. At the government office I submitted a request for the title document. The official's terse "return next week" gave me little confidence the document would be prepared in time. I wanted to pull the chocolate bar out of my bag as a thank-you gesture, but my conscience rattled me as though it were an illegal drug deal. My heart raced with nervousness. I looked around to confirm there were no video cameras, then quietly placed the chocolate bar on the table and discretely whispered, "This is for your tea."

I thought the transaction was just between us two. He took the chocolate bar, smiled at me, then announced to coworkers, "Everybody, look at what this guy gave me!" He thanked me lavishly and publicly. (He obviously knew how the culture worked!) My heart sank. I was afraid that others would accuse me of bribery and corruption for giving a chocolate bar, but the opposite took place. The colleagues came over in jolly spirits to greet me and admired the fine chocolate. (When they offered me a piece of the chocolate, I found it rather unpleasant tasting. But fortunately, the interaction depended on the status conferred by the chocolate more than its actual flavor!)

Amid the celebratory work break, the government official voluntarily called his superior in the back office to get immediate approval. "Come back in two days!" Such customer service shocked me; the motto in post-Soviet countries tends to be "the customer is always *wrong*." When I returned in two days, there was a long line for receiving documents. I made eye contact with the previous official, and he promptly walked over to retrieve the document for me. I walked out of the office amazed, thinking, *I have lived here nine years, and just now figured out how to navigate the bureaucracy!*

My gift to the official publicly implied, "You are somebody worthy of respect. I choose to recognize your power and prestige. Now could you please show your authority by helping me?" Where institutions and governments are unreliable, people barter honor to form relationships and access new networks of influence. A gift overcomes the dehumanizing commodification of anonymous transactions in our modern world. Gifts assert a person's unique worth. (One must be cautious not to conflate gifts and bribes. A gift seeks to relationally honor people with customary presents, whereas bribes manipulate a person to pervert justice through abnormal contributions.)

Remember that gifts are symbolic—the point is the relationship and the social exchange, not the actual object. So give gifts of symbolic value. Whether it is with a new refugee family at your church, your ESL students or neighbors in your apartment building, gifts are a great way to foster relationships crossculturally. Part of gift giving also includes graciously receiving gifts, even in moments when the gift appears too excessive and grandiose in light of the giver's modest income.

Honoring people with a gift for their accomplishments or to form a relationship is fine and appropriate. But Christians must realize that people merit honor because they are created in the image of God, not for what they can do. There is a place for simply honoring people because they are present with us. People's presence, as a reflection of God's presence through the *imago Dei*, is something to be honored in its own right.[4] This is where Christ's followers can go beyond the normal rules of gift exchange and bear witness to the reality of God's kingdom.

Gifting in honor-shame cultures can establish a variety of relational models, so it is important to know what a gift means. A gift to a superior functions as a client's thanks to a benefactor. If the recipient is a social equal, a gift reaffirms your common group membership and peer relationship. But giving a gift to a person unable to repay establishes you as a patron helping a client, and may even create an overwhelming sense of obligation to repay. In some instances it may be better to not give gifts because people are so calculated about keeping things balanced. For example, I (Mark) have temporarily stopped giving oranges from our tree to the Mexican family next door, because every time I do they appear to feel obligated to give something in return. (But the Mexican/Salvadorans on the other side do not.) The same gift can carry different significance in different contexts. By properly understanding these social undercurrents, a Christian worker committed to stewarding their resources can use gifts to appropriately honor people of all classes.

Be a Patron

Brian and his family were Americans called to ministry in Africa. As their family integrated into local life, their African friends began asking for material help. Each story had a unique reason, but they typically ended with an appeal for money. As their relational network grew, more and more people asked for material assistance. Though Brian always desired to help, the persistent requests became exhausting—emotionally, financially and relationally. He even began to notice physiological effects whenever he heard a knock at the gate; he dreaded the encounters. Years of financial requests created unbearable levels of stress and anxiety.

Brian's situation is hardly unique. Many Westerners find themselves caught in systems of patronage, and are never quite sure how to navigate the financial requests and relationships. Westerners are viewed as potential patrons from the moment they arrive, whether they realize it or not.[5] Their wealth and status makes them the new "Big Man" from whom people come to expect things. This new role leads to relational confusion, tension and stress in relationships with locals. I (Jayson) recall feeling used when people asked for money, so would get resentful and angry toward them. From within my Western schema, I never considered the requests for money as opportunities for deeper relationships and mutual honor. Since patronage is the primary structure of relationships and economics in Majority World cultures, one must understand the mechanics of the patronage systems.

Social etiquette prescribes a protocol for potential clients seeking benefaction. To prepare the way for a positive response from the patron, clients must pay their respects to a patron by visiting and offering token gifts. This allows time for both sides to properly vet each other, sort of like dating. After an acceptable period of paying respects, the potential client asks for material help. A contribution from the patron formalizes a long-term patron-client relationship.[6] This is the patron-client dance. So, if someone offers you a gift, expect a relational opportunity (i.e., patronage) to follow! Granting every request is not recommended, even if feasible. Christians are never obligated to fulfill expectations of patronage, but we are freed from sin to serve others through socially accepted channels of honors such as generous patronage.

Being a patron is not just handing out gifts like Santa Claus. Patronage involves fulfilling a multifaceted social role. Patrons are expected to do many things: adjudicate community problems, lead conversations, initiate relationships, host large events, as well as pedestrian things like dressing respectfully and sitting at the correct seat at a meal. A patron is not a sugar daddy, but a respected person in the community who acts accordingly.

Tim was an American missionary who founded a business-development center. After the staff Christmas celebration at the business center, everybody began cleaning up the dining room by clearing the tables and putting everything away. Wanting to help out, Tim grabbed the sponge and began washing the dishes. Upon seeing him, the cook employed at the business center gasped in horror and demanded he stop. Surprised by the cook's forcefulness and shock, Tim handed over the sponge and stepped aside.

Tim intended to communicate appreciation by helping with the dishes, but his actions were viewed quite differently. For the boss/patron to do manual labor suggested she had failed at work; she felt quite embarrassed that Tim had to do her job. In hindsight, Tim realized he could have shown his appreciation and honored her through the honor-shame dynamic of patronage. For example, noting her diligent work before colleagues or hiring a taxi to drive her home that night might have better communicated appreciation and honor to her. Patronage means using the role of respected leader who blesses and benefits other people.

The story above invites the question: Would it be sufficient for Tim to adopt the cultural systems (approach two) to communicate honor? Or does the kingdom of God point to something else, to a particular focus on honoring the person in ways beyond the cultural system (approach three)? Jesus' example of washing the disciples' feet seems instructive here (Jn 13:3-20). At that time foot-washing was a task reserved for non-Jewish slaves, not a respected teacher such as Jesus. It was shameful and humbling to wash another person's feet. For Peter the thought of Jesus washing his feet was unacceptable. "You shall never wash my feet." Being fully aware of those social dynamics, Jesus washed their feet to demonstrate his love and set an example of servanthood. Jesus even told them, "What I am doing you do not understand now" (Jn 13:7; cf. Jn 13:12), but Jesus nevertheless instructed the disciples to follow his example of washing one another's feet. How does such kingdom humility and servanthood properly translate in contemporary situations? There is no simple universal answer, but we think it is important to ask. Sometimes it means choosing approach two, other times choosing approach three. Tim's situation, at the least, points to the need of some verbal explanation, rather than simply assuming that an honor-shame native will interpret the action positively through a Western, egalitarian framework.

Approach three does not necessarily mean rejecting the patron-client dynamic, but it can mean being a different kind of patron. To employ household help is to enter a type of patron-client relationship. In Honduras the patron is expected to provide a meal for the worker. Generally hired people ate in the kitchen or on the back steps. My (Mark's) family fulfilled this expectation of a meal, but we purposefully invited the maid or gardener to join us at the family table at mealtime. We continued in a patron-client relationship, but

through subversive table fellowship we also cultivated deep friendships that
continue to this day.

Antonio was a Honduran friend and partner in ministry. Through participating in various workshops and experimentation on his own small
farm, he had become a gifted community-development worker in the area
of sustainable agriculture—something I knew next to nothing about. We
lent and gave him money at various points. He clearly felt indebted to us in
a patron-client way. I did not openly reject his comments or actions that
treated me as patron. I did, however, intentionally seek ways to level the
relationship by treating him as my gardening consultant. Every time he
would visit, I would take him to look at my compost pile and garden. I asked
him for direction and advice. I always thanked him and underlined that any
success in the garden was due to his guidance. When we visited him I would
always ask for a tour of his farm and inquire about new methods. I told him
he was my teacher and sought to take the posture of student, as a different
kind of patron.

Jesus called his followers to go beyond patron-client reciprocity. One way
to do this is to transform the aim of patronage. The world uses social capital
from patronage to promote their own honor (e.g., build public monuments
in their name, or leverage it for political gain). But Christians should cre-
atively use patronage for authentic relationships and kingdom purposes.
Sharing financial resources and meeting materials needs cultivates relationships for God's glory. Benefaction is stewarding God's finances for God's
purposes. Instead of receiving the praise and honor for themselves, Christian
patrons should direct clients' loyalties to Jesus so his name is honored as the
ultimate Patron.

Paul illustrates this very approach in Philippians 4. Recall the situation:
the Philippians provided a generous financial gift to Paul's ministry. Paul
acknowledges their exceptional generosity (Phil 4:10, 14-15), but clearly
qualifies his gratitude in order to reframe the relationship (Phil 4:11-13). Paul
transforms the paradigm of patronage by bringing a third party into the
picture—namely, God. This effectively counters any temptation the Philippians may have to position themselves as patrons who deserve "repayment"
from Paul. Philippians 4:17-20 directs the Philippians toward a God-centered
view of patronage in four ways. First, the return for the Philippians' gift is

not Paul's clientage but the spiritual fruit God credits to their account. Giving involves its own spiritual reward (Phil 4:17), which happens to be far greater than any Paul could repay. Second, their gift was not simply a financial contribution to Paul, but "a fragrant offering, a sacrifice acceptable and pleasing to God" (Phil 4:18). The Philippians were giving to God, not Paul. Third, the Philippians were not big-shot patrons distributing largesse, but were themselves recipients of God's benefaction "according to his riches in glory in Christ Jesus" (Phil 4:19). The Philippians were kindly thanked as mediators of God's provision, not praised as the original source of the gift. And fourth, all the praise and glory from the financial transaction belongs to God (Phil 4:20). For he, and not the Philippians, is the ultimate patron who deserves all the praise. Paul demonstrates how true patronage among Christians should be radically God centered. All benefactions begin with God's provision and end with God's glory. Such a reframing of the financial transaction does not dismiss the patronal qualities of the relationship, but rightly locates it in the broader context of God's purposes.

A key part of functioning as a patron is learning to accept various forms of repayment from clients. Instead of expecting people to repay financially, we must consider the assets they can offer. After several years in Central Asia I realized people were unlikely to repay a loan financially, but they could repay me in other ways. After I gave Erkin (a skilled handyman) an old computer to practice his English, I called him to fix a broken pipe in the basement of our apartment building. Upon completion, I asked him how much his services cost. He said, "If all your neighbors are paying together, the rate is thirty dollars. But if only you are paying then it is nothing; I owe you." Erkin was glad to repay me with his time and talents. Along the same vein, the greatest asset people in collectivistic societies possess is their network of acquaintances. If you are traveling to a new town, ask one of your "borrowers" if they have a relative in that town who could help you. Even if they do not know of a relative there, they will likely find someone to meet you. Granting you access to their social web expresses their thanks and loyalty for your patronage.

Westerners must recognize the nonmaterial assets people do possess—wealth is not just financial in nature. If you find yourself to be the patron, ask the question—what could this person offer to others (or to the kingdom)? In the context of a relationship, this question dignifies by affirming the innate assets and abilities people do possess. This may involve opening ways for people to repay you. Edgardo was a very poor Honduran. When crisis came he would ask us to borrow money, but there was little hope of his paying it back. We suggested that Edgardo wash our car as a form of repayment. Any time he came to our house we would let him wash the car. (In those years the car got washed much more than normal!) The point was not having a clean car, but affirming Edgardo's dignity. He had something to offer to the relationship. (Of note, years later when Edgardo finally got a good job, he borrowed a much greater amount of money from us to start building a house. He paid it all back, borrowed again twice more and paid it all back again.)

Patronage is also vital in discipleship relationships with Christians. When you enter patron-client relationships by helping people materially, they become more open to your spiritual influence. Patronage creates access into people's lives. This allows Christian patrons to instruct and mentor other believers. Christian clients become the patron's spiritual "children" (see 1 Cor 4:14). Patronage offers a framework for transmitting values to disciples in many non-Western societies. It is the "indigenous style of discipleship practiced naturally by many national leaders."[7]

Danyar was a young Christian whom I (Jayson) thought I was discipling. We would meet weekly over tea to read the Bible and pray together. He was happy to read the Bible, but subtle mentions of financial needs gave me the impression he was more interested in material things than spiritual things. After several weeks of our meeting together, Danyar asked for a significant amount of money to pay his college tuition. Feeling uncomfortable mixing money with discipleship, I declined the request and suggested he rely on family for the money. After that conversation he stopped appearing for our weekly discipleship meetings. At the time this confirmed my suspicions about Danyar's insincere motives; I thought, *He really was only interested in my money.* In hindsight I realize my actions likely surprised Danyar. He probably walked away wondering, *I thought we agreed to be friends. Why is he reneging on our relationship now? If he purposefully shamed me like that, I guess Jayson does not want to associate with me any more.* Being naively unaware of patron-client dynamics affected my discipleship relationship with Danyar.

There are certainly potential dangers of mixing patronage with discipleship. Without an actual relationship between people, the system can easily produce "rice Christians"—people jumping through the patron's "Christian" hoops for material rewards. This unhelpful dependency undermines mutual dignity. Another legitimate concern about patronage is the typically low level of accountability. Clients often feel obliged to overlook sins or malpractices to preserve the patron's image and maintain access to resources. Patronage is a structure for relationships, but never an excuse to skirt problems.

These common issues often cause Westerners to dimly associate patronage with corruption and abuse. Patronage should not be rejected as a deplorable system of dependence, but an acceptable model of interdependence (which, like all social systems, gets warped by sin). Jesus said, "The kings of the Gentiles lord it over them; and those in authority over them are called benefactors. But not so with you" (Lk 22:25-26). These words do not condemn patronage in its entirety, but the self-promoting abuses. The patronal system of that day flowed down from the Roman emperor; Jesus pointed toward a transformed patronal system that flowed from the ultimate patron—God as merciful Father.

The Bible tells us about several good patrons. God functioned as a patron toward Israel. As discussed in chapter four, the covenant at Sinai established a suzerain-vassal (i.e., patron-client) relationship between Yahweh and his people. Jesus' ministry was also benefaction.[8] One of Peter's sermons in Acts summarizes Jesus' life like this: "He went about doing good and healing" (Acts 10:38). The word for "doing good" (Greek *euergeteō*) was commonly used in Greco-Roman inscriptions for public benefactors. In fact, the Greek word for "savior"—a common New Testament title for Jesus—was synonymous with "benefactor" in the ancient world.[9] And in the early church, key Gentile leaders served as patrons by opening their large homes for gatherings and financing Paul's ministry (e.g., Rom 16:2). Paul and Peter even encouraged affluent Christians to benefact by promising them public recognition (Rom 13:3; 1 Pet 2:14).[10] Multiple figures in the Bible, including Yahweh and Jesus, utilized patronage systems to mediate salvation to the world, and this practice was advocated by the apostles. Serving as a patron can sometimes (not always) be a means to exemplify God's kingdom. These social dynamics are essential for properly using one's influence and resources for God's purposes in honor-shame contexts.

BE PURE

Oscar ministered to Asian refugees in America. One day he ran across the street of his apartment complex without putting shoes on to visit a Nepali neighbor. The host was dismayed. He glanced at Oscar's feet and said in broken English, "You are shameful. You cannot come in." Oscar realized walking barefoot was unclean, so he wisely began wearing shoes. Disregarding purity concerns risks shaming you and others, so is a significant area of consideration for our relationships.

Purity matters, particularly in Muslim and Hindu contexts. Society often defines people (and their message) based on their personal cleanliness. Christians in ministry must account for this cultural reality. Your appearance reveals the value of your message, so present yourself accordingly. Collectivistic cultures think holistically, so do not separate the message from the messenger. A Muslim student group in Jayson's city tried to discredit Christianity by telling fellow students that Christians wore dirty shoes. In their minds the logic was simple—because they do not clean their shoes, Christians are dirty people and unclean in God's eyes; therefore, Muslims should not associate with such dishonorable people lest they risk becoming defiled themselves. This cultural logic associated cleanness with truthfulness. Western culture rarely makes this connection, but the link between cleanliness and godliness is notable in purity-observant cultures.

Americans commonly observe the *public* filth in other counties: trash, smog, roaming animals, dirt floors and so on. Ironically, Americans' *personal* uncleanliness often surprises people in the Majority World. They reason, "If they are from a rich country with big homes and fancy cars, why do they wear T-shirts and old jeans? Are they homeless?" Paul Hiebert says Westerners need to learn to understand how other cultures see purity and pollution, and to reexamine their beliefs of "clean" and "dirty" to be more culturally sensitive. This typically means combing your hair, not sitting on the ground, dressing decently and washing your hands before meals.[11] The point is not to behave like pompous royalty, but to carry yourself respectfully. It may also be prudent to abstain from "unclean foods," as defined by the host culture. For example, Christians in Muslim contexts often refrain from pork for the sake of gospel witness.

Personally observing cultural purity rules can be important for relationships and ministry (approach two), but Christians can point to an even deeper level of purity and cleanness. My (Jayson's) wife hosted a gathering for Christian ladies. Kulfuza, a new believer, was asked to share her Christian testimony. As she recounted her conversion story, she specifically praised God for the newfound ability to ride public transportation without judging people based on the cleanliness of their shoes. For her, only a miraculous regeneration of her heart could override the cultural circuitry equating dusty shoes with dishonorable people! As God's Spirit cleansed her heart as a Christian, she was able to look beyond the surface-level dirt into matters of the heart to see people as God sees them.

The question of whether Christians should observe purity regulations of other religions is controversial. We do not pretend to resolve the issue here, but only suggest a greater awareness of the honor-shame dynamics associated with purity practices. To categorically reject all the purity codes of one's pre-Christian religion could turn Christian converts into social lepers. Violating social taboos risks dishonoring cultural identities and alienating Christians from their birth community.

A contextualization model that strives to honor people *and* honor God seems wise and biblical. For example, Jesus grew "in *charis* [i.e., favor, grace] with God and man" (Lk 2:52 NIV; cf. Prov 3:3-4). Paul took pains "to do what is *kalos* [i.e., beautiful, proper, good], not only in the eyes of the Lord but also in the eyes of man" (2 Cor 8:21 NIV). One missionary emphasizes, "If Christians living in Southeast Asia are going to faithfully honor God, they will need to understand how to live honorably in their local community."[12]

Navigating the tensions is rarely easy. Even the earlier church struggled to define acceptable purity lines. The first church in Jerusalem needed over a decade to work out acceptable dietary and circumcision practices for Gentile Christians (Acts 11–15). The process of defining what purity codes are acceptable for Christians to practice should follow this biblical rubric— it honors God (Rom 14:6) and honors people (by not distancing them from community, cf. Rom 14:13-21). For example, a church-planting team working among observant Muslims decided to offer containers of water for people to perform ablutions before prayer, but clearly taught that such ablutions were not "a meritorious requirement in Christianity."[13] This maintained the balance of not dishonoring or defiling people in their cultural milieu, while also honoring God as ultimate source of ultimate purity and cleanliness.

Regardless of Christians' convictions about contextualization, we must never conflate ritual purity with spiritual purity. The only thing making someone pure and clean before God is being in Christ. God declares all believers in Jesus clean (Acts 10:28). Only Jesus—the Holy One of Israel—makes a person pure. Observing social purity codes never affects one's standing before God, but it can eliminate potential stumbling blocks in our witness of the gospel.

Give Face

We were having visa problems, so I (Jayson) went with our administrator to the department of migration for an official meeting. As we talked with the government official our administrator noticed one of her former students interning in the office. To score a few social points, she pointed out, "Oh, I taught her. I bet she does a great job for you!" The official's next words were shocking to me. With the intern sitting nearby, the official went off in a loud, overbearing tone, "Her? She is awful! She can't even write her name! She doesn't even know how to use the copy machine, and it only has one button! She doesn't know anything!"

What provoked such a harsh outburst? Many interactions in honor-shame cultures function like gladiatorial contests for securing and displaying honor. People engage in matches of verbal jousting to win honor. When a person's status is threatened, they must respond to defend their honor. In this situation the government official maintained her social precedence by making it public how she did not benefit from us. She was the superior in the relationship, and we were dependent on her for favor. Such "challenge-response" interactions highlight a feature of honor-shame cultures—communication is about face, not just facts. The goal is not to efficiently relay information or complete a task, but to procure status.

When Westerners understand how status or face is the goal, they can better interpret social interactions that otherwise confound. These include public fistfights, tit-for-tat blood revenge, politicians humiliating inferiors on national television or Christian pastors outlining all their spiritual qualifications during an introduction. Reflect on an incident or two that seemed strange or confusing—do you think face played a role in it? Recognizing the social dynamic of face is important for understanding culture, but also engaging people. Christians can also be intentional to communicate face in personal interactions with people. We mention three examples of "giving face."

When Jayson's team finally found a buyer to purchase our building, we made a startling discovery. The title documents we had for the building were bogus. A government worker had given us unregistered documents and kept all the money. Through a long process, our friend Erkant sacrificed greatly to help us resolve the problem and retain the building. We wanted to thank him appropriately, so deliberately considered how to communicate honor. At the farewell banquet for all of the business's employees, we called Erkant up to the front. Before everyone, I commented on his strength (he was a competitive bodybuilder), highlighted his fruitful ministry, noted his sacrificial help, thanked him for being our "roof" (the slang term for patron), then presented him with a gift. As we presented the gift from the newest store in town, everyone oohed and aahed. We tried to communicate more than appreciation; we purposefully honored his generosity and friendship. Whether in formal meetings in an office or casual conversations on the street, intentionally communicating face goes a long way.

Sam was an American missionary teaching at a Bible college in Haiti. One day a local student came into his yard looking quite sick. When Sam asked what happened, the young man recounted how he felt disrespected by another missionary. His disgrace was visibly palpable as he said, "I can go three days without food, but without respect, I can't live." In that moment, Sam prayed with the Haitian student and shared how Jesus restores his honor. His face went from being totally downcast to brilliant after the prayer, and he left with the biggest smile. Sam wisely realized the root problem was a lack of face and respect. Restoration and healing came as Sam shared God's Face with the Haitian student.

In chapter five we mentioned the *60 Minutes* episode featuring the *Africa Mercy* ship to explain the full significance of Jesus' healings. The patients who arrive onto the hospital ship suffer from severe facial deformities because of tooth enamel that does not stop growing. *Africa Mercy* performs reconstructive surgery to remove the tumor and, quite literally, give people a new face. The relationships between medical staff and disfigured patients extends beyond the typical cultural calculus of observing society proprieties, and bears witness to radical kingdom values (approach three). The countercultural element of the medical ministry is plainly evident. CBS journalist Scott Pelley tells the nurse, "You know that there are some people who are watching this interview who are saying to themselves, 'I could never do what she does. Those poor people are terribly disfigured. I can't look at them.'" With a tear in her eye, the nurse responses with full conviction, "People have been saying that to these people their whole lives. And someone has to look at them. Someone has to look them in the eyes and tell them that you're human and I recognize that in you. It gets to the point where you don't see that anymore. You don't see the tumor. You can just see the person's eyes. Of if they only have one eye because the other one is a tumor, you find their eye and find a way to connect with them."[14] The way *Africa Mercy*'s ministry gives face to people goes beyond society expectations to expresses kingdom realities.

GOOD HONOR AND BAD HONOR

We have tried to outline the main "rules" of relationships in honor-shame cultures. Hopefully these guiding principles equip readers to relationally mediate God's honor to Majority World peoples. However, navigating cross-cultural relationships is challenging. Knowing how and when to observe cultural rules is often quite confusing. Sometimes you should "be a patron"; other times you should "be a client." Sometimes you should give a gift; sometimes you should withhold the gift. It takes time (as well as mistakes) to develop an intuitive sense for how to act. Despite these challenges we have found people are often gracious when they perceive love and sincerity. So take heart!

Learning about honor and shame sometimes handcuffs crosscultural Christian workers. They always strive to avoid offending other people. But simply avoiding all offense is not the ultimate goal of Christian ministry. The goal of our authentic relationships is not to give people any type of honor, but God's true honor. We must distinguish between "good honor" and "bad honor."

Good honor is a gift of God's common grace for those who live wisely. "The wise will inherit honor, but stubborn fools, disgrace" (Prov 3:35; cf. Prov 3:3-4; 21:21). People in Central Asia often "boasted" of the beauty of their country, their large family size or their self-built house. These are all good things we should affirm as legitimate grounds of honor, since they edify other people and develop community. God himself thinks highly of honor and wants to bless people with it, assuming they use it for the common good.

Bad honor comes at the expense of other people. Status derived by subjugating or marginalizing others is false and illegitimate in God's eyes. Bad honor not only degrades other people but also dishonors God by disrespecting his creation. When people claim such a false honor for themselves, it should be confronted. In chapter four (Old Testament) we discussed how God's hand of judgment involves both honoring and shaming. In the Gospels, Jesus not only blesses people with honor (Mt 5) but also curses the Pharisees with shame (Mt 23). Though it must be done with humility and wisdom, an aspect of our vocation as gospel bearers is calling out, or shaming, bad honor.

Ken was a Christian development worker living in Central Asia who was led by God to confront bad honor during a taxi ride between two cities. In the car with Ken was the driver and two other men. Then a young girl occupied the fifth and final seat. As they drove along, the three men began talking about the various women in their lives, which naturally made the young gal uncomfortable.

Then they addressed her, "Come to my house. I will feed you. It will be a relaxing time." They began discussing among themselves how good it would be to stop the car and spend time with the girl. She was visibly uncomfortable. Proud of their manly intentions, they turned toward Ken and asked, "So what do you think? Do you like that idea?"

Ken replied, "Well you could do that if you want to. It's your choice. But it reminds me of a riddle."

"Oh yeah?" they asked. "What riddle?" And Ken told them this story:

> So he walks out of his house onto the street. As he's walking along confidently, he looks over and he says to himself, "Wow, she looks good. I think I'll have her." So he goes over and does his thing with her. He keeps strutting down the street, and he sees another and says, "Mmm, I like her. I think I'll have her too." So he goes over and fulfills his desires with her. Then he sees some unclaimed food, so takes some for himself. Then a third time he sees a good looking one, takes her, and then carries on. Who is he?"

At this point the three men are glowing in anticipation, naturally thinking, "Wow, what a real man!"

Then Ken revealed, "He is a dog!"

Immediately the car was silent. "So, you can choose what you do and how you live. As for me, God created me a human, and I'm choosing to live like one." There was no more salacious talk.

The parable challenged the passengers' basic worldview by redefining their notions of honor and shame. Ken did not just reactively shame the shamers by saying something like, "You perverts are losers! Stop bothering her!" By helping them reinterpret their own codes of honor, Ken invited them to leave behind their degrading passions and become honorable people themselves. He subverted the prevailing system of false honor, and challenged them to realign their cultural honor code with God's (à la Jesus' parable of the wicked tenants in the vineyard in Mk 12:1-12). Knowing when, and how, to confront false honor requires great wisdom and boldness, as Ken's story illustrates.

The social context and God's Spirit help Christians determine when and how to properly honor people. Sometimes they should "play the game"; other times they should "leave the game." Yet Christians must remain aware of the rules and know the relational consequences of their choices.

Our primary objective is for Western readers to grow aware of these social guidelines for relationships, as they are often unwritten and uncertain. Observing the social rules all the time is never an obligation, but honoring people *is* a commandment from God, and that must be done in a way that makes sense to people. Building relationships in culturally appropriate ways is a freedom and blessing we possess as God's children.

Although what we have described in this chapter is of fundamental importance, much more is needed. For instance, the examples in this chapter focus on personal relationships with individuals. In chapter eleven we will examine honor-shame themes in the church—a community of believers. Also, Christians are called to do more than simply avoid shaming, build relationships and honor others. Having explained "good honor" and "bad honor," we must introduce a third type of honor—the "eternal honor" that only comes from being in God's family through Jesus. How can Christians proclaim God's eternal honor as good news to people? We now turn to evangelism in honor-shame contexts.

DISCUSSION AND APPLICATION QUESTIONS

1. What tangible gestures communicate "face" to people in your context?

2. In light of the above suggestions, what is the most challenging aspect of crosscultural relationships for you?

3. Recall a time when money and finances became an issue in a crosscultural relationship. How did the realities of honor-shame and patronage affect that situation?

4. Recall a time when you had conflict in a crosscultural relationship. How did notions of "face" and honor influence the reconciliation process? Should you have responded differently?

8

EVANGELISM

[God] adorned [his children] with so many honors
as to render their condition not far inferior
to divine and celestial glory.

JOHN CALVIN

Whoever believes in him will not be put to shame. . . .
So the honor is for you who believe. . . .
But you are a chosen race, a royal priesthood,
a holy nation, a people for his own possession.

1 PETER 2:6-7, 9 ESV

AYSON MET FARHAD, A YOUNG CENTRAL ASIAN MAN, at a local language institute. One day after class we were standing outside having a conversation about God. There was an open door to share the gospel, so I said something like, "Your sins make you guilty before God, but Jesus died so your sins could be forgiven and you could escape punishment." While speaking, I could tell something was not right. Farhad's eyebrows bunched up with a look of sincere confusion, as if I were speaking an entirely different language.

Like most people in Central Asia, Farhad hardly sensed personal guilt for doing something wrong, so he was not seeking forgiveness in his life. This explanation of the gospel did not resonate at the personal, emotional level. Couching the work of Christ in a legal framework (i.e., guilt, punishment, forgiveness) was difficult for Farhad to comprehend. The courts in Central Asia are notoriously corrupt—verdicts depend much more on who people know than what actually happened. So the imagery of a courtroom to explain how God saves sounded strange to him.

This common evangelistic approach confuses the hearer and frustrates the evangelist. Many Christians, however, know of no other option than to continue repeating the guilt-oriented explanation of the gospel. Assuming a strictly legal framework for the gospel functionally requires non-Western peoples to understand the gospel in the foreign language of guilt-innocence terms. So consequently, people in honor-shame cultures must adopt a guilt-innocence outlook to properly understand "the gospel." However, we believe the gospel can be explained and experienced within an honor-shame framework.

People very well may benefit from an articulation of the gospel in terms of guilt and innocence, but for many people, that does not reach to the deepest lostness and alienation they experience. For example, I (Mark) regularly share the gospel in terms of guilt with men in the county jail. If forgiveness, however, was the only element of the gospel they experienced, they would still carry a burden of shame. As Job said, "Even if I am innocent, I cannot lift my head, for I am full of shame" (Job 10:15 NIV). Or a Muslim cleric trained in Islamic theology might likely understand religious salvation in terms of deeds and merits yet be heavily influenced by the reality of shame in his community. Proclaiming biblical salvation in honor-shame terms is not over or against other gospel explanations but contributes to a fuller explanation of God's multifaceted saving work. To articulate the gospel in guilt-innocence terms is true, and often appropriate, but it is not the only facet of God's salvation.

Recently Mark's Japanese friend recounted how he became a Christian.[1] He was a university student following the path he desired and the one expected of him. Yet his life lacked meaning and purpose. He had never gone to a church, but visited one hoping to find more meaning for his life. The warmth and acceptance he felt there drew him back. He continued to attend. Although the pastor explained to him the plan of salvation, how to become a Christian, it was hard to comprehend. The concept of sin's guilt was foreign to him. The pastor, however, kept explaining it to him. Finally after a few months of repeated explanations he grasped enough to understand that Jesus died to forgive his sins. After listening to his story I asked my friend, "Wouldn't it have been helpful if the pastor would have described salvation to you in a way that connected with concepts and experiences you would have readily understood, such as shame and honor?" He responded, "That would have been wonderful." Rather than trying to teach Japanese how to understand the cross and salvation using foreign concepts of guilt and justice, how might things have changed if the pastor instead talked about sin and the cross in terms of shame?

This story illustrates our approach to evangelism—though God's Spirit is the ultimate agent causing spiritual regeneration in people, how Christians explain salvation does influence the evangelistic process. While acknowledging God's sovereignty, we explain the human element of evangelism to help Christians best steward the relationships and opportunities God has granted.

Honor-shame is not a "magic key" for evangelism, but it can reduce cultural friction. Even though a person may likely understand sin and salvation better when hearing the gospel in honor-shame terms, that may not automatically produce saving faith. Someone may cognitively understand the gospel yet deny Christ to avoid disgracing their family.

Chapters four and five set forth many theological elements of honor-shame in Scripture. As we apply those truths to evangelism, we purposefully do not offer a one-size-fits-all evangelism technique for all cultures. No single evangelism method can apply to all honor-shame cultures, as every context and every person is unique. We do mention several evangelistic presentations from specific contexts, but more as examples than as patterns. Understanding the biblical, relational and social facets of how God saves will help readers discern and catalyze the process of salvation.

BUILDING BRIDGES OF HONOR

The first step in the evangelism process is meeting people. In honor-shame cultures it is particularly important to form relational bridges that honor people. As we proclaim a God who removes shame and restores honor, we must concretely embody that message in our own actions and lives. People will hardly hear from us what they do not see in us. From our initial encounters with people our actions should correspond with our words. Naturally people will be more receptive to hearing about God's honor if they experience honoring interactions with us. Here is a negative example.

I (Jayson) started a video club to teach English at a local university to meet college students. I decided to watch *24*—the Fox television series featuring Agent Jack Bauer. I chose the entertaining show because it features ethical dilemmas worth discussing. After weekly meetings of the video club I would invite the students from club to tea, hoping to pivot the conversation to the person of Jesus. I labored as best as I knew at the time, but in hindsight I realize a significant flaw in my approach to meeting people. The bridges I developed to make relationships implicitly shamed people. In the show *24* the "bad guys" are usually Russians or Muslims. The students attending were Muslims who grew up as part of the Soviet Union. The Hollywood-created plots for *24* accentuated the standard stereotypes—"Muslims are evil terrorists," and "Russians plot world destruction." Hosting an English club that propagated these stereotypes was not an honoring way to relationally connect with young adults in Central Asia. It was akin to telling a Polish joke in Poland.

The means of our ministry (i.e., relational structures and bridges) must cohere with our ends (i.e., spiritual objective of making disciples). Martin Luther King Jr.'s words regarding the relationship between means and ends (originally in the context of nonviolent resistance) shed light on this aspect of evangelism.

> Ends are not cut off from means, because the means represent the ideal in the making, and the end in process, and ultimately you can't reach good ends through separate means, because the means represent the seed and the end represents the tree.
>
> . . . Means and ends must cohere because the end is preexistent in the means.[2]

In our evangelism, the means and ends cohere when the end of God's honor preexists in the ways we share that news. Since people *see* the gospel as much as they *hear* the gospel, our relational interactions with nonbelievers are vital aspects of the evangelism process. Two of Jesus' common relational bridges were eating with people and miraculous healings—both acts that removed social stigma and embodied the divine honor he taught about. Jesus' ministry sets an example for how his church continues God's mission of bringing honor to a world of shame.

What are practical ways Christians working in honor-shame cultures can *embody* the gospel of God's honor? As you ask this question, it is important to answer it from the vantage point of the host culture—"What are ways *they* would sense honor?" All cultures communicate (and receive) honor uniquely.

In the previous chapter we mentioned ways to honor people in personal relationships. Here are some examples of how Jayson's team reformulated some relational bridges and ministry structures to better account for the honor-shame realities.

I continued to teach English, but adopted an ESL curriculum focusing on trauma recovery to address wounds in our ethnically divided context.[3] Instead of merely entertaining or improving linguistic fluency, it fostered healing from traumatic shame and a conversation about the nature of ethnicity and true community.

I continued to spend time with the university students by inviting them to join me in volunteering at a local orphanage. Our attempts to play games with the children were chaotic, but provided a regular way to engage life on the margins. I don't want to overplay the impact of those afternoons, but our times developed a sense of mutual honor—the orphaned boys were always eager to be around older guys, and my student-friends overcame the false stigmas they associated with orphans. In a small way, we all experienced a taste of true honor in those courtyard soccer games. Those times helped everyone recalibrate his or her notions of honor to better align with God's.

In micro-enterprise development, our objective transitioned from simply job creation and business training to "honorification." We refocused business activities and structures to promote a healthy sense of personal and cultural honor for both employees and customers. Leveraging the natural inclination toward honor in the society improved the business, our relationships and overall impact.

Westerners in foreign countries often encounter the simple question, "What do you do?" In restricted-access countries, answering this question can be very challenging—how could I be honest about my spiritual aim without pegging myself as a proselytizer? I was often unsure of how to navigate social introductions. As we discerned the centrality of honor and made it a prominent factor in our ministry, I began saying, "God called us to Central Asia to *complete* people's honor, socially and spiritually, through various projects." Naturally, that provoked conversations about our projects and the nature of honor itself. We were intentional to use a verb that implied Central Asians already had dignity. Our objective was not to import honor from the West, but to highlight and uncover the glory they would eventually bring into heaven (Rev 21:26). Central Asians themselves are rather preoccupied about acquiring honor for themselves, their family and their nation, so were pleased to hear about a foreigner (and God) who shared a parallel interest.

When Christians employ honoring channels to engage people, their social identity naturally aligns with their spiritual objective. There is integrity. In honor-shame cultures the channel through which people meet you as a Christian will influence how they interpret the message you share with them. The message cannot be separated from the messenger. So we must purposefully make our relational structures honoring.

Building honoring relational bridges is a vital element of the evangelistic process, but only one element. Verbal proclamation of eternal honor from Jesus Christ is necessary. Working toward a healthy sense of social honor will be incomplete if people do not experience God's honor that saves people from spiritual shame. Social honor is part of God's common grace; eternal honor is God's saving grace.[4] In examining the nature of that eternal honor in Christ, we address two questions for honor-shame contexts: What is the gospel? and, How can we best explain the gospel?

METAPHORS OF STATUS REVERSAL

What happens when a person is saved? What is the state of a person before, and then after, they come into relationship with God? How does the Bible define salvation? We begin with these questions about salvation since soteriology (i.e., our theology of salvation) shapes evangelism (i.e., our proclamation of salvation). This fact requires us to consider the nature of biblical salvation before discussing evangelistic approaches.

Status reversal and group incorporation are two central aspects of biblical salvation. These two salvation motifs are prevalent throughout the Bible and relevant for non-Western cultures today. Examining each one moves us toward a biblical model of evangelism for contemporary honor-shame settings. First, we discuss status reversal.

God reverses our status from one of shame to one of honor. Salvation from God overturns previous measures of status. He reverses our identity. The gospel is a message of "salvation-as-reversal, of status transposition, of outsiders becoming insiders, and grace for unexpected people."[5] All humans are sinners in need of God's salvation. Salvation reverses the condition of spiritual shame that was brought on by a person's own sin. Status reversal includes an element of recognizing and turning from shameful behavior—such as Zacchaeus. Salvation also includes status reversal for those sinned against—people shamed and excluded by distorted honor systems, something every human experiences to some degree. Examples in the Gospels would be the lepers or the woman with the flow of blood. God's status-reversing salvation fully saves us from sin.

Observe how these verses portray salvation as the removal of shame and restoration of honor.

> I [God] will change their shame into praise
>   and renown in all the earth. . . .
> I will make you renowned and praised
>   among all the peoples of the earth,
> when I restore your fortunes
>   before your eyes, says the LORD. (Zeph 3:19-20)

> Instead of your shame
>   you will receive a double portion,
> and instead of disgrace
>   you will rejoice in your inheritance. (Is 61:7 NIV)

> The glory that you have given me I have given them. (Jn 17:22)

> "Behold, I am laying in Zion a stone,
>   a cornerstone chosen and precious,
> and whoever believes in him [Jesus] will not be put to shame."
>   So the honor is for you who believe. (1 Pet 2:6-7 ESV)

Biblical writers also utilize metaphors to explain the reversal of our status through Jesus. Metaphors attribute status and identity by projecting the characteristics from something known to something unknown. Metaphors are more than just communication aids or literary devices; they are powerful tools for shaping social reality and defining identity. Social anthropologists note that peoples' identities are often based on the metaphors they use.[6] English speakers, for example, use animals as metaphors in communication. Imagine if were playing a basketball game and I told you, "Watch out for John, he's a *snake!*" That intuitively means something entirely different than if I say, "Watch out for John, he's a *beast!*" When I mention a certain animal, your brain projects a specific meaning and identify onto John. That is how metaphors work. For this reason, biblical authors use social categories as metaphors to explain the radical transformation taking place in the heavenly realms when someone associates with Jesus Christ. This follows Aristotle's rhetorical advice: "To adorn borrow metaphor from things superior, to disparage from things inferior."[7]

In Ephesians 2:19 Paul leverages metaphors in just this way: "So then you are no longer *strangers* and *aliens*, but you are *citizens* with the saints and also *members* of the household of God" (Eph 2:19). Before Christ we were "strangers" and "aliens"—shameful people outside of the established community. But now we are "citizens" and "members"—honorable people within the group, accepted into the community. The words *honor* or *shame* are not present in this passage, but the honor-shame values ooze out of this text through the metaphors.

Because honor and shame are abstract notions, the Bible uses images and realities from regular life to explain how God transposes people from shame to honor. We list twenty-eight metaphors of status reversal. In moving people from shame to honor, God does the following:

- He purifies the defiled (Mk 5; 7:14-23; Acts 10:15; Heb 9:13-14).

- He clothes the naked (Gen 3:21; Is 61:10; Lk 15:22; 2 Cor 5:1-5; Rev 19:8).

- He enriches the poor (1 Sam 2:8; Lk 6:20).

- He cleanses the dirty (Mt 8:2-3; 1 Jn 1:7; Rev 7:14).

- He returns the exiled (Jer 29:10-14; Lk 15:22-24).

- He strengthens the weak (Is 40:29-31; 2 Cor 12:9; 13:4; 1 Pet 5:10).

- He heals the sick (Ex 23:25; Mt 9:27-35; 11:4-6; Rev 21:4).

- He raises the dead (Jn 11:23-44; Rom 4:17; 1 Cor 15:42-43).

- He exalts the humbled (Prov 3:34; Lk 1:52; Phil 2:8-9; Jas 4:10).

- He adopts the orphans (Ezek 16:1-10; Rom 9:25-26; Gal 4:1-6).

- He blesses the cursed (Ps 109:28; Gal 3:13-14).

- He makes wise the foolish (Jas 1:5; 1 Cor 2:6-12).

- He liberates the oppressed (Gen 41; Lk 4:18; Acts 16:25-26).

- He frees the slaves (Ex 6:6; Rom 6:15-23; Gal 4:7-9).

- He enlightens the darkened (Acts 26:18; Col 1:13).

- He accepts the rejected (Mt 9:10; Acts 10:35).

- He befriends the enemy (John 15:14-15; Rom 5:10).

- He draws near to the distant (Is 57:19; Eph 2:17-18).

- He enthrones the powerless (1 Sam 2:8; Eph 2:6; Rev 2:26-27).

- He marries the adulterer (Hos 3; Rev 19:7).

- He finds the lost (Lk 15:4; 19:10).

- He hosts the hungry (Ps 23:5; Lk 15:23; Rev 19:9).

- He raises the lowly (1 Sam 2:8; Mt 20:16).

- He remembers the forgotten (1 Sam 1:11).

- He gives victory to the defeated (Rom 8:37; Rev 12:11).

- He gives life to the barren (Gen 21:1-7; Ps 113:9; Is 54:1-5).

- He gives citizenship to the foreigner (Ruth 1:1–4:22; Eph 2:12, 19; Phil 4:20).

- He gives an inheritance to those without a birthright (Is 61:7; Eph 1:11-18; 1 Pet 1:4).

The honoring replicated in the above images reveals how God saves people from concrete ignominy, but those images serve as a metaphorical depictions of believer's spiritual transformation. When someone trusts in Christ, this is what happens in the heavenly realms. Biblical authors adeptly used culturally relevant metaphors to communicate our salvation from shame to honor.

Metaphors of status reversal are not simply the content of the gospel we proclaim, but also a biblical pattern to communicate salvation in culturally relevant terms. Metaphors inform hermeneutics *and* evangelism. Metaphors play a prominent role in biblical theology, so Christians contextualizing the gospel crossculturally must be adroit at utilizing metaphors in evangelism. This is how people can understand the honor they can have in Christ. We will now discuss how to use metaphors as a key evangelistic tool for proclaiming the gospel of status reversal.

EXPLAINING STATUS REVERSAL

Pragmatically speaking, the theological reality of status reversal must eventually be shaped into a reproducible evangelistic method. What is a concise, simple way you would explain how Christ removes shame and restores honor? The diversity of honor-shame cultures means Christian witness must be contextualized into the language and cultural symbols of your particular cultural setting. Every soil is unique. To aid readers in the process of developing a practical tool for evangelism, we offer this three-phase process. Please note, this process is not a five-minute activity you do individually, but an ongoing dialogue.[8]

1. Analyze culture: Learn the culture's language and grammar for attributing honor and shame. Here are some questions for mining the honor-shame elements in a culture. What common terms, idioms or euphemisms refer to the concepts of honor and shame? What are the primary symbols and images of honor and shame? When someone is disgraced, how do they try to restore their honor? What cultural rituals and practices confer status (high or low)? What words (e.g., phrases, metaphors, adjectives) communicate respect or disrespect? What verbs are used with the social metaphors of "face" and "name"? What objects are associated with honor and shame? What commonly known stories or characters embody the cultural notions of honor-shame? The answers to these questions become the metaphoric language for explaining biblical salvation—that is, evangelism.

2. Research Scripture: What verses, stories and images in the Bible parallel cultural notions of honor and shame? What aspects of the Bible will easily

resonate and naturally make sense to people? What biblical metaphors of status reversal listed above would be particularly meaningful? (Each metaphor of status reversal is a biblical motif one could easily use to frame the gospel, once you have a good grasp on the biblical metaphor.)

3. Create a tool: Develop a contextually meaningful tool that uses the cultural language and logic of honor-shame (phase one) to explain God's salvation (phase two). Avoid the tendency to distill the good news of status reversal into propositional statements. People of honor-shame cultures tend to be oral and concrete learners, so narrative articulations of the gospel resonate better. Lean toward parables and stories. Think imaginatively; convey believer's transposition from shame to honor visually and concretely using the arts. Experiment and explore, developing a biblical, relevant and concise evangelistic tool will likely be a process of trial and error. Since this is a creative act, collaborate with others to field the best ideas.

We feature three distinct evangelistic examples from honor-shame contexts. Their diversity in both content and form display a promising range of evangelistic approaches. All three approaches are extended metaphors of status reversals; they access cultural imagery to communicate how Christ restores honor. The first example comes from East Asia. Paul Sadler, a missionary-pastor in Japan, shares a metaphorical parable involving the Japanese *kotatsu* table. The following is excerpted from his *Evangelical Missions Quarterly* article "A Japanese Gospel Message."[9]

The *"kotatsu"* is a low table with an electric heat element in the bottom to warm those who sit around it. It is one of the most precious means of fellowship in Japanese society. Life in Japan can often be quite cold emotionally, but the *kotatsu* is a symbol of warmth, intimacy, and security. These are the values the Japanese long for and to which the Bible speaks to powerfully.

. . . The metaphor of the *kotatsu* can be used to show that it is a prior and more fundamental lack of security before God that makes people so vulnerable to the threat of shame from people. . . .

When sharing the gospel using the metaphor of the kotatsu, I start by telling a story of a young boy who would gather with other neighborhood children after school around a large warm kotatsu and talk about the day's events with his grandfather. I paint the scene of a welcoming grandfather who serves fresh mandarin oranges and barley tea and laughs and plays card games with the children.

Crisis comes one day when the boy, trying to make his friends laugh, makes fun of his grandfather, only to realize that he is standing right behind him. Seeing his grandfather's obvious sadness at the insult, he rushes from his home in embarrassment. After school the next day, he walks home as usual, but as he approaches his grandfather's house and hears the sound of laughter, he crosses over to the other side of the road, not wanting to be reminded of what he had done.

His avoidance continues, and over time he thinks less and less of his grandfather. He looks for new ways to spend time after school and convinces himself that he really isn't missing anything. But inside he is disappointed with himself and tries to make up for it by excelling in school and in sports. But he can't help but feel a sense of shame, inner loneliness, and anxiety. His grandfather sees the changes taking place in his grandson's heart and refuses to give up on him.

If he doesn't act, he knows his grandson will be lost to him forever. So, together with his son, he devises a plan to cover his grandson's shame, and restore him to a place of honor and acceptance at his *kotatsu*.

. . . The grandson's story is in fact our own. His story points to the reason the world often feels so cold and insecure. . . . Separated from God, the world becomes a cold place. It is in God's presence that humanity fosters qualities of love and acceptance, grace and kindness. Separated from it, we look to the world for warmth and intimacy, but often have to compete for acceptance, face harsh control and unkindness from the various groups we commit to, and in turn often feel a sense of powerlessness and anxiety.

Just as the boy avoided his grandfather, many people avoid God perhaps because thoughts of him bring up buried feelings of shame and unmet obligation. But God is filled with love for us and feels anguish over the pain and anxiety caused by our separation from him. While he will not overlook our actions, he developed a plan to restore us to a place of honor before him (Luke 13:34).

I explain how Jesus, in a sense, left the warmth of heaven's *kotatsu* and entered the coldness of our world. He willingly endured the things that cause us anxiety and shame for our sakes, in order to show us how a return to God could provide us with the warmth to thrive in a cold world. He was born in disgrace in a stable, raised in a poor family, rejected by his friends and relatives, betrayed by his own disciple, and finally crucified by the very people he came to love (John 1:11, Mark 14:64, Luke 23:34).

But Jesus' death was not just a demonstration of humanity's shame, but also a triumph of God's love. Jesus died for us. Like a parent who takes responsibility for the insult his or her child has caused a neighbor, or the president who resigns to bear the responsibility for the company's offences, Jesus took our shame upon himself. He took responsibility for our offences, and died in our place on the cross. In so doing, he opened up a seat of honor and acceptance for us before God (2 Cor. 5:21). We can return to the warmth of the kotatsu, and enjoy its security for all eternity.

Sadler's gospel parable revolves not simply around the *kotatsu* table, but also around the intrafamily relationships common in Japanese society. The family dynamic of shame is a contextual metaphor explaining the nature of our relationship with God. Overall, the concise story nicely explains the work of Christ in Japan's cultural language of honor-shame.

The second evangelistic approach—"Back to God's Village"—retells the biblical story using images and values from a Central Asian village.[10] Jayson's team developed it as an oral parable (hence its conversational tone).

God is like an honorable elder living in a grand two-story yurt—respected and prestigious. He is perfectly clean, without a single wrinkle on his suit or a speck of dust on his shoes. God is perfectly faithful to do everything he promised; he always keeps his word and helps his family—like the rich uncle who everyone wishes they had.

To show his glory, God created the Tien Shan Mountains and fresh rivers. Then God created Adam and Eve from dirt. "I will grant you my family name and authority to rule over my creation as respected princes." They were God's children living in God's village, crowned with honor and glory. In fact, they had so much honor that they walked around naked and were not even ashamed of it. Could you imagine!

But Satan seduced Eve and Adam with more glory. They ignored God's word and ate the fruit. For the first time they felt shame and disgrace, like disloyal children. God appeared, saying, "You once ruled the earth, but now you will become a slave to the earth." Then came the greatest shame—"Leave my village. Because you shamed yourself and me, you must go die elsewhere." God preserved his honor by banishing shame, like parents who disown a beggar son, or people who keep dirty animals outside their home.

In the new village Adam and Eve began a family. Do you know what it means that we are their children? We inherit their shame. If your grandfather defected during war, others would think less of you, right? Before God, we were born in a shameful family in a shameful village. And then our own sin adds more shamefulness. Before God, our status as sinners is like a crazy, barren, demon-possessed, naked, homeless person. For this reason, we can't be a part of God's family, so live on the shameful side of the river.

One day in the shameful village someone had an idea: "Let's create our own honor! We don't need God's honor! Let's create rules and traditions for everyone on this side of the river to keep, and whoever keeps them will get honor." Adam's descendants broke into several groups, each with their own cultural system to cover shame and grant honor. For example, one group said you had to pray five times a day and wear fancy, black suits. But no matter how hard they tried to make a name for themselves, they still couldn't get back to God's village.

So to help his distant children, God became a human and crossed into the shameful village. Jesus came straight from heaven, so is completely pure and without shame. Could you imagine a big-shot politician leaving his prestigious house to live in a trash dump? Jesus did exactly that!

Jesus' life was amazing. Jesus was so full of divine honor, anyone became clean and honorable the instant Jesus touched them—even a woman who discharged blood for twelve years. In his teaching, Jesus told stories of how the shamed would be honored in the final day: "One day, God the Father is going to have a big feast on that side of the river in his own yurt, but only invite the shamed and rejected."

But not everyone liked Jesus because he shamed the honored and honored the shamed. So they publicly shamed him by killing him on a cross. Can you imagine, the only perfectly honorable person being put to such shame! Why? The answer is simple: the shame Jesus bore was not his own, but ours. You know how if you use a rag to remove the dirt from your shoes, the rag becomes dirty. Well, Jesus was like a big white towel that wiped clean everyone's dirt and shame.

But even more incredible, Jesus rose from death to life. He was raised from the ultimate shame of death, crossed back to God's village, received a great name, and sat in the honored seat. Jesus' resurrection from the dead built a new bridge to God's village so people could leave their shame.

But even after a new bridge was built to the other side of the river, some people did not want to return. The powerful people felt content: "Why would I need God's honor? I already have enough honor here." Others approached the bridge, but then second-guessed themselves. "I'm too shameful to enter God's village. As soon as I set foot on that side, I will be exposed!"

But some decided to follow Jesus to the honorable side. As they crossed the bridge into God's honorable village, God himself dashed out from his yurt with great joy to embrace each person. God gave everyone who followed Jesus a new golden robe without wrinkle, inheritance documents, and a most honorable seat in his yurt. People finally had real honor. They were freed to love and serve other people, and to be the loyal, honoring child that God always desired.

However, the bridge that Jesus built is only temporary. In the future, Jesus will come again to cleanse the shameful village of all dishonor and impurity. Those who do not follow Jesus and receive God's honor will be stripped naked and banished to everlasting shame.

The narrative "Back to God's Village" leverages the village themes of family and purity to explain parallel biblical ideas. No parable or metaphor lines up exactly with the Bible, but this parable includes many key biblical themes in a relatively short span. A number of points will need further explanation—including how one crosses the bridge. But it communicates in honor-shame terms the reality of human lostness, that God has acted to provide salvation, a sense of what that salvation is and that a decision is required.

The final evangelistic example is from Nabeel Jabbour's book *The Crescent Through the Eyes of the Cross*. On a trip to a Third World Muslim country, Jabbour, an Arab American Christian, was invited to speak to a group of forty Muslim villagers for two hours. After praying, he decided to use the three relevant stories about Jesus in Mark 5. Sitting on the floor, with men on one side and women on the other, he shared these stories.[11]

The first story (Mk 5:1-20) was about Jesus healing the wild, demon-possessed man. Being controlled and enslaved by spirits brought years of shame and isolation to this man. The listeners were amazed that the demonized man recognized and respected Jesus' status—he bows down before Jesus, saying, "What do you want with me, Jesus, Son of the Most High God?" Jabbour explains the Muslim listeners' thoughts: "Everyone in the room knew that the demon-possessed man was worthless. He was a menace to the town and to the neighboring village. Why did Jesus give him worth and cast the demons out into the pigs?"[12]

The second story (Mt 5:21-34) was about Jesus' willingness to heal the hemorrhaging woman. The illness had depleted her physically, financially and socially. She would have had a low status in the Jewish town. To show

how the woman violated cultural norms by approaching, let alone touching, Jesus, Jabbour read Leviticus 12:1-5 and Leviticus 15:19-23—the Old Testament passages explaining how menstruating women defiled whatever they touched. His Muslim audience practiced ablutions to cleanse before ceremonial prayers, so the story "was addressing their felt need of longing to be clean so they could be acceptable to God."[13] In Mark 7 Jesus explains that it is relational sins of the heart, not ceremonial defilement, that make a person unclean before God. Jabbour suggests that Jesus exposed the woman— "Who touched my clothes?"—to give her assurance of complete healing and cleansing—"Daughter, your faith has healed you. Go in peace and be freed from your suffering."

The third story was Jesus raising Jairus's twelve-year-old daughter. Death in many cultures brings about a state of ultimate defilement and separation— as the act of burying someone in the ground indicates. Upon finishing his teaching presentation, the first question came from one of the women. She raised her finger, made a statement, then asked, "I want to believe in Jesus. How do I do it?"

Jabbour's teaching experience shows the power of simply retelling biblical stories in evangelistic situations. The natural similarities between ancient Jewish culture and daily life in many honor-shame cultures create an easy interpretive bridge. Listeners in the Muslim village naturally understood the honor-shame aspects of salvation intrinsic to the stories. Many cultures intuitively associate demon possession, defilement and death with shame. The three healing stories prove Jesus' authority to bestow the honor of spiritual freedom, purity and life. The experiences of the healed people in Mark 5 illustrated the nature of biblical salvation as status reversal to Jabbour's audience from a Muslim village.

Salvation as Group Membership

A second motif of salvation in the Bible is inclusion into the group of God's honored people. God bestows an honorable status on the excluded by welcoming and including them into his new community. Outsiders are now insiders. Kwame Bediako explains this communal element of salvation: "The redeemed now belong within the community of the living God, in the joyful company of the faithful of all ages and climes. They are united through their union with Christ, in a fellowship infinitely righter than the mere social bonds of lineage, clean, tribe or nation that exclude the stranger as a virtual enemy."[14] Paul's words in Ephesians 2:12-14 explain this collective reality.

> Remember that you were at that time without Christ, being aliens from the commonwealth of Israel, and strangers to the covenants of promise, having no hope and without God in the world. But now in Christ Jesus you who once were far off have been brought near by the blood of Christ. For he is our peace; in his flesh he has made both groups into one and has broken down the dividing wall.

Since the cultural milieu of the early church was predominantly collectivistic, we should expect New Testament epistles to show concern for group identity. In fact, the group-oriented question, who are God's *people*? animates the New Testament writings more than, how can *I* be saved? The individualistic proclivity of Western theologians misreads the communal elements of biblical writings. Krister Stendahl explains, "Where Paul was concerned about the possibility for Gentiles to be included in the messianic community, his statements are now read as answers to the quest for assurance about man's salvation out of a common human predicament."[15]

The honor derived from joining God's prestigious family is good news for people afflicted by shame. Regardless of what false social mechanisms of exclusion they fall victim to, those in Christ are eternally honored and accepted as members in the people of God, with full rights, privileges and status. This new group status *is* salvation itself. Paul's letter to the Romans articulates the good news of group membership using a variety of terminology: "justification/righteousness" (Rom 3), "children of Abraham" (Rom 4), "sons/heirs of God" (Rom 8) and "Israel/olive tree" (Rom 9–11).[16]

The language of "justification" and "righteousness" (Rom 3:21-31; cf. Gal 2:11-20; and our discussion in chap. 5) is one way of articulating a person's entrance into God's covenant community. People who respond to the gospel by faith are considered *dikaios*, "righteous," and "within the covenant."[17] The term "justification by faith" is a shorthand way of declaring whom God now considers his true community; faith in the Messiah, not observing Jewish cultural distinctives, marks a person in God's family (i.e., "justified").[18]

Romans 4 redefines descent from Abraham—the father of all who believe.[19] The question of Abrahamic descent is significant because God promised that Abraham's children would become an honored group (Gen 12:2-3). Through Abraham-like faith in the Creator, and not through being ethnic Israel (Rom 9:6-8), we obtain the honorable heritage of Abraham, which is to become the people of God's promise and possessors of a great inheritance.[20]

Romans 8 (cf. Gal 4) uses the powerful family language of adoption and inheritance to define those in Christ. Believers are considered rightful co-heirs with Christ of God's promises (Rom 8:17). Inheritance symbolizes honor by affirming the boundaries of worthy descendants; it assumes a kinship relationship. Once orphans without a name, we have become children of God adopted into his family (Rom 8:16-21). In honor-shame cultures, one's family determines one's status; so divine adoption through the Spirit grants a new status and a prestigious future of glory.

The longest explanation of God's redefined, new-covenant people is Romans 9–11. Without disregarding the uniqueness of ethnic Israel, Paul says of Gentiles, "Those who were not my people I will call 'my people.' . . . They shall be called children of the living God" (Rom 9:25-26). In other words, Gentile believers in Christ are "grafted into the olive tree" cultivated by God (Rom 11:17-24). Longtime outsiders are now members of the group!

In Romans Paul expounds this gospel: God worked decisively in Jesus to create his own family, and salvific inclusion into this honored community is available to people from all groups. Salvation *is* group membership. Salvation in Romans is more about entrance into God's covenant community than entrance into heaven. Even Paul's incorporative phrase "in Christ" speaks of the new honorable status of belonging to the Messiah's community. This salvation is mediated through grace—God's acceptance of the shamed. Salvation from God trivializes every group's false claim to honor, whether based on Jewish Torah observance, Roman imperial power or Greek wisdom. Only in being honored by God through Christ's shameful death on behalf of the shameful can humans be integrated into God's community and bear eternal honor (Rom 2:7; 9:23; 10:13).[21] *This* is the good news!

First Peter articulates such salvation this way: "But you are a chosen race, a royal priesthood, a holy nation, a people for his own possession. . . . Once you were not a people, but now you are God's people" (1 Pet 2:9-10 ESV).

Telling the Story of Group Membership

So how can Christians today practically communicate the gospel as incorporation into God's family? The short answer: use relational and communal language. To address the issue of shame in evangelistic encounters, one should explain salvation using the conceptual metaphors of family, relationships and community. Sin is fundamentally a relational problem, and salvation is a restoration of broken relationships, so they must be communicated accordingly. The following words represent group language for explaining the gospel:

Loyalty	Mediator	Family	Father
Community	Child	Harmony	Threat
Public	Alliance	Allegiance	Feast
Inheritance	Adoption	(Dis)grace	Respect
Unity	Defilement	Inclusion	Hospitality
Humiliation	Face	Reputation	Worth
Reverence	Identity	Acceptance	Dignity
Alienation	Disgrace	Unclean	Approval
Patron(age)	Worthy	Glory	
Purity	Envy	Dishonor	

Telling the story of salvation (i.e., creation-fall-Israel-Jesus-salvation) using the above word set will probably feel like speaking a second language, a bit unnatural and strained. For Western Christians, legal language is the default language for communicating theology; it comes out automatically. These judicial words commonly appear in evangelistic presentations:

Law	Transgression	Judgment	Works
Judge	Right/wrong	Rules	Acquittal
Correction	Condemnation	Innocence	Penalty
Punishment	Forgiveness	Payment	
Personal	Merit	Debt	
Commands	Wrath	Guilt	
Justice	Pardon		

Of the two word sets above, which is more theologically familiar to you? We have observed that many Western Christians portray salvation as a courtroom scene. Note the judicial terminology (in italics) in this gospel summary: We are *guilty* of *violating* the *law*. Since God is *just*, he must *judge* sin (i.e., *personal wrongdoing*). *Restitution* must be made to *right* a *wrong*. Jesus pays our *penalty* and appeases *wrath* so *justice is satisfied*. We are *forgiven* of our *transgressions*, our sins are *pardoned* and we are made *innocent*.

We note the strong legal emphasis of most evangelistic presentations not to imply that all legal-oriented evangelism is wrong, but to increase self-awareness. The first step toward articulating the gospel relevantly in honor-shame contexts is becoming aware of your own default language in spiritual conversations. Learning a second language often requires a new understanding of your first language. For people coming from a Western mentality, communicating the gospel from an honor-shame perspective is an acquired skill. One must be intentional to learn and practice it, or will likely resort to the default language.

The various forms of gospel proclamation originating from Western contexts (e.g., printed tract, personal testimony, oral sermon) follow a common pattern—transgression, guilt, restitution, confession and forgiveness. This basic paradigm corresponds to the guilt-innocence narrative structure explained in chapter four. As expected, this evangelistic framework employs judicial and legal imagery. Table 8.1 compares this traditional approach with an honor-shame alternative.

Table 8.1. Two paradigms of salvation

Process of Salvation	Guilt Based	Shame Based
Problem of sin	**Transgression** People have broken God's law through a particular action.	**Unfaithfulness** People have broken the relationship with God by being disloyal.
Dilemma of humans	**Guilt** Our moral violations merit punishment.	**Shame** Our disgrace merits banishment.
Solution of Jesus	**Restitution** Jesus satisfies the legal requirements of justice by enduring retribution for us.	**Restoration** Jesus bears shame to reconcile the relationship by repairing honor.
Response of faith	**Confession** People must acknowledge their wrongdoing.	**Allegiance** People must be loyal to honoring God.
Result of salvation	**Forgiveness** God pardons wrongdoings and declares lawbreakers to be innocent.	**Honor** God makes outcasts his children and exalts people to eternal glory.

The column on the far right suggests an alternative way to structure the gospel in honor-shame terms—unfaithfulness, shame, restoration, allegiance and then honor. Relational and communal language explains how Jesus rescues people from spiritual shame before God. As you develop reproducible methods of evangelism, or share informally with people, you may consider this basic framework to structure evangelistic presentations.

Contextualizing evangelism involves more than just repackaging evangelistic presentations. The social realities of honor and shame affect our understanding of the entire conversion process. Verbal explanation of the gospel in honor-shame is only one aspect of Christian witness. The means by which we proclaim the gospel must also be adapted to the cultural context. Contextualizing the gospel means adapting the *process*, not just *content*, of our evangelism to account for hearers' honor-shame tendencies, as we discuss in the next chapter, about conversion.

DISCUSSION AND APPLICATION QUESTIONS

1. In your cultural setting, what are the primary causes and sources of honor and/or shame?

2. What are the primary ways you encounter and meet nonbelievers? Do those relational bridges communicate dignity and honor to people?

3. In three or four sentences, how would you explain the gospel in honor-shame terms?

9

CONVERSION

*Shame can be overcome only when the original unity
is restored, when man is once again clothed by God.*

DIETRICH BONHOEFFER, *ETHICS*

*How can you believe when you accept glory
from one another and do not seek the glory
that comes from the one who alone is God?*

JOHN 5:44

*W*ESTERN CULTURAL VALUES SHAPE NOT ONLY *what* we communicate but also *how* we communicate. Missiologists commonly describe Western methods of ministry as a "truth encounter." Western missions, developed in a cultural setting emphasizing legality and justice, employs courtroom methods for evangelism. Truth encounter presents the gospel as truth—ideas and facts one must believe as true to know God. Since truth is viewed propositionally, as either right or wrong, evangelism appeals to rationality and reason. Evangelism involves logically presenting divine truth and defending potential objections, akin to a courtroom lawyer. Conversion is viewed as cognitively adopting a new belief set as true.

Without neglecting the fact that Christian witness always involves verbally proclaiming the gospel as truth, Majority World peoples may better encounter the gospel of God's salvation as *community*, not just *ideas*. While

Christian witness is both/and, we propose approaching evangelism as a "community encounter" in honor-shame settings.

The Approach of "Community Encounter"

In honor-shame contexts, Christian mission brings people to encounter true community.[1] A community encounter redefines a person's primary group identity through genuine relationships. Entrance into a new community transforms one's spiritual status. Conversion means granting loyalty and allegiance to a new group—God and his people. Through a community encounter, unbelievers come to redefine their court of reputation (i.e., who decides which people are honorable) and honor code (i.e., what is truly honorable and shameful) in light of God's honor. A biblical communal encounter involves the interface of three communities: the Trinity, the church and the family.

In Acts 16 Paul and Silas sat in the Philippian prison singing and praying to God. Suddenly, an earthquake rattled the prison doors open and unshackled their handcuffs. The jailer on duty awoke to the chaos and drew his sword to kill himself, having failed his duties. Paul shouted just in time, "Stop! We are here!" After the situation settled down, the jailer and his household came to believe in the Lord Jesus for salvation, then enjoyed an evening of fellowship together with Paul and Silas. The Philippian jailer's family believed in Jesus when they encountered the gospel as community. The following sections draw out principles of community encounter from the story of the Philippian jailor.

The Trinity. Christian mission leads people to encounter the Most Honorable and Glorious. Honor is reoriented around the triune community. Father, Son and Spirit replace family, ethnicity and tribe as the community of honor. The Father welcomes home the shamed with a gracious acceptance and honor. The Son now functions as our honorable Brother, saving a seat of honor for us in heaven. The Spirit comes as a down payment of our future inheritance of glory. True face only comes from encountering the Face of God. Relationally knowing God's Face, as revealed in the face of Jesus, is the only definitive source for gaining a new and esteemed status.[2]

The Philippian jailer sought to kill himself to cover his shameful failure on the job. He acted to preserve the honor of his people by sacrificing his own life. People in honor-shame cultures must come to acknowledge the falseness of social shame, even though initially it may be very painful. With his sword drawn, the Philippian jailer paused long enough to reconsider how God's honor outweighs all possible social shame.

Andrew Mbuvi explains, "By clearly directing people to the correct dimension of honor and shame as the *vertical* relationship with God, rather than the *horizontal* relationship with man, we can affirm that God is the true 'significant other' who ascribes honor to us even when we do not deserve it."[3] Eternal glory comes solely through God's Son (Jn 17:22), because only God's opinion will last forever. When people reject God as the lone source and arbiter of honor, they choose finite honor over infinite glory (Jn 12:42-43). Christian witness replaces false shame ("I am a worthless nobody") and false honor ("My group is best!") with true honor from God, by bringing people into direct relationship with God himself.

The Church. To save the jailer's life, Paul yelled out, "We are here!" The church, as the earthly body of Christ, is the primary community in which unbelievers encounter the gospel. While ultimate honor comes from God, participation in God's family on earth is where honor is remade, affirmed and expressed. The church functions as a surrogate family whose gracious welcome frees people to unmask their shame.

Church-planting strategies typically proceed as such: evangelism, discipleship and then community. First you get individuals to make a decision for Christ, then disciple them into maturity and then gather people into the church. But the conversion process in honor-shame cultures is often the exact opposite: community, discipleship and then evangelism (see table 9.1).

Table 9.1. Church-planting patterns

Western ministry model:	Evangelism	→	Discipleship	→	Community
Majority World reality:	Community	→	Discipleship	→	Evangelism

Group-oriented people view conversion as transferring loyalty and identity to a new group, so they must experience the group before choosing to join it. So participation in the body of Christ is the first step in the evangelistic process. As people associate with believers (community) their lives begin to change (discipleship), and then they come to publicly profess Jesus as Lord (evangelism). Or in other words, people "belong," "behave" and then "believe." Relationships and community are obviously important for ministry in all cultures, but even more so in honor-shame cultures. Community is how people experience God's honor and liberation from shame.

Various aspects of the evangelistic process can be adapted to communicate honoring implicitly. This is critical because shaming people, even unintentionally, contradicts the gospel of God's honor. In chapter seven we suggested ways Christians can relationally proclaim God's honor—an essential element of Christian witness. These additional ideas are specific to the evangelism process. First, simply eat with unbelievers. In Acts 16 Paul and Silas accepted the jailer's invitation to eat with his family. Sharing a meal is one effective way to honor others, since it forms a relational bond. Table fellowship was a central way Jesus honored people in the Gospels. A shared table preaches God's honor as loudly as a sermon in collectivistic societies. Second, seek opportunities to pray with people for their honor. This communicates genuine care for their deepest desires, and plants the seed truth that people must rely on God for true honor (Ps 63:7). Third, incorporate local proverbs or narratives. This implicitly honors their collective identity. And fourth, speak gracefully; combative rhetoric not only is obnoxious but is also viewed as threatening. People avoid contact with those who appear to be attacking their identity and honor. Arguing may win the argument but will likely lose the relationship. These ideas reflect possible ways people may tangibly sense God's honor during evangelism, and so naturally deepen the relational bonds.

The Family. In collectivistic cultures, conversion to Christianity may shame one's biological family and neighboring community. Many unreached people do not reject Christianity for theological reasons but because of social and cultural forces that disgrace one's family. For collectivistic people, choosing their religion in isolation from the group implies rejection of the group itself. An unbeliever may be open to following Jesus, but nevertheless remain unwilling to jeopardize their community standing or family's reputation to follow Jesus. The idea of group (or family) conversion might mitigate the shame of social dislocation.

While faith in Christ is always personal and might include rejecting group obligations, there are New Testament examples of family conversions. Paul's invitation for the jailer's entire family to be saved avoided the scandal of one person disgracing the rest of the family. The idea of "group conversion" does not ignore individual faith and repentance but understands that some people prefer to make decisions in a group setting, interdependently and simultaneously.[4]

The notion of interdependent decisions for Christ affects our evangelism. For example, if a young person indicates interest in Jesus, it may be prudent to invite the entire family into the conversation. By sharing with the household leader and anticipating a family decision to follow Christ, we can limit the social upheaval of extracting an individual from their relational network. A missiological approach of community encounter involves helping people encounter Jesus as a community, not just individually.

Nevertheless, some people in honor-shame societies will individually decide to follow Christ. This often produces family arguments, angry threats and community gossip. Amid those challenging circumstances, there may be long-term advantages to encouraging new believers to remain in their family as a light and not reject social identities. Family networks are the most natural channels for transmitting the gospel in honor-shame contexts, so they should be maintained whenever possible.

Jatagul, a university student in Central Asia, heard the gospel and believed. When Jatagul explained to her Muslim parents that she followed Jesus, her dad lashed out strongly, threatening to kill Jatagul if she did not renounce Jesus and read the Qur'an. He likely feared how her conversion would mar his reputation as a family leader once neighbors began hearing about his daughter's decision. After one particular outburst of rage, Jatagul came to our house visually shaken up and seeking counsel on how to flee the country. Once she explained the situation, I called the local church leaders. After praying and talking, Jatagul agreed with the unanimous counsel of the local church to return home.

The local pastor, himself from a rural community, explained to me, "If Jatagul leaves her family, then the word *Christian* in that village will mean 'someone who dishonors their family and abandons their community.' That gives Jesus a bad name." The church's recommendation for Jatagul was not merely to curry good public relationships with the majority culture, but was for the advance of the gospel. In Central Asia, we discovered that nearly 70 percent of Christians came to Jesus through a believing relative. Another study in Thailand concluded that the odds of an unbeliever becoming a Christian are 229 times higher if they have a Christian relative.[5] So if Jatagul removed herself from her community, how would her community ever hear the gospel? Extracting new converts from their social networks to avoid immediate threats may limit their long-term influence as believers. When Christians share the gospel with an individual, they should actively choose practices "to facilitate the spreading of the gospel message through the seeker's existing social networks even before that person becomes a believer."[6] This is one aspect of helping people encounter the gospel as community.

Viewing Christian witness as a community encounter reshapes evangelism among group-oriented peoples. When honor and shame are predominant values, people meaningfully experience the gospel by encountering the divine and ecclesial community from within their social networks.

Honor-shame cultures are notoriously diverse. For this reason, we hesitate to prescribe universal methods for evangelism. Our approach has been to articulate a biblical soteriology, outline general principles about evangelism and conversion in honor-shame contexts, and highlight positive case studies in order to fuel your imagination for how to contextualize the gospel, in both content and form, to bear greater fruit for the kingdom. The following section showcases three diverse examples of community encounter— Arab ESL students in America, gang members in Honduras and African Christians in Benin—to illustrate some ways honor-shame shapes the process of evangelism and conversion.

EXAMPLES OF COMMUNITY ENCOUNTER

Steven intentionally connected with young Arabs studying English in the United States. Steven realized through his relationships that Arabs were highly group oriented. (In fact, some young adults from the Middle East had never conversed with any nonrelatives before visiting the US.) Steven adjusted certain practices to account for this social dynamic.

When reading the Bible with Arabs, he always tried to gather students into groups. Rather than meeting individually, Steven would ask spiritually open students to bring friends along. Doing something without a group can create a sense of anxiety—"What will others think of me doing this?" The group setting created a more comfortable setting to explore the Bible. Students reasoned, "If others are joining me, then it must be okay."

Steven also talked with the students' parents back home through Skype, which brought honor in multiple ways. This communicated genuine interest in them as people, and it allowed the students to display their English skills as they translated to their parents. Making himself known to the students' broader social networks minimized false stereotypes of him as an American and as a Christian. Steven related to Arab students as members of a family, not simply isolated individuals.

While Steven adapted his approach to evangelism to account for honor-shame realities, he knew no approach to disciple making among Arabs would avoid all sources of shame. For this reason, he purposefully communicated that suffering shame and persecution were inevitable aspects of following Jesus. In all, Steven's approach removed unessential stumbling blocks to the gospel, yet without skirting "the shame of the cross."

The second case study is about Pancho, a Honduran who carried a stigma of shame from a young age. In his own words, "When I was five years old my mother became ashamed of me and left me to grow up with my grandmother."[7] His father was not involved in his life, and he never really had a family. Sometimes Pancho lived with his grandmother, other times with uncles. Not only did these uncles treat him as inferior to their children, but they also beat and verbally abused him. Days like Mother's Day and Father's Day heightened his shame when he observed other children with their parents. At age eleven he was hanging out with gang members—attracted to their status and the sense of solidarity and belonging. By the age of twelve he was formally a gang member—exuding a sense of pride and confidence he had never had before. Gang life allowed him to mask his shame.

Pancho's experience is not unique. In a fascinating book, *Homies and Hermanos: God and Gangs in Central America*, sociologist Robert Brenneman uncovers the key role shame plays in propelling young people to join gangs. In one sense Pancho gained respect and honor through the gang. He achieved honor within the gang and was feared by others. Yet he was trapped; he had burned his bridges with society—following the honor code of the gang made him a despised outsider, less than human, to the rest of society.[8]

At one point a judge sentenced Pancho to an evangelical rehab center. He was planning his escape when a visiting pastor delivered a prophetic warning regarding his future if he escaped. Pancho remembers,

> When the pastor said this to me my whole body began to shake and shake and [I started] to cry . . . and the truth, man, is that I hadn't cried in approximately eleven years. . . . I began crying man, like a baby and asking for forgiveness from God, right? For everything I'd done, for all that had happened, right? And for the damage I'd caused my family and then everybody was shocked, man, from watching how I cried.[9]

With the pastor praying for him, he continued crying for about four hours. Pancho decided not to escape and stayed at the center. Just as Pancho's shame-driven entry into a gang was not unique, his conversion experience out of the gang was also not unique. Brenneman observes that stepping away from masking shame and emotionally acknowledging it before others was a common element of conversion from homie to *hermano* (brother). The display of emotion itself "involved trespassing a deeply gendered feeling rule of the gang—homies don't cry. Therefore, the experience came to mark a biographical 'moment zero' dating the conversion and allowing the convert a sense of security in moving forward with the project of personal reform."[10]

The public and communal aspect of Pancho's conversion was of notable significance. The experience of emotional vulnerability was a step away from the gang's definition of honor and manliness toward the church's definition; it allowed him to "try on" the experience of acknowledging shame before others.[11] When God moved in his life in that moment, Pancho and others observed the reality of conversion. This was much more than giving mental assent to some truths about God; it was a visceral confession of and release from shame.

Also, Brenneman observes that by acknowledging "past wrongdoings and by agreeing to stay at the [rehab] center rather than escape [Pancho] took an important first step in repairing social bonds to non-gang society that had been allowed to deteriorate for eleven years."[12] Because of the public nature of his conversion experience, others immediately began embracing and supporting him and thus replacing the gang community he lost.

Brenneman summarizes his research on gang conversions with these remarkable words on group incorporation.

> What is new and surprising is the extent to which evangelical conversion and participation in an evangelical congregation helps violent, heavily stigmatized "outsiders" like the Central American gang homies find acceptance and reintegration in communities that have come to fear and loathe them. In effect, evangelical congregations provide an entire resocialization program free of charge.[13]

Our final example of community encounter comes from Mathieu Gnonhossou—an African evangelist in Benin, West Africa.[14] Here is the story in his words:

> For several years I've worked as an evangelist with other brothers and sisters in Benin. Mahugnon was a leader in a mainline church community, whom we perceived to be a nominal believer because he did not break from the mainline community and affirm an "evangelical" faith. Christians in mainline churches incorporate indigenous protective practices in syncretistic ways. Mahugnon himself sees this as problematic, yet he remains in that church. Our evangelistic efforts sought to extract Mahugnon from that community to join a breakaway community. We took his resistance to cut relational ties with his church as proof he was not yet born again.
>
> Elements of our approach shamed and dishonored him. His displeasure was evident. For instance, a house church met in his home. It was an unofficial subgroup of his main church. His own children helped lead the group. But since Mahugnon did not clearly confess faith, the leaders decided to stop meeting there.
>
> Also, almost all of Mahugnon's biological children involved in that house church became uncaring toward Mahugnon. Evangelists commonly

disrespected non-believing family members in this way. Once when Mahugnon was sick, none of his children knew for four weeks because they had
not asked about their father. To think that this would happen in African
culture is unbelievable.

With a new understanding of faith formation, I began encouraging our
evangelism partners to change approaches. I was not initially successful in
persuading my co-workers to change approaches, so I changed my personal
attitude and actions toward Mahugnon. Whenever I encountered or visited
him I expressed interest by asking about his family and church friends. Mahugnon reported those greetings to the church, and I began getting personal
greetings back from those church members and leaders. Oral reports came
from their midst that I was different because I *"no do yeyi go na me"* (lit.
"make people beautiful," i.e., honor or respect people).

Mahugnon missed having the house church meetings in his home. Although he maintained his membership at the original mainline church, he
occasionally attended worship services at the house church's new meeting
place. One day he confided to me, "I don't oppose your preaching. I admire
it. But I can't wipe away a long history of relationships with people I have
known for decades by leaving them at once and joining you." Mahugnon
understood he did not have to leave his friends to follow Jesus or be a blessing.

I even began attending some of the worship services at Mahugnon's church,
and they invited me to teach their youth. From conversations, I realized our
past approach was *"mansin ba do mego"* (lit., "pouring vegetables' dirty liquid
onto people," i.e., making people dirty, or shameful). Mahugnon understood
evangelicals' level of commitment, but dreaded leaving people who never
wronged him. The evangelism approach needed to consider Jesus' own
method—"Go home to your friends, and tell them how much the Lord has
done for you, and what mercy he has shown you" (Mark 5:19).

With time, Mahugnon involved me in the primary school built by his
mainline church and hopes we will make a positive impact on the children.
Mahugnon also began regularly attending the house church, and provided
guidance and insight for our evangelism team. Mahugnon is also involved in
resolving a leadership conflict that threatens to break this church community
led by the same people who evangelized him. It's amazing to see him helping
to find a reconciling pathway out of the mess.

Seeing the new direction in our relationship, some of the leaders of the
new breakaway community have adopted this new approach to evangelism.

Mahugnon's story shows he is open to Christian faith in a new way without necessarily breaking his human connections. He recognizes the syncretistic practices must be addressed with the Christian faith, but does not believe in severing ties with his community. According to the narrative Mahugnon is now living by, he values past relationships, communal living, honor, and respect. An evangelism approach that does not antagonize the gospel and those values better assists Mahugnon and his socio-religious network towards the paths of discipleship and disciplemaking.

THE DYNAMICS OF CONVERSION

When someone is moved by the gospel, how should they respond? What is a biblical response to the gospel in terms of honor and shame? How does conversion happen in collectivistic contexts? These questions lead us towards a theology of conversion. Communicating the gospel is only half of the process, as the message must also be received and appropriated by the hearer. The above section on community encounter set forth *social* realities influencing one's conversion to Christ, whereas here we address the *theological* realities involved in conversion to Christ. For this, we examine key aspects of conversion—conviction, false righteousness, conscience, repentance and faith—to develop a biblical theology of conversion in honor-shame terms.

Our explanations do not unfold the entire biblical meaning of these concepts, but highlight those aspects most relevant for honor-shame contexts. We aim to complement, not replace, existing theological paradigms associated with evangelism and conversion. So our comments about Western theological views are meant as a comparison, not a critique. With that stated, we begin by noting Western assumptions about religious conversion.

Zeba Crook, in his book *Reconceptualising Conversion*, observes, "Psychology, with its emphasis on emotional and introspective features of human experience, provides the default framework within which the modern West tends to analyze and describe conversion."[15] This psychological perspective of conversion begins with an individual emotionally crippled with a burdened conscience over personal shortcomings; the soul is existentially divided and troubled by guilt. Conversion is a personal choice made by an individual governed by their own psychological needs—a "personal religious quest" of sorts. People in crisis convert when they "see the light"—a euphemism for religious conversion as a psychological breakthrough. Salvation means coming to peace with yourself, feeling assured you will go to heaven. Yet this psychological view of conversion (i.e., individualistic and internal) is not the universal human experience, but rather cultural.[16] Western culture assumes this psychological pattern of religious conversion is global, and that assumption shapes our soteriology and our methods of evangelism.

Western approaches to evangelism presuppose that people must sense a conviction of guilt and dread of impending wrath before converting. The opening move of many evangelistic presentations focuses on moral failure and person guilt—"Despite your good works, no one is morally perfect. No matter how good or moral you are, just one bad deed makes you guilty before God." The aim is to undercut an individual's pride in their own moral goodness. But as many missionaries know from experience, making people in honor-shame cultures feel guilty about their misdeeds is quite challenging. Western evangelistic practices address the problem of "works right-eousness"—that is, doing enough good works to counterbalance bad deeds and earn one's way into heaven. However, a more common form of false righteousness in honor-shame contexts is "group righteousness"—a claim to superiority over other peoples because of one's group identity.

In the New Testament, some Jewish Christians lived as if part of their right standing with God depended on their participation in a special group (and consequently, separation from outsiders, see Gal 2:1-14). They thought Jews were more honorable then Gentiles, so they scrupulously observed ethnic distinctives such as sabbath and circumcision to maintain that social distinction. Such "group righteousness" is still a common expression of sin in collectivistic cultures; people feel worthy of honor for being in the right social group. Honor-shame cultures are more likely to construct a false and idolatrous identity based on their group associations (e.g., family name, neighborhood, ethnic group, economic class), than on good moral deeds. The gospel deconstructs this false group honor (as well as false moral pride). Addressing false group-based righteousness in evangelism could sound like this: "Despite your group identity, no one is entirely honorable before God. No matter who your family is, every person and every group bears shame for dishonoring God. Everyone inherits Adam and Eve's shame and compounds that shame by being disloyal to God."[17] People are more likely to acknowledge their need for God when they view their group, and by extension themselves, as honorless and shameful before God.

Speaking about shame is often challenging; nobody naturally wants to discuss the topic of shame. People strive to hide their shame, not expose it, so broaching the topic is relationally dicey. Here are some starting suggestions for discussing shame.

1. Be vulnerable and share your own shame. Recount a time where you struggled with shame, or tell your testimony in terms of honor and shame. People long for release from shame but carry the burden alone because they fear being exposed. When people trust you will not think less of them or gossip to others, they are more likely to make their deepest vulnerabilities known.

2. Tell a Bible story of a shameful person who experienced God's salvation. The narratives of Mephibosheth, Tamar, the bleeding women or the prodigal son invite people to identify with the main characters.

3. Speak generally about our inheritance of shame as descendants of Adam and Eve. Because the first couple acted shamefully in Genesis 3, the entire human family faces shame. Frame the problem of shame as a universal problem we all share.

These suggestions broach the topic of shame by discussing it in the life of someone else, and subtly invite nonbelievers to process their own shame. This discussion on eliciting shame in evangelistic conversations raises the question of conviction and conscience—How do people become aware of their problem before God?

CONVICTION OF SIN

To state the obvious, people's behavior in honor-shame cultures is governed by honor and shame, not guilt and innocence. Their existential problem is not so much a plagued introspective conscience (i.e., internal guilt), but public disgrace (i.e., external shame). Because shame and honor are communal qualities, moral conviction tends to be external, not internal. So when the Holy Spirit convicts the world (Jn 16), he does so through internal conviction (guilt) *and* external conviction (shame). In fact, "scholars generally agree that the Holy Spirit convicted biblical characters through external, not internal, voices."[18] One example is how the prophet Nathan was a tool of the Spirit to convict King David (1 Sam 12).[19]

We should not limit the Holy Spirit's work of conviction to the "the inner voice" of one's internal moral faculty (i.e., guilt); we should include "the outer voice" of the community (i.e., shame). Conviction includes a corporate reality as well. We learn about our sin from other people; this is often the voice of shame. The New Testament word translated as "conscience" (Greek *syneidon*) does not strictly refer to an inward moral compass, but a general awareness of something—"consciousness."[20] The *syneidon* that convicts people involves a "social awareness" of how our actions are perceived by others. The awareness of how God and his people regard us (i.e., consciousness) makes us feel ashamed ("convicted") of our sin, and consequently pursue honorable conduct. "Pray for us; we are sure that we have a clear conscience, desiring to act honorably in all things" (Heb 13:18).

Perceiving shame as the Spirit's conviction affects evangelism. We ought not dismiss shame as some elementary insecurity or irrational "people pleasing." The shame people feel not only represents a surface-level "felt need" but also illustrates their sinfulness before God. While a nonbeliever may not be aware of it, their anxiety over communal shame is ultimately rooted in their shame before God. One reason people may feel shame is because they have actually sinned.[21] Shame may be a legitimate starting point in evangelism. Theologian Dietrich Bonhoeffer said shame "gives reluctant witness" to our disunion with God.[22] People's experience of shame testifies, in part, to the reality of and need for the gospel. Christian witness does not invite nonbelievers to throw away the mask of shame, but to discern the underlying spiritual reality behind the mask. Shame, not just guilt, is God's piercing voice making people aware of their need for salvation.

So then, once a person is conscious of their spiritual shamefulness before God and desires to follow Jesus as Lord, how should they respond to be saved? The answer is Jesus' summons in Mark 1:15—"Repent, and believe in the good news." People must "repent" and "believe" to acquire a new honorable status and join God's group. What does it mean to "repent" and "believe" in collectivistic and honor-shame cultures, such as those of the Bible?

REPENTANCE AND FAITH

In first-century Israel the shame of Roman occupation weighed on the people. They longed for restored glory. The various types of Jewish groups (e.g., Zealots, Essenes, Pharisees) sought restored glory through different means. Yet in that setting Jesus called people to forego efforts, whether violent or otherwise, to remove Israel's shame and restore national honor. To experience the kingdom of God in fullness, Jesus said (in various ways) that people must turn from those warped ideologies of status accrual and begin following him. Repentance involves exclusive allegiance and adherence to Jesus himself.[23]

Conversion involves changing allegiances, abandoning the agenda of one group for another, turning from the honor code of one group for that of another. Or in simple terms, conversion means entering a new family. The call to repentance summons people to desist from the cultural game of exalting their own name and instead to come live under God's name. Repentance is not so much a change of ideology from one set of beliefs to another, but a change of alliance from one group to another. Jesus' command to repent could be paraphrased as "Stop trying to accrue honor through that group, and join my group to obtain the glory of God's kingdom!" This repentance Jesus spoke of "offered membership in the renewed people of the covenant god."[24]

In the throes of everyday life, repentance means different things for people depending on their position in the social hierarchy. On one hand, the marginalized and scorned must repent from their hopelessness in failing to trust God's power to remove shame; they turn from false shame. On the other hand, for the privileged and proud, repentance means abandoning humanly concocted efforts of procuring status and constructing face; they turn from false honor. But regardless of whether one is a social outcast or a social elite, repentance involves a movement toward God and his true honor.

While conversion is primarily a transfer of allegiance to Jesus, moral change remains an essential component of conversion. As one becomes a member of the new group, naturally certain behavior is expected of them to demonstrate their allegiance. This is indeed true for believers in God's family. (In chapters ten and eleven we will discuss Christian morality and ethics in honor-shame terms.)

Along with repenting, a person must have *pistis*. This Greek word *pistis* (commonly translated as "belief" or "faith") carries the sense of personal "loyalty," or "fidelity," to a relationship, similar to the Latin word *fides*.[25] Biblical *pistis* is not primarily internal emotions or cognitive ascent, but a sense of relational loyalty—that is, faithfulness. A person's *pistis* is a publicly demonstrated commitment to the group and its leader. Such loyalty brings honor to a superior. *Pistis* is a pledge to remain faithful to the relational covenant, and purposefully seeks to promote the honor of a superior via obedience to their authority.

People of honor-shame cultures can easily understand this covenantal meaning of *pistis*, as they already place a high value on relational loyalty and commitment to the group leader. Families are tightly knit kinship groups where individual members are expected to advance the group's reputation. One example of this is Asian American families—young adults are expected to choose careers that reflect positively on their parents; there is a strong sense of familial loyalty; children's obedience brings honor to their parents. This strongly relational notion of group loyalty best approximates the meaning of *pistis*, not the common Western idea of "my personal faith." Such faithfulness toward the Lord enhances his name and renown by demonstrating allegiance.

The structure of patron-client relationships could be a helpful model for understanding conversion in honor-shame cultures. Following Jesus is not merely a "personal religious experience," but "allegiance to a new patron." The frequent New Testament words *savior*, *faith* and *grace* were all common terms in the rhetoric of benefaction in the Greco-Roman world. We've discussed patron-client relationship in human relationships (chaps. 3 and 7), but the ancient honor-shame cultures of the Bible commonly understood conversion as transferring their loyalties to a new patron-client relationship—humans receive divine salvation from their Patron, and he gets glory, praise, loyalty and allegiance from us, the grateful clients.

As people come to believe in Jesus Christ as Lord, the question arises—How do people follow Jesus in an honor-shame context? Our final chapters look at Christian discipleship, ethics and community from an honor-shame perspective.

Discussion and Application Questions

1. Reflect on your own conversion experience. What were the primary factors leading to Christ? At that time, how did you understand your decision to follow Jesus?

2. Since a common pattern of conversion in honor-shame contexts is "community → discipleship → evangelism," what are practical ways you could integrate nonbelievers into your existing community of believers?

3. What are some ways you could talk about shame with unbelievers?

10

ETHICS

*Honor is very important in bringing
about change in the world.*

ANTHONY APPIAH

*Love one another with mutual affection;
outdo one another in showing honor.*

ROMANS 12:10

*A*MINA WAS EIGHTEEN YEARS OLD WHEN her family in Kabul, Afghanistan, forcibly betrothed her. She did not want to marry the man her family had selected, so she ran away from home and took refuge at a women's shelter.[1] The women's shelter contacted Amina's parents to mediate restoration with her family. After her brother and uncle signed and video recorded guarantees that she would not be harmed, Amina agreed to return to her family. She left the women's shelter, but never reached home. Allegedly, armed men stormed the car and shot her to death, though nobody else was harmed. Amina was the victim of an "honor killing" to eradicate family shame.

In conservative honor cultures such as Afghanistan, community pressure to preserve traditions leads families to violently expel a member who has brought shame or disgrace on the family. The honor of men (as father, husband or brother) is linked to the sexual purity of the women in their family. The victims of honor killings, and other forms of honor violence, are often younger family members whose lives do not meet community expectations. Honor killings make little sense to people in the West. The bizarre and unintelligible social practice appalls Western minds.

To curb the occurrences of honor killings, one response has been to pass new laws criminalizing the behavior. The United States alone spent $904 million in Afghanistan between 2002 and 2010 to fund the "rule of law and justice" and to "develop effective justice sector institutions."[2] But as one might suspect, creating new rules and laws has hardly changed moral behavior in Afghanistan's rural and tribal regions. The *New York Times* article telling Amina's story is titled "In Spite of the Law, Afghan 'Honor Killings' of Women Continue." The reason new laws have not prevented honor killings is rather simple—people take honor far more seriously than the law. As one Iraqi man explained, "It's about honor. Honor is more important for us than religion."[3]

While honor killings represent an extreme tendency of honor-shame cultures, we find the surrounding ethical discussion relevant for Christian ethics and discipleship in collectivistic societies. How is morality changed in honor-shame contexts? The reflex of Westerners, whether Christian missionaries or secular diplomats, is to double down on laws and justice, but this exacerbates the frustration, as reflected in the common refrain, "It doesn't matter what the law says, they only feel bad if someone finds out!" So if laws and justice do not uproot deep-seated honor codes and change moral behavior, what does? What is the best approach to reforming morality?

In his book *The Honor Code: How Moral Revolutions Happen,* Princeton philosophy professor Anthony Appiah suggests the best weapon for changing moral norms is—honor and shame.[4] Appiah notes how the historic practices of Chinese foot binding, gentlemen's dueling in England and Transatlantic slave trading all ceased once they became associated with shame and dishonor. When moral decisions are propelled by a sense of honor, social norms will change only as people begin defining particular behavior as honorable or shameful, not legal or illegal. Therefore, changing ethical norms requires reshaping the honor code.

Interestingly, the New Testament letters employ this same approach and strive to reform believers' honor codes. The New Testament makes honor a key foundation for moral and ethical behavior, especially 1 Peter.

The New Honor Code (1 Peter)

The epistle of 1 Peter provides believers with a new honor code to guide their personal conduct. The overall literary structure of the letter is worth noting, as it provides a logical framework for contemporary discipleship. The opening one and a half chapters (1 Pet 1:3–2:10) theologically affirm believers' divine honor; then the final three and a half chapters (1 Pet 2:13–5:11) outline how Christians are to live out that divine honor in everyday life. The admonition of 1 Peter 2:11-12 transitions the letter from theology to ethics, explaining how Christians live honorably in the face of shame. Our paraphrase draws out the honor-shame nuances of these verses.

> Those cherished and honored by God,
> I urge you as marginalized and scorned social outcasts,
> refrain from cultural mechanisms to establish your own reputation
> (because that actually demeans your worth before God).
> Rather, make sure your behavior among the pagans is honorable.
> So, even though they scorn you and spoil your reputation,
> Eventually they will see your respectable behavior and honor God
> when he returns to publicly evaluate all people. (1 Pet 2:11-12 authors' paraphrase)

As Peter reshapes notions of honor and shame for readers, he does not speak in theological generalities, but offers a new honor code for specific aspects of life in 1 Peter 2:13–5:11. Below are eight areas in which Peter restructures the honor code, so as to keep Christians on the track of God's honor. Note the honor-shame language (italicized) in each admonition.

- Government (1 Pet 2:13-17): "*For the Lord's sake* accept the authority of every human institution . . . as sent by him to punish those who do wrong and to *praise* those who do right. . . . *Honor* everyone. *Love* the family of believers. *Fear* God. *Honor* the emperor." To honor the emperor was normal, expected of all; Peter adds to this, "honor everyone" (1 Pet 2:17).

- Work (1 Pet 2:18-20): "Slaves, *accept the authority* of your masters *with all deference.* . . . If you endure when you do right and suffer for it, you have *God's approval.*"

- Marriage (1 Pet 3:1-7): "Wives, in the same way, accept the authority of your husbands, so that . . . they may be won over . . . when they see the *purity* and *reverence* of your lives. . . . Let your adornment be the inner self with the lasting beauty of a gentle and quiet spirit, which is *very precious* in *God's sight*. . . . Husbands, in the same way, *show consideration* for your wives in your life together, *paying honor* to the woman."

- Community (1 Pet 4:8-11): "Above all, maintain *constant love* for one another, for love covers a multitude of sins. *Be hospitable* to one another. . . . *Serve* one another with whatever *gift* each of you has received . . . so that *God may be glorified* in all things through Jesus Christ."

- Persecution (1 Pet 4:13-16): "But rejoice insofar as you are sharing Christ's *sufferings*, so that you may also be glad and shout for joy when his *glory is revealed*. If you are *reviled* for the *name* of Christ, you are *blessed*, because the spirit of *glory*, which is the *Spirit of God*, is resting on you. . . . Yet if any of you *suffers* as a Christian, do not consider it a *disgrace*, but *glorify* God because you *bear this name*."

- Leadership (1 Pet 5:1-4): "As one who shares in *the glory to be revealed*, I exhort the *elders* among you to tend the flock of God. . . . *Do not lord it over* those in your charge, but be examples to the flock. And when the *chief shepherd* appears, *you will win the crown of glory that never fades away*."

- Followership (1 Pet 5:5a): "In the same way, you who are *younger* must *accept the authority* of the *elders*."

- Social stratification (1 Pet 5:5b-6): "And all of you must *clothe yourselves with humility* in your dealings with one another, for 'God *opposes the proud*, but *gives grace to the humble*.' *Humble yourselves* therefore *under* the *mighty hand of God*, so that he may *exalt* you in due time."

    People proudly displayed their social position by wearing garments that identified their social position. To suggest they all wear the same garment negates such social distinctions. Yet Peter goes a step further when he suggests the common garment they all wear is humility. "A world built around social stratification works only if those who are of high status exhibit disrespect toward those of lower status *and* if those of low status esteem those of higher status."[5] If everyone takes a posture of humility of self and esteem of others, then that system crumbles. By pairing the two, Peter flattens the status pyramid of the Roman world.

Peter's key to discipleship in honor-shame contexts is profoundly theological and deeply rooted in Jesus' shame-removing and honor-restoring life. John Elliott writes, "In Christian communities at odds with their environments and pressured to conform and assimilate, honor and shame are theologically redefined and reckoned according to the calculus of divine reversal preeminently expressed in God's honoring of the shamed Messiah."[6] This countervailing honor from God reconceptualizes relationships and ethics in all spheres of life.

The topics 1 Peter broaches are hardly random or accidental. In our experiences, these are significant areas of life in which sub-biblical honor codes can so easily entangle Christians. If a believer's honor code is not reoriented toward God's, then major parts of a believer's life will be determined by the default values of cultures. They will resort to cultural mechanisms to avoid shame and accrue honor. Marriage and leadership are keys areas where God's honor code reshapes prevailing norms.

BIBLICAL MARRIAGE

Erdo and Jakul, both believers, were newly married. A few months after their wedding, Erdo's relatives visited their house. Jakul spent the day preparing and cooking for her in-laws. When the guests arrived, Erdo sat with them in the main living space while Jakul served the food, as was customary. When Jakul did not attend to Erdo amid the busyness, one of the relatives commented to Erdo, "Did you see how your wife disrespected you? Why don't you have control of your house like a man?" The comment was public, challenging Erdo to assert his honor by scolding and beating his wife before the group. In such a moment, Peter's radical instruction recalibrates notions of honor and shame—"Husbands, in the same way, show consideration for your wives in your life together, paying honor to the woman" (1 Pet 3:7). Erdo's relative's comments display vividly the challenge for believers navigating two conflicting honor codes.

At a wedding dinner in Malaysia, Dave (a Western Christian) explained this new honor code regarding marriage.[7] Here is his story:

Some of the Malay men have more than one wife, and it is common here for the guys to "joke" about taking a second wife. My wife and I went to a Malay wedding. We were sitting at a round table with four other couples. After eating the men started joking about taking second wives; the women fell silent with somber faces. Even though the men do this in a humorous tone, it seems they are sending a clear message to their wives. The "jokes" remind the wives that if they do not "toe the line," the husband does have the option of taking another wife, which of course is humiliating to the first wife.

After a few minutes they were curious to know my thoughts on taking a second wife. I told them, "Like Adam and Eve, I believe my wife is God's gift to me, and I need to look after her. God never gave Adam a second wife, and that is the example of a marriage to aspire to." The ladies started to smile and look up. "Later it was written in the New Testament that husbands should love their wives like Jesus loved the church (his followers). We Christians believe Jesus voluntarily gave up his life for his followers. This means that I should think of my wife and put her needs before mine, and if I do that my wife will gladly respect and follow me." By this time the smiles of the wives were pretty broad. The message I wanted them to hear is that God honors them as women and wives. The men were quiet. If they felt dishonor for honoring their wives, that is something they should learn to overcome.

BIBLICAL LEADERSHIP

Honor-shame cultures distribute leadership power unequally.[8] Leaders enjoy unique privileges and unequal rights; subordinates generally accept the hierarchical authority and fulfill their subordinate role. While power tends to corrupt people in every culture, the disproportionate power of leaders in collectivistic cultures often leads to unbiblical expressions and abuses of leadership. For this reason, God's new honor code transforms ideals of leadership for Christians.

Leaders in contexts prizing honor often seek to leverage power for personal and relational gain. For example, government leaders often turn the state into a family business, extracting wealth from others (and everybody expects it). These leaders acquire the key status symbols to indicate their significance—an important title, a large entourage, an expensive car and so on. Leaders coalesce decision-making authority into their own hands and publicly scold subordinates to demonstrate power. They become "the Big

Man" controlling resources, the patron who provides in exchange for praise and loyalty. Leaders project strength and power to garner honor, or at least to instill a fear of retaliation for not honoring. This characterization of leadership—honor grasping and honor abusing—is most visible in the political world, but also occurs in the workplace, home and church. If this is the modus operandi of leaders (especially in honor-shame contexts), how does God's honor redefine and transform kingdom leadership? How can Christian leaders and ministers counteract the innate honor-grabbing reflex found in every human heart? Some ancient examples help us answer these questions.

About two thousand years ago, Marius Valens was a leader in the Roman military colony of Philippi. Like other residents of the highly stratified community, Marius Valens sought honor. He felt compelled to publicly proclaim his social distinction and importance. So he inscribed his biographical reasons for honor (*cursus honorum*) in stone, then publicly displayed it for every passerby in Philippi to see. Filled with honorific terms and titles, the actual inscription boasts:

> Publius Marius Valens, son of Publius, of the tribe of Voltinia, honored with
> the insignia of rank of a member of the town council, aedile, also a decurión
> of Philippi, flamen of the divine Antonius Pius, duovir, organizer of the glad-
> iatorial games.[9]

Marius Valens boldly publicized his claim to honor as a Philippian leader. New Testament scholar Joseph Hellerman notes, "Excavations at Philippi have produced the most detailed inscriptions found anywhere in the Roman Empire outlining the civic and military honors of veteran colonists." This suggests Philippian citizens were particularly eager to display their superior rank and status.[10] In this context of widespread self-honoring, the Christians in the Philippian church "would hardly have been immune to these pressures" of boasting and claiming status, especially the leaders.[11] To help redefine leadership and power for these Philippian believers, the apostle Paul recounts the *cursus honorum* of two other leaders. Their radical examples subvert the traditional Roman idea of power and authority.

> Though he [Jesus Christ] was in the form of God,
> [he] did not regard equality with God
>   as something to be exploited,

but emptied himself,

taking the form of a slave,

being born in human likeness.

And being found in human form,

he humbled himself

and became obedient to the point of death—

even death on a cross. (Phil 2:6-8)

If anyone else has reason to be confident in the flesh, I [Paul] have more: circumcised on the eighth day, a member of the people of Israel, of the tribe of Benjamin, a Hebrew born of Hebrews; as to the law, a Pharisee; as to zeal, a persecutor of the church; as to righteousness under the law, blameless.

Yet whatever gains I had, these I have come to regard as loss because of Christ. More than that, I regard everything as loss because of the surpassing value of knowing Christ Jesus my Lord. For his sake I have suffered the loss of all things, and I regard them as rubbish, in order that I may gain Christ.... I want to know Christ and the power of his resurrection and the sharing of his sufferings by becoming like him in death. (Phil 3:4-8, 10)

The letter to the Philippians defines Christian leadership in terms of humility, not power. The words of Philippians 2:3-5 are likely familiar verses to you, the reader. But to sense the weight of Paul's admonition for humble servant leadership, read these verses through the eyes of Marius Valens (above), or a political/business leader in your context: "Do nothing from selfish ambition or conceit, but in humility regard others as better than yourselves. Let each of you look not to your own interests, but to the interests of others. Let the same mind be in you that was in Christ Jesus" (Phil 2:3-4).

Humility is the hallmark of Christian ministry. Leadership is not relinquishing all power to become the proverbial doormat to others, but using strength to serve, love and honor others. Humility is not relinquishing all influence in the name of modesty. Rather, humility "is *the noble choice to forego your status, deploy your resources or use your influence for the good of others before yourself.* More simply, you could say the humble person is marked by *a willingness to hold power in service of others.*"[12] Leadership is influence, and humility enhances influence because it is a winsome character trait of leaders.

Everybody regards humility as a virtue, but mostly for other people, not themselves! Biblical humility is a posture of the heart played out in countless ways in everyday life. Here are some identifiable ways it transforms leadership in honor-shame contexts. Christians can lead honorably by growing in their capacity to accept criticism, overcome jealousy and empower teamwork.

In hierarchical societies, correcting leaders is perceived as a challenge and even an insult. Leaders respond to critics by harshly shaming them to preserve face. When operating by the values of biblical humility, receiving criticism is honorable. Mature leaders accept correction graciously as an opportunity for growth (Heb 12:5-8).

Jealousy is another poison debilitating leaders. Envy of others' status leads to conflict and competition, as status is often viewed as a zero-sum game—your gain means my loss. But Christians operate with a surplus of honor. When the reservoirs of our souls are at full capacity with God's honor, we are free to bless others with honor; it overflows. A leader with Honor is not seduced by honor.

Last, humility allows leaders to empower teamwork. The purpose of a group must extend beyond making the leader appear prominent, to achieving the group's highest interest. Then the assets of each person, regardless of rank or status, contribute to the overall good of the group. Legitimate teamwork needs a benevolent leader who prioritizes the group's best. A leader who utilizes the giftings of each person brings flourishing to the entire group, not just fame to their own name.

CHRISTIANS' NEW HONOR CODE: GLORY, PURITY AND LOVE

The letter of 1 Peter reveals God's new honor code for first-century Christians, and we examined how God's countercultural honor code can operate in the areas of marriage and leadership. But as contemporary Christians in honor-shame contexts encounter new ethical situations, it becomes essential to develop a nuanced honor-based ethic. The Bible appeals to honor to guide Christians' moral decisions in several ways: Christians should glorify God, purify themselves and love others. These three principles provide a biblical rubric for ethical discernment in honor-shame contexts. The following examples will display how biblical ethics is "honor based."

As the Westminster Catechism famously begins, "Man's chief end is to glorify God." The ultimate aim of all Christian behavior is to bring honor to God. "So, whether you eat or drink, or whatever you do, do everything for the glory of God" (1 Cor 10:31; cf. Col. 3:17).

In Romans 14 Paul helps the congregation in Rome overcome divisions based on food convictions. Neither the "weak" nor the "strong" should despise or condemn (i.e., shame) the other because of dietary matters (Rom 14:1-5). Rather, "The one who eats, eats in honor of the Lord, since he gives thanks to God, while the one who abstains, abstains in honor of the Lord and gives thanks to God" (Rom 14:6 ESV). To guide the community, Paul does not offer specific commands for a particular behavior, but explains that right action is done "in honor of the Lord." Morality revolves around a God-honoring faith. Bringing honor and glory to God functions as the ethical standard. This implies there are situations in which people "sin" without ever breaking a rule or commandment (Rom 14:21-23). According to Romans 3:23 the target all humans miss is properly glorifying God, not an impersonal legal code of moral behavior. In Malachi, God critiques the priests because they did "not take it to heart to give honor to My name" (Mal 2:2 NASB), but have despised and profaned God's name with their polluted sacrifices (Mal 1:6-14). The aim of Christian ethics is to honor, or glorify, God.

Even God acts to enhance his own honor. God refers to his own name, praise and glory six times in this short passage.

> For *my name's sake* I defer my anger,
>   for the sake of *my praise* I restrain it for you. . . .
> For *my own sake*, for *my own sake*, I do it,
>   for why should *my name* be profaned?
> *My glory* I will not give to another. (Is 48:9, 11)

In Exodus 32 Moses appeals to God's public reputation to influence his actions. When Israel creates and worships a golden calf at Sinai, God vows to destroy the entire nation for their idolatry. Observe how Moses appeals to honor ("It would be *shameful!*") instead of justice ("It would be *wrong!*") to convince God otherwise:

> Why should the Egyptians say, "It was with evil intent that he brought them out to kill them in the mountains, and to consume them from the face of the earth"? Turn from your fierce wrath; change your mind and do not bring disaster on your people. Remember Abraham, Isaac, and Israel, your servants, how you swore to them by your own self. (Ex 32:12-13)

Destruction of Israel would be doubly shameful for God. One, the Egyptians would speak badly about his name. And two, God jeopardizes his honor and integrity if he breaks the promises he swore to by his own name. Apparently God found Moses' honor-based rationale convincing—"And the LORD changed his mind about the disaster that he planned" (Ex 32:14). Proper moral behavior is that which brings glory to God's name.

The Bible also appeals to a believer's own honor, using the language of holiness and purity to positively influence moral action. In 2 Timothy 2, Paul offers Timothy instructions for dealing with quarrelsome teachers in the church. In the middle of his specific instructions (2 Tim 2:14-26), Paul uses the metaphor of vessels to describe the basis of ethics—Timothy's *own* honor.

> Now in a great house there are not only vessels of gold and silver but also of wood and clay, some for honorable use, some for dishonorable. Therefore, if anyone cleanses himself from what is dishonorable, he will be a vessel for honorable use, set apart as holy, useful to the master of the house, ready for every good work. (2 Tim 2:20-21 ESV)

Paul here uses the term *vessel*—a common euphemism in Greek for the human body—to identify the different types of people in the church. Some are composed of valuable materials and so are for honorable purposes, while others consist of inferior materials suitable only for dishonorable tasks. Paul applies this imagery to the spiritual household of God. (Recall, these were the days before modern plumbing, so the "dishonorable vessels" typically carried bodily excrement out from the bathroom; see Deut 23:12-13.) Timothy therefore must distinguish himself from the dishonorable via moral separation and cleansing. As Timothy proves himself to be an honorable vessel by properly handling the church conflict as Paul instructs him, he will be considered a "holy" vessel capable of carrying out the Master's will. The motivation for godly behavior in Paul's instruction is to make oneself an honorable person worthy to be used for God's honorable purposes.

The language of purity, holiness and sanctification informs ethical instruction throughout the New Testament. The early church transformed Old Testament purity regulations into a new purity code in which separation from vice (not Gentiles) is the guiding principle. The revulsion once felt toward the "unclean" is now applied toward defining and influencing the morality of Jesus' followers.[13] "Since we have these promises, beloved, let us cleanse ourselves from every defilement of body and of spirit, making holiness perfect in the fear of God" (2 Cor 7:1). According to 1 Thessalonians 4:4, the will of God includes knowing "how to control your own body in holiness and honor." Personal (and corporate) holiness is an aim of the Christian life. God deems people who act appropriately to be morally clean and undefiled.

> Like obedient children, do not be conformed to the desires that you formerly had in ignorance. Instead, as he who called you is holy, be holy yourselves in all your conduct; for it is written, "You shall be holy, for I am holy."
> . . . You have purified your souls by your obedience to the truth so that you have genuine mutual love. (1 Pet 1:14-16, 22; cf. Lev 11:44; 20:26)

The New Testament appeal to become honorable people by virtue of holiness and moral purity reminds Christians that seeking and obtaining "honor" is not always sinful. Honor is a good thing when people seek it from God and use it for his glory. Christians should not abandon pursuit of honor. Rather they should passionately pursue the *right kind* of honor. The Gospel of John explains the issue in the clearest of terms: "How can you believe when you accept glory from one another and do not seek the glory that comes from the one who alone is God?" (Jn 5:44), and "They loved human glory more than the glory that comes from God" (Jn 12:43). The Pharisees are not condemned for pursuing glory, but for pursuing glory *incorrectly*. The Bible does not reject honor as an unworthy pursuit, but summons people to a higher, truer, eternal honor. The goal of discipleship is not to pivot people from shame-based morality to a guilt-based morality, but rather is to transform people's notions of honor and shame so they align with God's.

The third way the Bible develops an honor-based ethic is by making honor a central obligation we owe to fellow humans. The New Testament frequently makes "honor others" an imperative of Christian ethics. Note these examples:

> Honor everyone. (1 Pet 2:17)

> Outdo one another in showing honor. (Rom 12:10)

> Pay to all what is due them—taxes to whom taxes are due, revenue to whom revenue is due, respect to whom respect is due, honor to whom honor is due. (Rom 13:7)

And those members of the body that we think less honorable we clothe with greater honor, and our less respectable members are treated with greater respect. (1 Cor 12:23)

Honor widows. (1 Tim 5:3)

Let the elders who rule well be considered worthy of double honor. (1 Tim 5:17)

Let all who are under the yoke of slavery regard their masters as worthy of all honor. (1 Tim 6:1)[14]

One way the Bible speaks about properly extending honor and respect to other people is "love." Note the parallel between love and honor in Romans 12:10—"Love one another with mutual affection; outdo one another in showing honor." Loving people (i.e., considering them and their interests as more significant) is the centerpiece of Christian ethics (1 Cor 13). At several points in the New Testament, honor/love overshadows legal obedience as the leading moral virtue. When the Pharisees ask Jesus about the commandments of the law, he says all the law and the prophets hang on two commandments—love the Lord your God and love your neighbor as yourself (Mt 22:37-40). One's relational commitment to God is fulfilled by entirely loving God and one's neighbor. When the lawyer asks Jesus to clarify what this means, Jesus tells the story of the good Samaritan (Lk 10:25-37) to highlight how extending love and dignity to others overrides the laws concerning ceremonial defilement. In Galatians 5:13-14 Paul summarizes his communal instruction in similar terms—"Through love become slaves to one another. For the whole law is summed up in a single commandment, 'You shall love your neighbor as yourself.'" The measuring stick for ethics in the community marked out by God's Spirit is love, as expressed through servant-like service to others. Voluntarily undignifying oneself to esteem others captures the biblical meaning of love.

The Bible commonly grounds ethics in notions of honor. Glorying God, being an honorably pure person and honoring/loving others are core bases for Christian ethics. Unethical conduct brings dishonor to God's name, defiles oneself and disregards others. Despite the prominence of honor and shame in biblical morality and ethics, Western Christianity by and large neglects the re-formation of believers' honor code in training and discipleship.

HONORING RELATIONSHIPS AS MORALITY

Westerners often have the impression that honor-shame cultures do not believe in right and wrong. This is a false impression. Ghanaian theologian Kwame Bediako comments,

> Some suggest that ours is a "shame culture" and not a "guilt culture," on the grounds that public acceptance determines morality, and consequently a "sense of sin" is said to be absent. However, in our [African] tradition, the essence of sin is in its being an antisocial act. This makes sin basically injury to the interests of another person and damage to the collective life of the group.[15]

The belief that traditional peoples have no sense of sin originally came from Western evolutionary paradigms viewing shame-based cultures as morally inferior, even depraved, compared to guilt-based cultures.

Honor-shame cultures do have a moral sense of right and wrong, but their basis for right and wrong differs from Western culture. Honor-shame cultures define right and wrong relationally and communally, not abstractly or legally. What is best for relationships and people is morally right; what shames is morally wrong. The basis for ethics and morality is not an abstract legal code or impersonal sense of justice, but harmonious relationships and community (see 1 Pet 2:12-15). Victor Furnish in his study *Theology and Ethics in Paul* notes a similar perspective within Pauline ethics.

> This communal context of the believer's life is of the greatest importance for Paul's understanding of how the Christian is able to know what he ought to and ought not to do. . . . For [Paul], moral action is never a matter of an isolated actor choosing from among a variety of abstract ideas on the basis of how inherently "good" or "evil" each may be. Instead it is always a matter of choosing and doing what is good for the brother and what will upbuild the whole community of brethren.[16]

Ethics is ultimately the formation of Christian community—*ekklēsia*. Paul grounds his moral vision in the formation of God's new covenant people. New Testament scholar Richard Hays explains, "For [Paul] the primary sphere of moral concern is not the character of the individual, but the corporate obedience of the church. . . . He is consistently formulating the ethical mandate in ecclesial terms, seeking God's will not by asking first, 'What should I do?' but 'What should we, as God's people, do?'"[17]

A relationship-based ethic does not mean community preferences become the moral standard; quite the opposite. God's reality determines what is honorable and shameful. The Bible acknowledges that people in every context have unique ways of expressing honor and shame (Rom 14), but unequivocally affirms that only God defines true shamefulness and honorableness.

The letter of 1 Corinthians, in which Paul ad hoc addresses various ethical issues within the community, illustrates this community-centric ethic. Paul's vision for group unity shapes his pastoral admonitions. In 1 Corinthians, whether the issue is factions (1 Cor 1–4), incestuous relations (1 Cor 5), meat sacrificed to idols (1 Cor 8–10), the Lord's Supper (1 Cor 11:17-34) or public worship (1 Cor 12–14), the right action must be discerned with the needs and identity of the community in mind. Edifying relationships constitute Paul's foremost moral yardstick—"All things are lawful," but not all things build up. Do not seek your own advantage, but that of the other (1 Cor 10:23-24). In light of Paul's vision to form countercultural communities of Jesus followers around the Mediterranean, Paul's letters "should be read primarily as instruments of community formation. Their rhetoric consistently aims at reinforcing group cohesion and loyalty within the community of faith."[18]

This Pauline emphasis on community and relational harmony parallels the moral ideals of honor-shame cultures. New Testament ethics communicates morality through an honor-shame framework (e.g., glory, purity, community, relational harmony, honor code). However, sin distorts social systems of honor and shame and undermines relational harmony. In the Corinthian community, the pursuit of status distinction within the group caused divisions and demeaned others. Particular members claimed status based on their oratory skills, benefactions, appearances, wealth and even spiritual gifts. Their twisted pursuit of worldly honor produced shame, and thus required a recalibration of their honor code to align it with God's conceptions of honorableness and shamefulness. To restore unity, Paul counteracts all such boasting with God's sovereign, shame-erasing grace.

> Consider your own call, brothers and sisters: not many of you were wise by
> human standards, not many were powerful, not many were of noble birth. But

God chose what is foolish in the world to shame the wise; God chose what is weak in the world to shame the strong; God chose what is low and despised in the world, things that are not, to reduce to nothing things that are, so that no one might boast in the presence of God. He is the source of your life in Christ Jesus, who became for us wisdom from God, and righteousness and sanctification and redemption, in order that, as it is written, "Let the one who boasts, boast in the Lord." (1 Cor 1:26-31)

Believers derive honor solely from God's election and the sanctifying work of his Spirit in the believer, not any social status resulting from worldly accomplishments or spiritual giftings.[19] Consequently Christian ethics renounces honor competition and status distinction in favor of community edification, the construction of God's holy temple. The honor conferred by God enables genuine community (Jn 17:22; 1 Cor 12:23-25). The formation of God's *ekklēsia* is God's central focus in the current era of salvation history, and so stands as the center of new covenant ethics and morality.

Conclusion: Seeing the Light

How should Christians seek to bring about moral change in a socially redeeming and God-glorifying manner? How does the Holy Spirit guide a person to follow and obey Jesus? Following Jesus involves adopting his code of honor in all areas of life, making everyday decisions based on what God determines is honorable or shameful.

The Gospel of John uses this language of *darkness* and *light* to explain the transformation of honor codes. Darkness is basically a false code of honor. To be in darkness is to esteem all the wrong things, to misattribute glory and worth. Those in darkness are unable to perceive the glory manifested in Jesus, unlike Isaiah, who saw the glory (see Jn 12:37-41; Is 6:10).

When people come into the light, they can rightly perceive spiritual realities. Light allows people to see an object's true identity and worth. Such vision affords the correct granting of honor to objects of legitimate value. John's language about sight is another image about correctly perceiving identity and worth. In John 9 the blind man believes and worships Jesus upon receiving sight (Jn 9:30-33, 38). Jesus, as "the light of the world," allows humanity to discern who and what is truly honorable. In Jesus, the human family can see the face of Glory—"For it is the God who said, 'Let light shine out of darkness,' who has shone in our hearts to give the light of the knowledge of the glory of God in the face of Jesus Christ" (2 Cor 4:6). The gospel of Christ's glory sheds light on true honor.

Transforming the honor code is central to Christian discipleship in many ways. But ultimately, simply knowing God's honor code for life will not suffice. It must be lived out. The next chapter explores how the Christian community can aid people in living out God's honor code.

Discussion and Application Questions

1. What are aspects of the local honor code in your context that reflect God's will and common grace? What are some aspects of it that must be redeemed and transformed?

2. How could you communicate Christian ethics in terms of honor and shame?

3. In what moral situations should relationships be more important than rules for guiding behavior?

11

COMMUNITY

It is clear also what is the power
of honor and how it can cause party faction;
for men form factions both when they are themselves
dishonored and when they see others honored.

ARISTOTLE, *POLITICS* 5.2.4

The glory that you have given me I have given them,
so that they may be one, as we are one.

JOHN 17:22

*T*HE NEW HONOR CODE PROCLAIMED in the New Testament was radical. For example, Paul writes, "There is no longer Jew or Greek, there is no longer slave or free, there is no longer male and female; for all of you are one in Christ Jesus" (Gal 3:28). Yet these words do not shock Western Christians; Paul's statement generally coheres with Western egalitarian values. One cannot appreciate how radical something is without first knowing what is normal in that same setting.

Bruce Longenecker, a New Testament scholar, has written *The Lost Letters of Pergamum*.[1] His book is a narrative of historical fiction that helps the reader sense not only how concern for honor pervaded the world of the New Testament but also what was considered honorable. Longenecker's story portrays the "normal" of Paul's day, when society made marked distinctions between people and groups of people. To accentuate the contrast between Christian practices and the norms of Paul's day, Longenecker introduces us to how a non-Christian might have responded to a first-century church meeting. Antipas, a high-status nonbeliever, describes the gathering in a letter.

> One thing struck me from the moment of being welcomed among them: The gatherers are very diverse with regard to their social statures, ethnic backgrounds, and civic positions. . . . Moreover, at no point did those gathered seem particularly interested in regulating their behavior according to social codes. This was especially evident when the food was brought out from the kitchens. At that point, the gatherers simply assembled themselves in small groups throughout the house, without any special interest in arranging themselves according to social customs of honor. I have never seen members of associations act in that fashion.[2]

At the house-church gathering Antipas meets Simon, a tenant farmer who, after hitting hard times, had ended up sick and begging on the streets. Antonius, the host of the meeting, had picked up Simon the beggar and brought him into his house and the church group, and his health was restored. Antipas comments that despite his low status Simon had a kind of nobility in Antonius's eyes, something he finds incomprehensible. What nobleman would care for a diseased beggar? Antipas explains,

> Moreover, Antonius must certainly have compromised his public honor in the flagrant act of extending hospitality to an expendable such as Simon had been. All of my natural impulses are repelled by the thought of Antonius' action, and my instincts label it an impractical, irresponsible, and ultimately dishonorable action. And yet there was Simon, standing before me in Antonius' house, with honor in his eyes—a testament to Antonius' unprecedented benevolence.[3]

Intrigued by both the meal in Antonius's house and by a manuscript of Luke's Gospel that he was reading, Antipas returned to the house church. Again he reports with amazement how the group acts in ways contrary to the norms and values of the day. He noted that those attending treated Antonius with the respect reserved for one who is the patron of a meeting. On further thought, however, Antipas qualifies his observation: "Or perhaps it is better to say that all the people gathered there were treated with the respect ordinarily reserved for noblemen such as Antonius."[4] Antipas reports with amazement that Antonius and his wife Mania served food to local artisans and to servants from their household! He assumes that during the rest of the week they work as servants. "But when they gather as Christians, patterns of behavior are intentionally changed to reflect the fact that members of this group belong to a new order of society, or as they call it, the empire of god."[5]

In part we tell this story to feed your imagination of what it might look like for a Christian group to live out what the previous chapters have described—a redeemed understanding of honor. Yet just as importantly this story conveys what sort of ridicule and shaming a group of Christ followers might experience for doing things their neighbors consider nonsensical and dishonorable.

The contrasts between early Christians and their neighbors went beyond the gathering Antipas observed. Christians stopped participating in traditional rites and any dinner or civic function related to idols. They refused to honor the gods—something that was viewed as necessary for the well-being of the city and empire. An honor-shame society bestows honor and threatens shame as means of promoting desirable behavior and preventing undesirable behavior. Neighbors and city leaders would likely shame the Christians and threaten them with exclusion. The same thing often happens to Christians today. It is one thing to articulate an alternative honor code, as the previous chapter did, but it is something else to actually live it out and lose face in one's community. This chapter explores these questions: How can Christians live in such countercultural ways, even though people around them shame them for doing so? What is the church's role in helping them to do so? How can we develop church communities and Christian leaders who properly reflect and embody God's honor? Responses to these questions are multilayered, and so we explore various aspects of pastoral care and discipleship vital for developing healthy Christian communities in honor-shame contexts. We again begin with the letter of 1 Peter.

Shame-Resistance in 1 Peter

The text of 1 Peter makes clear first-century Christians were suffering. They were being slandered (1 Pet 2:12; 3:16), reviled (1 Pet 2:23; 3:9), maligned (1 Pet 4:4, 14) and persecuted (1 Pet 1:6; 2:19-20; 3:14, 17; 4:1, 12-16, 19; 5:10) because they are living as Christ followers. New Testament scholar John H. Elliott explains the social context of 1 Peter in this way:

> The chief weapon of attack employed by the [Christians' local neighbors] was a barrage of verbal abuse designed to shame, defame, demean, and discredit the believers as social and moral deviants endangering the common good. A strategy of public shaming was employed as a means of social control with the aim of pressuring the minority community to conform to conventional values and standards of conduct. The unrelenting abuse resulted in undeserved suffering on the part of the believers.[6]

The shaming of Christians that Peter describes and responds to is not an isolated problem in just one specific church. First Peter is a circular letter written to Christian groups in a number of regions (1 Pet 1:2), and we see similar verbal and physical attacks on Christians' honor in other epistles.[7]

Certainly this situation calls for Peter to offer comfort as they suffer slander and shame. That is not, however, the greatest need. The persecution is purposefully shaming; the dominant group seeks to stop this deviant behavior. As David deSilva states, "The Christians' neighbors were trying to reclaim, not destroy, these wayward members of their society."[8] Therefore Peter writes not just to comfort Christians but also to counter outside efforts to pull the Christians back to behaving in ways considered honorable in that society. The neighbors are shaming them, but offer the face-saving option of leaving the way of Jesus. Peter's strategic response to this challenging situation strengthens Christians to withstand shame and remain loyal to Jesus. He does so in multiple ways that we can also utilize today.[9]

Generally, the majority determines what is considered honorable in a society. But as Peter reminds the minority Christians, the majority is not always correct. At the time of the flood the tiny minority of eight people were the ones who were aligned with what was truly honorable (1 Pet 3:20). God's opinion, not majority opinion, is what ultimately matters. Also, "the example of Jesus provides definitive proof that the evaluation human beings form about a person can be dead wrong in God's sight."[10] First Peter 2:4 describes Jesus as "rejected by humans but in God's perspective elect, honored" (1 Pet 2:4).[11] Therefore Christians are not the ones living dishonorably; their neighbors are (1 Pet 4:3-4). The Christians should not be afraid of the shaming efforts of these neighbors (1 Pet 3:14). Peter reminds them they were called and have made a deliberate decision to leave that former way of life (1 Pet 1:2, 14; 2:9). So, "If they left their old life behind for good reasons why should they value their neighbor's evaluation of them?"[12]

Peter offers alternative perspectives of their shame and rejection that promote "perseverance *through* those experiences rather than backing down in the face of those experiences."[13] First, he interprets their trials as proving the genuineness of their trust and commitment to God, and as a way to attain greater glory and honor when Christ returns (1 Pet 1:6-7, 14). Society tells them their resistance will lead to greater shame, but Peter says the opposite—resistance becomes the path to "praise and glory and honor" at the revelation of Jesus (1 Pet 1:7; cf. 1 Pet 4:13; 5:4, 10). Second, Peter normalizes their experience by pointing to Jesus as a historical precedent. "The converts are urged to keep their focus fixed on Christ's norm and paradigm, assured that, as they share now in Christ's experience of enduring shame and rejection for the sake of God, they would come to share also in his honor and vindication before God"[14] (1 Pet 4:1-2, 12-13). Third, their suffering is not a sign that they are out of God's favor, but the opposite. They are moving in the direction God was leading (1 Pet 2:19-20; 4:14, 19). Their suffering is not from God; it is linked to the devil (1 Pet 5:8-9).

The method Peter proposes for defending one's honor is also countercultural. The instinctual norm in that setting was to retaliate or counter any insult or challenge to an individual or group's honor. Jesus did the opposite—"When he was abused, he did not return abuse" (1 Pet 2:23). Christians are called to not retaliate but instead offer a blessing and a gentle defense to accusations (1 Pet 3:9, 15-16). Beleaguered believers are to denounce the temptation to defend their honor with revenge and retaliation, but rejoice that they bear the badge of divine honor (1 Pet 4:13). Such a dignified response stems from solidarity with the shamed but divinely honored Lord Jesus Christ—the exemplar and enabler of all truly honorable conduct.

One significant strategy for shame resistance is redefining the circle of people whose opinion matters, and helping people see they are a part of a new honor-granting community. Peter underscores the honor Christians have through being part of God's family. He exhorts them to provide "social support and personal affirmation [to each other] that could keep individuals from crossing back into their former way of life and its networks of support"[15] (1 Pet 1:22; 3:8; 4:8-11; 5:3, 6). Peter practices this himself in the letter; he showers them with honorific titles (1 Pet 2:4-10). Both his words in the letter and what he encourages them to do establishes the church as the new honor community—the court of reputation reflecting God's estimation.

But not all is countercultural. Peter affirms that Christians hold honorable values in common with society at large. So although part of his strategy is to discredit the shaming authority of those causing their suffering, another aspect of his strategy is to encourage them to outdo themselves in living out the shared positive values. Their detractors may come to honor them for this behavior (1 Pet 2:12). But even if that does not happen, the Christians themselves can bolster their sense of healthy honor through living out these values.

By changing their way of life, Christians not only experience increased shame from their neighbors but also receive less honor from others in society. Peter seeks to address this lack of honor by outlining the honor they already possess. The honor believers possess through Christ is what enables a person to faithfully endure shaming. First Peter exhorts readers

> to an honorable way of life and honorable endurance of suffering by assuring the beleaguered readers in the opening section of the letter (1:1–2:10) of the several related ways in which they have already been honored by God, the ultimate conferrer and arbiter of honor and shame. . . . As children of God's family they too are honored with God's grace/favor, sanctification, rebirth, inheritance, praise, salvation, redemption, life, goodness, blessing, imperishable crown, exaltation, protection, and glory—all images of honor.[16]

Or, as 1 Peter 2:6-7 states, "'Whoever believes in him [Jesus] will not be put to shame.' So the honor is for you who believe" (ESV). Christians are now honored as members of "a chosen race, a royal priesthood, a holy nation, a people for his own possession" (1 Pet 2:9 ESV)—the very people of God himself. Persecution does not define Christians as shameful because God has defined them as honorable. Believers can resist social shame because they have received divine honor.

Peter's strategic pastoral moves are as applicable in honor-shame contexts today as they were in the first century. Perhaps the biggest lesson to take from 1 Peter is that dealing with the threat of losing face is a key aspect of discipleship in honor-shame contexts.

THE NEW COMMUNITY OF HONOR

In the first century, communities of believers did not flourish simply because they were given Jesus' teachings. It was not enough to simply know, for instance, that Jesus called his followers to open-handed sharing characteristic of family relationships. Rather, as we observed in 1 Peter, the apostles recognized that Christians would need support to live out a new honor code that would cause them to lose face with their neighbors. Since honor is a corporate and public dynamic, the church community is the key agent not just in providing information about ethics but also in honoring alternative behaviors practiced by converts and disciples. The church becomes an alternate court of reputation.

Machismo is a powerful honor code in Latin America that shapes men's behavior. It defines what "true" men do and what manly actions will make one gain status. Over the years I (Mark) had observed that Miguel did a number of things that went against machismo's definition of manliness. I recently had the opportunity to ask Miguel how he came to resist the dynamics of machoness. He first affirmed how strong the honor code of machismo is. For instance, one aspect of machismo is drinking. A commonly heard saying is "One who does not drink is not a complete man." In his teen years his friends started pressuring him to "be a man" and drink. He already felt shame for being poor, so to avoid more shame he began to drink. Some years later he got a job in a shoemaking shop and was surrounded by coworkers who were evangelical Christians. He never went to their church. He continued his macho ways, but he listened to them. One night he was drunk and got beat up. This left him thinking about his life, his wife and their baby daughter. He started attending church and five meetings later accepted Jesus as his Savior. The church had a clear rule against drinking. The rule may have informed him that he should stop, but it was not the rule itself that enabled him to change, even though he in fact wanted to stop drinking. The rule was not some sort of legal dictum imposed in an abstract way. It was, in essence, part of a counter-code of honor. The church honored those who followed the code. As Miguel reflected on how he stepped away from the ways of machismo, he mentioned three things. A man from the church, Hector, spent a lot of time with him offering support and affirmation. Second, the Christian men at work and the people at the church provided a counter-chorus. Old friends around him began ridiculing him and shaming him for becoming a Christian; they pressured him to continue in his macho ways. Christians countered these shaming comments of Miguel's friends by intentionally affirming him for his efforts to stop drinking. Last, as his new identity as a loved child of God grew, he felt increasing security to step away from other aspects of the machismo honor code and walk in the ways of the New Testament honor code. His church continued to affirm and honor him as he took these steps. The shaming comments of other men did not stop, but they do not have the power over him that they used to.

Another element in the machismo honor code, and in the honor code of many cultures, is the necessity of retaliation—seeking revenge for an attack on one's honor or family's honor. This drive to protect honor through revenge is strong among most men in Central America, but it is even more pronounced within the honor code of gangs. Yet the way of Jesus is exactly the opposite. Robert Brenneman recounts the experience of Roberto, a former gang member facing these conflicting honor codes, and points to the significance of the church community as an alternate court of reputation. Six years after his conversion Roberto is married with two children and remains active in his church. He currently serves as a worship leader.

> But it hasn't been easy. The church-related youth center where he had been employed . . . closed . . . and Roberto was without work for six months. During that time, friends from his former life contacted him and urged him to accept lucrative one-off jobs moving drugs for the Mexican drug cartels. He candidly admitted that turning down such offers was very, very difficult and he came especially close to accepting at least one offer—turning it down only at the last minute. Even more difficult was the recent murder of his younger brother whom he had recruited to join the gang many years earlier, but who had also

left the gang several years earlier. Such events place a recovering gang member in a difficult position. According to the moral logic of the street, a "good brother" defends the honor of his fallen kin by avenging his death with "payback." And indeed the offers for assistance in "making things right" came swiftly from Roberto's former associates. But just as quickly came the support and reminders of his new "brothers in Christ." "Violence only begets more violence," his pastor told him. "That's no way to respond." Roberto decided not to seek out vengeance and to relinquish his "right" to kill his brother's killers.[17]

Miguel and Roberto both received intentional and direct teaching that articulates how a Christian's behavior will differ from the society at large. That is as important in an honor-shame context as it is in a Western context. We would do well, however, to follow the example of the New Testament authors and use honor-shame terminology when offering ethical instruction. Miguel's and Roberto's stories also, however, point to the importance of not just making pronouncements in a sermon. There must be an alternative honoring community that accompanies the pronouncements of an alternative honor code. Honor is a public verdict, and as we observed in their stories the voices of others in the church served to counter the public verdict decreed by non-Christians.

Christopher Flanders summarizes these ideas using the language of face.

> Although God is the ultimate source of face, when we understand virtue as a proper basis for face, the Church becomes a face-generating community. We do this differently as we follow new face rules other than the scripts the dominant culture provides. But God's people, who bear his life and follow his ways, becomes a new source of face as it grants recognition, approval, and inclusion based upon the righteousness of God revealed in Jesus.[18]

CHURCH COMMUNITIES THAT INCREASE SHAME

Ana grew up in a town near Tegucigalpa, Honduras. She was the second of fourteen children. Her father inherited a large farm from his parents, but he spent more time drinking than working. He sold the property little by little to support his family and his drinking habit. Eventually the family experienced the shame of ending up in the street. A neighbor took pity on them and let them stay rent free in a house she owned. Ana's mother started working as a maid, and brought home food her employers gave her for the

family. Her unemployed father was so consumed with guarding his macho
sense of honor, when he caught her mother bringing the food home he would
throw it out, accusing her of getting the food by sleeping with other men.

Ana felt deep shame because of her father and the family situation; she
also lived in fear of her father. He beat all of them, including her mother,
with electrical wires. When he came home in a drunken rage Ana and her
siblings jumped out of bed and ran outside. Ana rushed home from school
each day, not because she was eager to be with her family, but to avoid possible punishment. To avoid saying something wrong and being ridiculed or
beaten, Ana learned to say as little as possible. She carried this practice with
her to school, where she talked much less than the other students, and
usually only participated in class if the teacher forced her to.

When she was in third grade a cousin told Ana's mother that she would
like to help Ana by letting her live at her house, giving Ana food, clothing
and covering her school expenses. The cousin lied. The cousin "rescued" Ana
only to make her a slave. She did not let her go to school, made her work all
day without payment and excluded her at the family table. She gave Ana the
leftovers, if there were any. Ana got up at four in the morning and ate secretly
because her cousin punished her whenever she caught her taking food.

Boys began showing interest in Ana when she turned fourteen. But the way
her father treated her mother made it hard for her to believe the boys' talk about
love. She ignored or rejected them. Ana learned how to survive. Her silence and
low profile protected her from more beatings, greater shame and rejection, but
over the years she gradually rejected herself and internalized the shame. She
could not imagine anyone would love her. Her shame was so deep she once
tried to kill herself by drinking pesticide, but she did not even get sick.

Ana eventually did trust a young man enough to want to start a family
with him. Her cousin ridiculed her, saying he was poor trash. But Ana ran
away from her cousin's home and eventually moved to Tegucigalpa with her
husband. As an adult and mother Ana joined a neighborhood church. She
came to church carrying a heavy burden of shame. Unfortunately, rather
than offering healing and removing the burden, the church added to her
shame. She strove to be a "true Christian" and live up to the group's expectations—and there were many. The church had rules about dress, women not
cutting their hair or using makeup, forbidden behaviors like dancing and

smoking, and required behaviors like attending church every evening. Ana went to church every night, followed the rules and worked hard in various projects to raise money to construct a church building. She did not, however, feel loved or cared for, and she observed the shame and exclusion others experienced when they failed to keep the rules. When one of her friends started going to night school to finish her high school degree, church leaders scolded her and forbade her to help lead worship if she only attended on weekends. Although Ana obeyed the rules, she fell short in other ways. She felt shame because she did not speak in tongues. The first time she shared in a church meeting, someone disapproved of her words. Feeling shamed, she returned to her childhood practice of remaining quiet.

All social groups, churches included, need a means of distinguishing those who belong from outsiders. Sadly, Ana's church practiced an approach to group identity that has a propensity for inappropriate and unnecessary shaming. Missionary anthropologist Paul Hiebert would call this a bounded church.[19]

Hiebert borrows from mathematical set theory to describe two ways society categorizes people into groups. One way of categorizing people is to list essential characteristics they must have to belong to the set. Such "bounded" sets have a clear boundary line that is static and allows for a uniform definition of those who are within the group, as in figure 11.1.

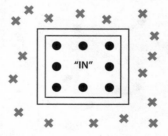

Figure 11.1. Bounded group

Using a bounded approach is appropriate for many groups in society: clubs, unions, sports teams, associations and so forth. But for churches to use a bounded approach is problematic. Bounded churches can use behaviors, rituals, spiritual experiences or beliefs as the basis for drawing lines that define insiders from outsiders. Shaming is a common and powerful method of encouraging compliance. A bounded church honors insiders and shames those who do not live up to the standards of the church. The nature of bounded churches inclines toward inappropriate shaming because they tend to prioritize the line of division over the welfare of the offending person. Complying with the boundary line is essential, lest one face shame or gossip from the community. Without a clear boundary individuals in the church lack security of identity, and the group may disintegrate. A bounded approach injures not only the excluded but those inside as well. The lines hinder transparency as members find it hard to express their struggles honestly for fear of losing face or standing in the church.[20] The boundary established to provide security becomes a wall of isolation. Fortunately, there is another way to identify a community of Christians.

CHURCH COMMUNITIES THAT LIBERATE FROM SHAME

Hiebert states that an alternative approach to defining a group focuses on how people relate to a common center. For instance, whereas an official fan club with dues and requirements functions as a bounded group, anyone who cheers for a particular team would be part of the centered group of that team's fans. Casual fans may be far from the center, but they are turned toward the center; therefore they are part of the centered group (see figure 11.2).

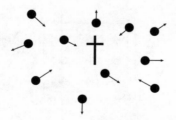

Figure 11.2. Centered group

Some people may have been active and passionate fans (close to the center), but after too many losing seasons they have switched their allegiance to another team. Thus they are moving away from the center and are not part of the centered group. The group is made up of all people moving toward the center. Those in the group will not necessarily be uniform in characteristics, but they will be heading the same direction. A distinction can still be made between those who are "in" and "out." This is done, however, by looking at the person's direction, their relation to the center, not by looking to see if they have met the standards of a particular boundary line. We can draw a line between those who belong to the group and those who do not (see diagram below).

"In centered-set thinking, greater emphasis is placed on the center and relationships than on maintaining a boundary, because there is no need to maintain the boundary in order to maintain the set."[21] In figure 11.3 we could remove the line and nothing would change because the line does not define the group. The group emerges as those related to the center are distinct from those not related to the center.

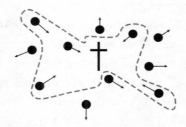

Figure 11.3. Centered group with boundary

In a centered church, the center, God, is the focus—not the boundary. People are disciplined by the community not for rule breaking or boundary crossing, but for turning their backs to God, walking away from the relationship. Therefore the critical question is, To whom does the person offer his or her worship and allegiance? A centered church does make a distinction between Christians and non-Christians. Yet Hiebert observes that the emphasis "would be on exhorting people to follow Christ, rather than on excluding others to preserve the purity of the set."[22] A centered church paradigm has two types of change. The first is conversion and repentance, entering the group by turning around and heading a different direction. The second is movement toward the center. Conversion is a definite event followed by an ongoing process of discipleship.

Centered churches facilitate sincere and deep relationship because unity comes not from uniformity but from common relationship with the center.

There is space to struggle and even fail, since automatic shameful exclusion is not a threat. All recognize they are in process—moving closer to the center. Since their security is in the center, the centered approach naturally leads people to focus on the center—Christ. A bounded approach does the opposite. A bounded church may talk of God being the center of all, but the paradigm itself naturally pulls peoples' focus to the boundary line that defines the group and provides their security.

The advantages of a centered approach are particularly important in an honor-shame context. In social settings that use shame to regulate behavior, the inclination of bounded-set communities toward inappropriate shaming is especially problematic—they are likely to honor and shame people for the wrong reasons; their honor code rarely aligns with God's. And in the same setting, the centered approach is especially beneficial. Its directional focus and relational priority decrease the likelihood of inappropriate shaming and facilitates healthy, appropriate shaming (something we explore below).

It is important to clarify a few points. First, a centered approach is not "Christianity-Lite."[23] Following Jesus, facing and heading toward the center, has significant implications; one will look radically different from others in society. Second, a centered church does not practice universal inclusion. In contrast to the spirit of rejection and exclusion that emanates from a bounded church, a centered church has an invitational character. But it has a center, and relationship to the center matters. Those who have turned toward the center are included, others are invited, but until they repent and change direction, they are not seen as part of the family of faith. Third, Hiebert is not saying that using any boundary lines makes a church a bounded group. For instance, a centered church can still articulate what we might call boundary lines between appropriate and inappropriate behavior. What differs is how the groups discern and define who is part of a group—in a directional way related to a center, or in a static way defined by a line.

An example from sports helps to illustrate these three points. A soccer team that is part of a league would likely be a bounded group. It may have tryouts to select the best players. The players must come to practices and wear the team's uniform in games. Those who do not have the ability or do not fulfill the obligations are not part of the team. In contrast, a centered approach might be to announce that anyone who wants to play soccer is invited to come to the park Saturday at two in the afternoon. Everyone can play. If there are too many for one game, a second will be started. To come will demonstrate an interest in playing soccer (an arrow turned toward the center). If, however, someone picks up the ball and runs with it, others will say, "You can't do that. This is not rugby." If the person continues, eventually the others will tell that person they cannot participate until they are willing to play by the rules. That player was not centered on soccer. So too a centered church invites all, but does not include all regardless of their relationship with Jesus Christ, the center.

Today Ana is a confident mother and grandmother; she shares her ideas in Bible studies, visits others who are hurting and in need, and often leads the women's meeting at her church. Light shines from her eyes. She has had the courage to go against society's definition of a "good woman." For example, she worked alongside her husband in a shoemaking shop—an all-male profession in Honduras. How did this happen? Ana was released from shame to live more as the woman God had created her to be through a long process that included the following.

Ana no longer attends a bounded church. She became part of a new church—Amor Fe y Vida. Through studying Galatians the people of Amor Fe y Vida came to recognize the inappropriate and unnecessary shaming that was a fruit of their legalistic practices. They worked to shift from a bounded approach to ethics and community that focused on drawing lines of distinction, to a centered approach that focused on whether they were getting closer to Jesus himself.[24] Her experience at church shifted from adding shame to being in a place where she gradually felt safe to express herself and reveal her heart.

At the same time her church broadened their proclamation of the gospel from a narrow focus on release from guilt to include multiple aspects of Christ's salvation (discussed in chapter five). At an individual level Ana experienced God's loving embrace in a more profound way. She acquired a deeper sense of identity as a loved and honored child of God. She experienced release from the burden of shame she had carried for so many years. As she took off the mask she had hidden behind, her church family encouraged her and honored her for who she was and who she was becoming. At the corporate level she joined with others to reflect on the relationship between their own reality and seeing the cross and resurrection within the context of Jesus' life. They recognized that in the incarnation God embraced the very human finitude and vulnerability that the people in their squatter community tried to mask when following distorted definitions of "real men," "good women," "true Christians" and other imposed roles and status markers. Before, they had not imagined the possibility of living in other ways; but seeing the cross and resurrection as a victory over distorted systems of honor in Jesus' day opened up the possibility of saying no to these forces and developing new definitions of honor in their church community. These followers of Jesus formed a new code of honor and new court of reputation. The changing character of Amor Fe y Vida church led Ana to experience more love and acceptance *from* others, and in turn to express more love *to* others.

ADDRESSING SIN WITH REINTEGRATIVE SHAMING

In our world that has strayed from God's ways, many people like Ana are shamed inappropriately. Thus we have often written of liberation from misplaced shame and distorted honor codes through Jesus Christ. That does not, however, mean that using honor and shame to influence behavior is always wrong. Godly behavior should be encouraged, and sinful actions should be discouraged by the community. This chapter has illustrated a number of ways that honor can be used to support ethical behavior. But in addition, the communal role of the church family also includes shaming inappropriate behavior. For example, Paul plainly told the believers in Corinth, "I say this to your shame" (1 Cor 6:5; 15:34; cf. 2 Thess 3:14-15). Some behavior does deserve shame. So, what is the biblical role of shame in Christian community?

Insights from a criminologist, John Braithwaite, help guide our response to sin in the community of faith. Braithwaite contrasts two responses to inappropriate behavior in his book *Crime, Shame and Reintegration*— "*dis*integrative shaming" and "*re*integrative shaming." Disintegrative shaming focuses on ensuring the guilty violator gets what they deserve, and makes an example on the offender. It ultimately stigmatizes. Reintegrative shaming, on the other hand, acknowledges that the social bond has been damaged and draws attention to the shameful action, but does so with the purpose of healing relationships and reintegrating the person to the group. This approach recognizes the normative function of shame for building and strengthening social bonds between people.[25] Such a restorative approach focuses on addressing the relational obligations and fractures created by the wrongdoing, so as to promote a healthy community.[26] "Shaming that is reintegrative . . . shames while maintaining bonds of respect or love."[27]

What does reintegrative shaming look like?

Yuritzy Villasenor teaches first grade in Fresno, California. Her class is ethnically diverse, and none of the students are from the dominant culture. One child in the classroom regularly does not follow directions. On one particular day the child's behavior was worse than normal, including hitting classmates. As she considered how to respond, Yuritzy recalled a legend about an African tribe. According to the legend, when someone commits an offense the tribe gathers around the person and shares good things the offender has done as a step toward restoration.[28] This inspired Yuritzy to try an alternative approach to common disciplinary practices.

So Yuritzy called her class together to sit in a circle. She asked them to state things the offending child had done that day that they did not like. A number of classmates complained about being hit, and others confirmed these accounts. Meanwhile, the child in question, who had refused to join the circle, looked hurt and angry, and finally blurted out, "I am tired of you saying all these bad things about me." Yuritzy then spoke, affirming that she too had witnessed some of the episodes the children had mentioned. Then she asked, "What are kind things we can do for others?" All those in the circle shared ideas. Yuritzy turned to the offending student, who was stewing outside of the circle, and said, "I need you to come and sit in the middle of the circle." Then she said, "I want all of you to say something positive about your classmate sitting in the middle of the circle." She explained that they would go around the circle, but students could skip their turn and speak later if it was hard for them to think of something positive. At first they were a bit confused and found it hard to shift from words of accusation to words of affirmation. But after a few started the process, everybody eventually shared. The offender soaked in the kind words of affirmation and visibly changed. The child behaved much differently the rest of the day, having been reintegrated into the classroom community.[29]

Christian communities are clearly called to seek the restoration of sinners and thus to practice reintegrative shaming (Gal 6:1). How might we do so? Functioning from a centered approach does not guarantee that a church will practice reintegrative shaming, but it certainly increases the possibility. A centered approach facilitates focusing on the person, and thus strengthening relational bonds. And because the direction of movement is most important, a centered approach lends itself to shaming that will focus on healing relationships and reintegrating the person to the group.

Shaming, especially public shaming, is a powerful act that often goes the direction of disintegrative shaming. Robert Brenneman told us of an example he witnessed of a Guatemalan pastor transforming an event that easily could have been disintegrative shaming and instead making it reintegrative. It occurred in a church in Guatemala City that includes middle-class families as well as lower-class families from marginal neighborhoods. Leticia, a young woman on the lower end of the economic and class spectrum, was very involved in the church. Her becoming pregnant before being married devastated her family. We do not know the details of Leticia's personal conversations with the pastor, but we do know what the pastor, Roberto, did publicly. Near the close of a Sunday-morning service he called Leticia to the front of the church, put his arm around her and reported to the congregation that she was pregnant and that she was not married. He told them they had invited the father to come and be with her that day; he was not interested. Then Roberto said, "Well, what are we going to do? How do we respond to this situation?" The response was immediate. Members from the church, including those from a higher social class, started calling out, "We are going to support her! Yes! We are not going to gossip! Yes!" Leticia continued attending and started showing signs of pregnancy. There was nothing to gossip about; everyone already knew. When the baby arrived, the church took up a collection and bought a new stroller far nicer than Leticia or the father could have afforded. The baby got lots of attention and love and grew as a little boy in the church.

Although so directly addressing the issue in a public way may not be appropriate in all cultural contexts, this was a public issue—the pregnancy would become visible to all. Brenneman praises the wisdom and skill of the pastor. "He allowed the church to continue to say a firm 'No' to extra-marital sexuality without permanently shaming the person and in fact giving the congregation the possibility for consistently supporting life. Obviously, it also cut short the possibilities for gossip—which is essentially a powerful form of social control exercised by those who believe that the more formal or institutional forms of control are not working."[30] The pastor's intentionality was crucial in making this a reintegrative experience. Yet the pastor could not have done this alone. The church already had a centered character. A bounded church would have likely responded quite differently to his question. Practicing reintegrative shaming requires skill and wisdom in the moment, but also requires the long patient work of developing congregations that function in a centered way.

Healing and release from shame ultimately does not come simply from sermons or discipleship programs, but from community. The origin of shame is exclusion, rejection and isolation—a disunion with community, both divine and human. Therefore the solution for shame is not simply the theological idea of honor, but the realization of honor through genuine community. The social act of labeling deviants attaches a rather permanent stigma on the shamed. Reintegrating the stigmatized into community requires intentional acts of "delabeling" and "relabeling," which are done verbally and through nonverbal actions.[31] Christian sacraments such as confession, baptism and sharing the Eucharist as rituals that "wash clean" and "relabel" the sinner provide an ecclesial mechanism for deshaming sinners. The communal role of the church in overcoming shame and facilitating behavioral change involves communicating God's honor symbolically. These rituals performed in community contexts are means for discharging and escaping shame, and ceremonially reintegrate sinners into the Christian community.

CONFESSING AND CONFRONTING SIN

What is an appropriate way to acknowledge sin? If your friend says, "I confessed my sin," what do you imagine? When you read the word *confession*, what specific forms or experiences come to mind for you?

We lead with these questions because every culture acknowledges sin in a particular way. Cultural groups socialize members to prioritize specific responses to sin as genuine and authentic. Western Christianity views confession as verbalizing wrongdoing and requesting forgiveness. While noble and sincere in its own context, this reflects certain Western cultural values, such as direct communication, sin as individual transgression and forgiveness as the solution. These cultural assumptions create expectations that all people should address sin in a similar fashion, thus opening the door for miscommunication crossculturally. The way non-Western Christians handle sin often leads Westerners to believe "they just sweep everything under the carpet and ignore it." In the Bible, Ezra provides a biblical example of confession rooted in honor-shame dynamics.

When Ezra learns how Israel has defiled themselves by giving their daughters in marriage to Gentiles, he confesses the nation's sin in this way:

> When I heard this, I tore my tunic and cloak, pulled hair from my head and beard and sat down appalled. Then everyone who trembled at the words of the God of Israel gathered around me because of this unfaithfulness of the exiles. And I sat there appalled until the evening sacrifice.
>
> Then, at the evening sacrifice, I rose from my self-abasement, with my tunic and cloak torn. (Ezra 9:3-5 NIV)

Confession in the Old Testament often involves disrobing, putting on sackcloth, sitting in ashes and weeping bitterly—all symbols of self-shaming and self-abasement. Observe how the narrator in Ezra 10:1 defines confession as weeping and falling prostrate—"Ezra prayed and made confession, weeping and throwing himself down before the house of God." This ritual visibly embodies the shamefulness of sin and renewed desire to live humbly under God's name.

When Ezra talks, he acknowledges shame, in word and posture. "[I] fell on my knees with my hands spread out to the Lord my God and prayed: 'I am too ashamed and disgraced, my God, to lift up my face to you, because our sins are higher than our heads and our guilt has reached to the heavens'" (Ezra 9:5-6 NIV).

Genuine confession does not necessitate Hebrew-style sackcloth and ashes. But neither is a look-'em-in-the-eyes verbalization of wrongdoing the only way to confess sin. Churches globally must draw from their local culture to communicate genuine repentance. As Ezra models, people of honor-shame cultures may acknowledge sin with symbolic displays of contrition, view the problem as disgrace and view the solution as restoration of relations and face (see Job 42:6).

This form of contrition is often hard for Western Christians to accept as sincere and efficacious. Consider how Christian parents in America teach their children to acknowledge sin—anything less than an explicit, "I am sorry I wronged you. I did *x y z*. Will you please forgive me?" does not count as true confession and repentance. This response to sin assumes the sinner retains a high degree of control to fix the problem on their own accord and seeks to prove the sinner does hold themselves accountable to justice. Meanwhile, interpersonal reconciliation in honor-shame contexts places the offender at the mercy of others and seeks to maintain face and harmony. For this reason, people in honor-shame contexts apologize in general terms—"If I've done anything wrong, please help me," or "I won't do it again."

A common Western application of Paul's admonition "Do not let the sun go down on your anger" (Eph 4:26) is to talk through the entire problem with your offender before bedtime until everything is hashed out. This application reflects the Western approach to issues of sin and conflict. The verse simply reads, "Do not let the sun go down on your anger," which some contexts may sincerely apply as "forget your offense." Addressing sin is wrought full of cultural, relational and spiritual challenges; there are no simple guidelines. Nevertheless, we mention two guiding principles for dealing with sin: (1) the goal is restoration of relationship and community; (2) realize that culture, whether non-Western or Western, strongly influences acceptable and genuine forms of confession, repentance and restoration.

Address the problem without exposing or disrespecting the person. Genuinely help people address their sin and spiritual shame, but without creating an insurmountable amount of social disgrace. Keep one eye on the relationship, and the other eye on the issue/sin. Or, in the words of Hebrews 12:14, "Pursue peace with everyone, *and* the holiness without which no one will see the Lord." In chapter seven we offered practical suggestions for making this happen in everyday relationships. Remember, the objective of pointing out another's fault is regaining and restoring the person's relationship (with God *and* people), not an admission of guilt per se. Note this point in Matthew 18:15 and Galatians 6:1: "If the member listens to you, *you have regained that one*"; "My friends, if anyone is detected in a transgression, you who have received the Spirit *should restore such a one* in a spirit of gentleness." The goal is restoring and reintegrating the person back to the community. Here is an example of addressing sin in a culture where the concept of justice is relational.

Mohammad lives in Sudan; he is often expected to mediate in legal disputes in his tribe where legal means something different in that context. Once there was a case in which a husband, having been absent from home for long time, returned and expected his wife to perform her marital duties. He was incensed when she refused. A small family dispute resulted and grew into a major family disruption between the two extended families. A husband's honor had been challenged, he felt disrespected and moved away.

At this point Mohammad's counsel was sought. Mohammad is a wise man, so quietly he approached the husband first which is proper etiquette, and asked if he had enquired from his wife if she was in her monthly period. It had been a long time since he had been home so he had completely forgotten to even consider this possibility. He sent an intermediary to enquire, indeed this was the case. Was Mohammad going to punish the wrongdoer? If you are wondering why the wife did not say anything, well this is appropriate honorable behavior in her context in which she has to preserver her place. Justice in this setting did not consist of punishing the husband for his lack of common sense, but in restoring the broken relationship. He counseled the man to publically uphold the honor of his wife by bringing home a lavish gift, a sum of money she could use at will. He may not have openly apologized, but his action spoke of his change of heart towards his wife. There was a big celebration, relationships were restored and justice and mercy were upheld.[32]

Ultimately the biblical response to sin is to be characterized by forgiveness. The dynamics of honor and shame (hospitality, generosity, collectivism, etc.) generally promote strong relationships and cohesive bonds in society. But in a rather ironic twist, honor and shame also stand behind the bitterness, offense and unforgiveness that destroy community and relationship. The destructive sin of unforgiveness is rooted in a warped longing for honor. People will break relationships over slight offenses, whether real or perceived. Men especially view forgiveness as a sign of weakness; it means releasing one's right to honor, which is unthinkable. A Chinese proverb says, "A murder may be forgiven, but an affront never." People respond to offenses with shaming tactics such as gossip and rejection when feeling disrespected. Without forgiveness, petty slights mushroom into intense rivalries. Sadly this happens within the church rather often.

Because unforgiveness is so disruptive to community, the New Testament reminds believers of the necessity of forgiveness (Mt 6:14-15; 18:21-35; 2 Cor 2:5-10; Col 3:13). Biblical forgiveness is more than pardoning offenders of the legally mandated punishment. Forgiveness involves releasing people from relational isolation and foregoing your claim to a certain respect. Forgiveness frees people from their social debt, and also frees the person forgiving from the bondage of sinful systems of honor acquisition. In honor-shame contexts, forgiveness bears profound witness to God's kingdom values—Christians need not "demand respect" from others because they have already been honored by God. Paul's concluding statement to the fractured church in Rome summarizes the issue—"Welcome one another, therefore, just as Christ has welcomed you, for the glory of God" (Rom 15:7).

We end this section on addressing sin with one more example, which displays missionaries practicing what has been described in the last two sections. In the previous chapter we recounted the story of Dave's table conversation at a wedding in Malaysia when he presented an alternative honor code to the common Malay practice of taking a second wife. He and his wife, Deborah, practiced reintegrative shaming when they confronted someone in relation to the same issue. To their surprise Abdul, a married business partner, brought a girlfriend on a joint trip. Dave and Deborah knew about the girlfriend, but they had been hesitant to confront Abdul directly because he would lose face. They now felt they must act. If they did not address the situation it would appear they were condoning his actions. Word would get back to their city. People there, including Abdul's wife Fathima, would assume they approved. So Dave and Deborah stated that they did not approve and insisted that the two women sleep in one room and the two men in another. Abdul at first defended himself to save face, but then became withdrawn. Dave and Deborah knew that Abdul assumed that this was the end of their relationship and their joint business activity. To counteract this they visited his home a couple days after they returned. They greeted Abdul and Fathima and spent time visiting together. They did not mention the incident with the girlfriend. They intentionally commented on some up-coming business tasks, asking Abdul to take on some of the responsibilities as usual. Although they did not speak explicit words of forgiveness, they communicated forgiveness and restoration of relationship through the visit and their words of continued cooperation. Dave and Deborah noted that their relationship with Abdul actually deepened after this. They sense that he realized their friendship could weather a confrontation, and that when they did confront him it was out of concern for him and the good of his family. He stepped back from his relationship with the girlfriend and paid noticeably more attention to his wife.

Transforming Leadership

In an honor-shame context leaders are key in helping Christians live out the countercultural ethic. Examples in this chapter, from 1 Peter to the present, portrayed the central role of leaders not just in communicating an alter-native honor code but also in supporting Christians as they face shame when living it out. This includes words and actions at the individual level and also the work of shaping a centered church that honors those walking in the way of Jesus and practices reintegrative shaming. Yet leaders themselves are not immune from the pressure of alternative honor codes. Christian leaders also feel the shaming pressures of the surrounding society. They too need support to live according to God's honor code.

Khalid, a Muslim-background believer, leads the campus ministry of an international Christian organization. He is respected as a mentor and gifted at discipling other believers into maturity. At home, Khalid has a healthy marriage and the blessing of multiple children. Moreover, as a former wres-tling champion and bodybuilder, his physical stature causes others to respect him. And as the grandson of a famous khan, people instantly recognize his family name and grant deference to him as coming from an important family. For these reasons, Khalid is respected by Christians and non-Christians alike. So I (Jayson) was surprised to learn that Khalid regularly struggled with feelings of disgrace and shame.

Khalid and I met regularly to pray and encourage each other in ministry. Because the honor-shame dynamics affected so many aspects of Christian ministry in Central Asia, our conversation often touched on the subject. We would discuss the nature of honor and shame in culture, our personal life and the Bible—seeking how God was working to reveal his honor in and through us. Then during one meeting, his demeanor changed as he began to share his feelings of being a worthless person. Whenever he visited his home village, neighbors would comment, "You are almost thirty years old, and you don't have a car. What kind of man are you? You need to buy a piece of land and build a house so you can take care of your parents." Khalid sensed embarrassment when walking (instead of driving) around town, and not being able to buy land for a house. The feelings of inadequacy were heavy as he recounted the evaluations of former classmates and neighbors, and how those judgments scarred him. This shame occasionally prompted him to regret entering full-time ministry; for his salary precluded the typical status symbols for men his age, like a car and home. Throughout our months of mutual discipleship, Khalid learned to counteract the messages of shame with the truth of God's honor. He has persevered in ministry through the seasons of shaming by resting assured in the honor God has promised. The fact that the above conversation occurred after a year of our meeting together highlights the deep-seated nature of shame, even for Christian leaders. Such issues will likely not surface in initial conversations, so require ongoing affirmation of the scriptural truth of God's honor for Christian leaders.

Many Christian leaders in non-Western contexts face perpetual shame for a host of reasons. Often they are the target during times of persecution, lack university education because they studied at unaccredited Bible colleges, have relatively limited material possessions and/or are deemed traitors by their own family members. Andrew Mbuvi echoes this: "On the whole, the African pastor is the embodiment of poverty. In a society where honor is judged by material wealth and power, he finds himself rather inadequate to confront the powerful politicians or businessmen who boast of more wealth, better education, and a more influential position."[33] In some ways, social shame is an inherent part of Christian leadership. Jesus instructed his followers to put themselves in a low position and purposefully "undignify" themselves (Lk 22:26). The apostle Paul viewed himself as God's "slave," and constantly faced shameful circumstances in his ministry (see 2 Cor 4:7-11; 11:21-33). How can Christian leaders and ministers withstand the constant shaming brought on through these circumstances? The solution is ultimately God's honor, which Christian leaders experience in three ways.

Christians who serve God (in professional or vocational ministry contexts) receive unique honor before God. Jesus directly promises, "Whoever serves me, the Father will honor" (Jn 12:26). Peter instructed the church elders, "Do not lord it over those in your charge, but be examples to the flock. And when the chief shepherd appears, *you will win the crown of glory that never fades away*" (1 Pet 5:3-4). Christians who lead from a humble posture receive the ultimate recognition of honor—God's unfading crown. They are recognized by God (see Mt 25:23). The hope of eschatological honor pulls Christian leaders through the swamps of shame and redefines leadership.

Nursultan assumed the role of team leader, overseeing a ministry center and leading staff members. With the new responsibilities came the inevitable temptation to leverage the new position for personal status. In his culture, authoritarianism and nepotism are common management strategies for people in leadership positions. Within a few months of becoming leader, God used the story of Eli's sons (1 Sam 2:12-36) to help Nursultan assume a different posture of leadership. Through the story, Nursultan realized that God actually shames leaders who abuse their privileges and power for distinction and gain. Eli's sons stole the choicest portions of temple sacrifices and suffered the consequences of honoring themselves above God. Not wanting to be like them, Nursultan realized God had blessed him to serve others and steward resources for God's honor. For this was the path to ultimate honor before God. God tells leaders, "Those who honor me I will honor, and those who despise me shall be lightly esteemed" (1 Sam 2:30 ESV). Today Nursultan is trusted by Christians and Muslims in the community for his consistently selfless and servant-hearted leadership. While it is encouraging how Nursultan encountered God's honor through his own devotional reading of the Bible, many Christian leaders in honor-shame contexts have not had this type of experience. Therefore it is important to intentionally point Christian leaders toward this truth.

Moreover, God desires his leaders to experience honor also in the present, not just the future age. One way the church functions as an alternative honor community is by granting honor to its leaders. "Let the elders who rule well be considered worthy of double honor" (1 Tim 5:17). This honor that elders experience in the local community comes not by virtue of their position, but by virtue of their character. In fact being an honorable person is a primary prerequisite for church leadership.

> [A bishop] must also have a good reputation with outsiders, so that he will not fall into disgrace and into the devil's trap.
> In the same way, deacons are to be worthy of respect. . . .
> In the same way, the women are to be worthy of respect. (1 Tim 3:7-8, 11 NIV)

As honorable people assume leadership roles, the local church must appropriately honor them.

From Jayson's experience in Central Asia, understanding biblical *followership* was just as vital as biblical *leadership* for the church family to become a healthy honoring community. Decades of Soviet-government strong-arm tactics created a culture of disrespect toward leaders. People offered platitudes when face-to-face with leaders (out of fear of reprisal, not genuine respect), then spoke critically and maliciously about them when among friends. Raised in this pattern of followership, Christians were quick to gossip and malign church leaders, then would justify their critique with the proverb "A fish rots from the head first." This pattern made capable leaders hesitant to assume leadership positions. They felt demeaned and insulted, not honored. In contrast, we observed some biblical followers who intentionally affirmed their leaders and refrained from slander, which in turn enabled their leaders to lead with conviction and passion. Discipling followers, not just leaders, to relate according to God's code of honor is essential for healthy Christian community (see Phil 2:29; 1 Pet 5:5-6; Heb 13:17).

Finally, Christian leaders experience divine honor by virtue of their mediatory role in God's mission. Consider the important role of mediator in collectivistic cultures. To meet a top-level person you must personally know someone to advocate for you. The mediator brokers the flow of benefactions, and consequently receives honor for brokering the relationship. Being the person who knows someone who can help is noble and respected.

In a similar vein, David deSilva states that Christ's disciples are brokers of divine favor.[34] We know "Someone" who can help. Christians are the very means by which God's salvation is realized in the world. Observe the mediatorial function of these biblical metaphors: we are "vessels" of God's glory, the "body" of Christ and "ambassadors" of God's righteousness. God's people broker God's benefactions and mediate his salvation to all nations. Through Christians, people encounter and experience God's salvation (2 Cor 2:14–5:21; Col 1:24-27). There is great honor in being God's unique messengers and workers. The sent one bears the status of the sender. Christopher Wright explains this connection in *The Mission of God's People*.

> The person who is sent embodies the presence and authority of the person who sends. This was true even of ordinary human sending. To treat messengers with respect or with humiliation was effectively to honour or shame the person who sent them. The way you responded to messengers was taken as your response to their sender and treated accordingly (1 Sam. 25:39-41; contrast 2 Sam. 10:1-5).[35]

Christian ministry includes being an honorable mediator and ambassador of God's salvific blessings. When God called Abraham, he effectively positioned him as universal broker of divine blessings.[36] God blessed Abraham with a great family and great name *so that* he would bless all the families of the earth (Gen 12:2-3). The apostle Paul viewed himself in a similar manner.[37] Having been called by God's grace to make the mystery of salvation known to all Gentiles, Paul mediated blessings from God to the nations. Paul viewed his ministry as "the grace given me by God to be a minister of Christ Jesus to the Gentiles in the priestly service of the gospel of God, so that the offering of the Gentiles may be acceptable, sanctified by the Holy Spirit. In Christ Jesus, then, *I have reason to boast of my work for God*" (Rom 15:15-17; cf. Phil 2:16). Because of this priestly role of connecting people with God, Paul rightfully claims honor. God's people are the very channel of the King's salvation and blessings, an unspeakable honor.

Ahmed Ali Haile worked most of his career as a peacemaker among warring clans destroying his native country of Somalia. Even after a grenade nearly took his life, he continued his journey of peacemaking, always inviting leaders from conflicting factions to drink tea together. Ahmed, whose name means "a person worthy of honor," opens his memoir *Tea Time in Mogadishu* by saying, "Five decades ago God honored me by calling me to be an emissary of peace."[38] God's calling to be his representative ambassador is one of the greatest honors of the Christian life.

CONCLUSION

The church is God's chosen instrument for bearing his glory and reflecting his honor. As people participate in the community of God's people, notions of honor and shame are transformed to reflect God's honor code in all areas of life. The forces of this world pressure us with the stick of false shame and tempt us with the carrot of temporary honor. Nevertheless, Christians must be firmly rooted in the honor of God. Experiencing God's gracious honor empowers believers to bear witness to God's salvation among the nations.

The subject of this book—Christian mission in honor-shame contxts—is hardly novel. God has repeatedly revealed himself in and through honor-shame cultures—in the days of Abraham, Moses, David, Jesus and the early church. God's salvation from shame and unto honor is a predominant motif in the Bible. Consequently our task of mediating this divine salvation among the honor-shame cultures of today's world has a solid biblical precedent in the Scriptures.

We pray this book provides you with helpful trail markers to guide you on the path of mission in honor-shame contexts. The theme of each chapter, however, calls for more work. We invite you to join us in probing deeper, asking further questions and bringing others into the conversation. May you have God's wisdom and blessing as you seek to apply the general guidelines of the book in your particular context. May many meet Jesus and walk in his ways, and may Christian communities living according to God's honor code be agents of transformation.

To God be the glory forever. Amen.

DISCUSSION AND APPLICATION QUESTIONS

1. Ana's story illustrates how some communities are prone to shame people while others are more inclined to affirm and honor members. In your life, when have you experienced either kind of community?

2. What is one thing your community of fellowship can do to become more centered and less bounded in its interactions?

3. What leaders do you know who serve humbly and honor others? What empowers them to forgo worldly honor?

Appendix 1

KEY SCRIPTURES
ON HONOR-SHAME

CRUCIAL ELEMENT OF UNDERSTANDING honor and shame in Christian mission is simply seeing the themes in Scripture. We have compiled a list of prominent honor-shame verses for your reference. The biblical teaching on honor-shame is vast and extensive, so we have only cherry-picked the most notable verses. Because honor-shame cultures tend to communicate truth via orality (e.g., proverbs, songs and narratives), we emphasize verses from Proverbs and Psalms.

As you read the Bible, remember that the *realities* of honor and shame are far greater than the actual *words* of *honor* and *shame*. For example, the words *face, name, glory, boasting, purity, praise* and others are best interpreted in the honor-shame, collectivistic framework of biblical societies. The pervasiveness of honor and shame in the biblical world means we should not limit ourselves to reading only verses with honor-shame terminology, and also read them in context with the surrounding verses and themes.

OLD TESTAMENT

And the man and his wife were both naked, and were not ashamed. (Gen 2:25, the last sentence of the creation account)

Then the eyes of both were opened, and they knew that they were naked; and they sewed fig leaves together and made loincloths for themselves.

They heard the sound of the LORD God walking in the garden at the time of the evening breeze, and the man and his wife hid themselves from the presence of the LORD God among the trees of the garden. (Gen 3:7-8, Adam and Eve after eating the fruit)

Today the LORD has obtained your agreement: to be his treasured people, as he promised you, and to keep his commandments; for him to set you high above all nations that he has made, in praise and in fame and in honor; and for you to be a people holy to the LORD your God, as he promised. (Deut 26:18-19, God's covenant with Israel)

Therefore the LORD the God of Israel declares: "I promised that your family and the family of your ancestor should go in and out before me forever"; but now the LORD declares: "Far be it from me; for those who honor me I will honor, and those who despise me shall be treated with contempt." (1 Sam 2:30, God addressing Eli's disobedient sons)

All the makers of idols will be put to shame and disgraced;
   they will go off into disgrace together.
But Israel will be saved by the LORD
   with an everlasting salvation;
you will never be put to shame or disgraced,
   to ages everlasting. (Is 45:16-17 NIV)
Do not fear, for you will not be ashamed;
   do not be discouraged, for you will not suffer disgrace;
for you will forget the shame of your youth,
   and the disgrace of your widowhood you will remember no more.
For your Maker is your husband,
   the LORD of hosts is his name;
the Holy One of Israel is your Redeemer,
   the God of the whole earth he is called. (Is 54:4-5, to Israel in exile)

Instead of your shame
   you will receive a double portion,
and instead of disgrace
   you will rejoice in your inheritance.
And so you will inherit a double portion in your land,
   and everlasting joy will be yours. (Is 61:7 NIV)

The nations will see your vindication,
   and all kings your glory;
you will be called by a new name

that the mouth of the LORD will bestow.
You will be a crown of splendor in the LORD's hand,
    a royal diadem in the hand of your God. (Is 62:2-3 NIV)

And my people shall never again be put to shame.
You shall know that I am in the midst of Israel,
    and that I, the LORD, am your God and there is no other.
And my people shall never again be put to shame. (Joel 2:26-27)

I will deal with all your oppressors
    at that time.
And I will save the lame
    and gather the outcast,
and I will change their shame into praise
    and renown in all the earth.
At that time I will bring you home,
    at the time when I gather you;
for I will make you renowned and praised
    among all the peoples of the earth,
when I restore your fortunes
    before your eyes, says the LORD. (Zeph 3:19-20, God speaking to Judeans
        as they faced upcoming exile)

PROVERBS

A person is praised according to their prudence,
    and one with a warped mind is despised. (Prov 12:8 NIV)

Righteousness exalts a nation,
    but sin is a disgrace to any people. (Prov 14:34 NASB)

It is to one's glory to overlook an offense. (Prov 19:11 NIV)

[God] mocks proud mockers
    but shows favor to the humble and oppressed.
The wise inherit honor,
    but fools get only shame. (Prov 3:34-35 NIV)

A person's pride will bring humiliation,
    but one who is lowly in spirit will obtain honor. (Prov 29:23)

It is not good to eat much honey,
    or to seek honor on top of honor. (Prov 25:27)

Like snow in summer or rain in harvest,
> so honor is not fitting for a fool. (Prov 26:1)

Whoever disregards discipline comes to poverty and shame,
> but whoever heeds correction is honored. (Prov 13:18 NIV)

When wickedness comes, contempt comes also;
> and with dishonor comes disgrace. (Prov 18:3)

Blows and disgrace are his lot,
> and his shame will never be wiped away. (Prov 6:33 NIV, speaking about
> an adulterous man)

Whoever oppresses the poor shows contempt for their Maker,
> but whoever is kind to the needy honors God. (Prov 14:31 NIV;
> cf. Prov 17:5)

Let love and faithfulness never leave you. . . .
Then you will win favor and a good name
> in the sight of God and man. (Prov 3:3-4 NIV)

A good name is more desirable than great riches;
> to be esteemed is better than silver or gold. (Prov 22:1 NIV)

Better to be a nobody and yet have a servant
> than pretend to be somebody and have no food. (Prov 12:9 NIV)

Prize her highly, and she will exalt you;
> she will honor you if you embrace her.
She will place on your head a fair garland;
> she will bestow on you a beautiful crown. (Prov 4:8-9, speaking about
> Wisdom herself)

With me are riches and honor,
> enduring wealth and prosperity. (Prov 8:18 NIV, Wisdom speaking)

The eye that mocks a father
> and scorns to obey a mother
will be pecked out by the ravens of the valley
> and eaten by the vultures. (Prov 30:17)

A wife of noble character is her husband's crown,
> but a disgraceful wife is like decay in his bones. (Prov 12:4 NIV)

The glory of young men is their strength,
   gray hair the splendor of the old. (Prov 20:29 NIV)

Children's children are a crown to the aged,
   and parents are the pride of their children. (Prov 17:6 NIV)

Whoever robs their father and drives out their mother
   is a child who brings shame and disgrace. (Prov 19:26 NIV)

Otherwise, I may have too much and disown you
   and say, "Who is the Lord?"
Or I may become poor and steal,
   and so dishonor the name of the my God. (Prov 30:9 NIV)

Do you see those who are skillful in their work?
   They will serve kings;
   they will not serve common people. (Prov 22:29)

PSALMS

But you, O LORD, are a shield around me,
   my glory, and the one who lifts up my head. (Ps 3:3)

All my enemies shall be ashamed and struck with terror;
   they shall turn back, and in a moment be put to shame. (Ps 6:10)

What are human beings that you are mindful of them,
   mortals that you care for them?
Yet you have made them a little lower than God,
   and crowned them with glory and honor. (Ps 8:4-6, commentary
      on creation)

His glory is great through your help;
   splendor and majesty you bestow on him. (Ps 21:5, regarding Israel's
      king; cf. Ps 89:27; 132:18)

Do not let those who wait for you be put to shame;
   let them be ashamed who are wantonly treacherous. (Ps 25:3)

Ascribe to the LORD the glory of his name;
   worship the LORD in holy splendor. (Ps 29:2)

In you, O LORD, I seek refuge;
   do not let me ever be put to shame;
in your righteousness deliver me. (Ps 31:1)

Let all those who rejoice at my calamity
    be put to shame and confusion;
let those who exalt themselves against me
    be clothed with shame and dishonor. (Ps 35:26)

On God rests my deliverance and my honor;
    my mighty rock, my refuge is in God. (Ps 62:7)

Do not let those who seek you be dishonored because of me,
    O God of Israel.
It is for your sake that I have borne reproach,
    that shame has covered my face.
I have become a stranger to my kindred,
    an alien to my mother's children. . . .
You know the insults I receive,
    and my shame and dishonor;
my foes are all known to you. (Ps 69:6-8, 19, David amid persecution)

You will increase my honor,
    and comfort me once again. (Ps 71:21)

But it is God who executes judgment,
    putting down one and lifting up another. (Ps 75:7)

Fill their faces with shame,
    so that they may seek your name, O LORD. (Ps 83:16, Israel about her
        attacking neighbors)

For the LORD God is a sun and shield;
    he bestows favor and honor. (Ps 84:11)

I cling to your decrees, O LORD;
    let me not be put to shame. (Ps 119:31)

For though the LORD is high, he regards the lowly;
    but the haughty he perceives from far away. (Ps 138:6)

For the LORD takes delight in his people;
    he crowns the humble with victory.
Let his faithful people rejoice in this honor. (Ps 149:4-5 NIV)

He humbled himself
and became obedient to the point of death—
even death on a cross.

Therefore God also highly exalted him
and gave him the name
that is above every name. (Phil 2:8-9)

For it stands in Scripture:

"Behold, I am laying in Zion a stone,
a cornerstone chosen and precious,
and whoever believes in him will not be put to shame."

So the honor is for you who believe, but for those who do not believe,

"The stone that the builders rejected
has become the cornerstone." (1 Pet 2:6-7 ESV)

But we do see Jesus, who for a little while was made lower than the angels, now crowned with glory and honor because of the suffering of death, so that by the grace of God he might taste death for everyone.

It was fitting that God, for whom and through whom all things exist, in bringing many children to glory, should make the pioneer of their salvation perfect through sufferings. (Heb 2:9-10)

Let us run with perseverance the race that is set before us, looking to Jesus the pioneer and perfecter of our faith, who for the sake of the joy that was set before him endured the cross, disregarding its shame, and has taken his seat at the right hand of the throne of God. (Heb 12:1-2)

And the city has no need of sun or moon to shine on it, for the glory of God is its light, and its lamp is the Lamb. The nations will walk by its light, and the kings of the earth will bring their glory into it. Its gates will never be shut by day—and there will be no night there. People will bring into it the glory and the honor of the nations. But nothing unclean will enter it. (Rev 21:23-27, about the new Jerusalem)

But the throne of God and of the Lamb will be in it, and his servants will worship him; they will see his face, and his name will be on their foreheads. (Rev 22:3-4)

Appendix 2

Biblical Stories
Addressing Honor-Shame

*T*HE MOST PROMINENT WAY BIBLICAL WRITERS communicate God's honor for the shamed is through stories. Narratives tell the story of God saving his people from disgrace and displaying his honor. In chapter four ("Old Testament") we explained the honor-shame structure of many biblical stories. This appendix lists key biblical stories in which honor and/or shame are prominent elements.

PATRIARCHS

Creation (Gen 1–2): God creates his honored vice regents from lowly dust, crowing them with honor and glory (see also Ps 8).

Adam and Eve (Gen 3): God's children disobey him, inducing feelings of shame and expulsion from God's presence.

Cain (Gen 4): After being disregarded by God, Cain's face falls and status envy prompts him to kill his own brother.

Babel (Gen 10): Humanity strives to build a name for themselves and exalt themselves to the heavens.

Abraham (Gen 12:1-3): God calls Abram to a position of grand prominence: a great nation, abundant family, divine blessing, mediation of universal blessing, etc.

Sinful woman (Lk 7): Jesus defends the scandalous actions of the sinful woman before the Pharisees.

Gerasene demoniac (Lk 8): Jesus cures a naked, demon-tormented man living in the tombs, thus greatly increasing Jesus' own fame.

Bleeding woman (Lk 8): Jesus heals and purifies a woman subjected to twelve years of incurable bleeding, and honors her with praise.

Zacchaeus (Lk 19): Jesus graces a short tax collector on the periphery with honor by entering his house.

Unexpected invitees (parable, Lk 14): When the regular folk are too busy to eat, the master invites all the poor, blind and lame—a picture of the messianic banquet Jesus was inaugurating.

Prodigal son (parable, Lk 15): The two shameful sons find reconciliation and welcome from their father. A picture of Jesus' radical table fellowship with shamed sinners before the Pharisees.

Wicked tenants (parable, Lk 20): The ungrateful tenants are expelled from the vineyard and the responsibility is given to outsiders. A picture of Israel's ethnic presumption and Gentile inclusion.

Controversies with leaders (Lk 20): In a series of public spats the Jewish leaders attempt to discredit Jesus, but his ripostes silence their challenges and garner more fame from the crowds

Jesus' foot washing (John 13): Aware of his authority before God, Jesus assumes the role of servant and washes his followers' dirty feet as a symbol of self-debasing love.

Jesus (Phil 2): God resurrects a crucified corpse to his right hand and grants him a name above all names.

Appendix 3

Recommended Resources

*T*HIS BRIEF LIST INCLUDES WORKS we consider most helpful for understanding honor-shame for Christian mission. It is organized by their primary emphasis. For a fuller list of resources, online articles, videos and websites, visit www.HonorShame.com/recommendations/.

BIBLE

Bailey, Kenneth E. *Jesus Through Middle Eastern Eyes: Cultural Studies in the Gospels.* Downers Grove, IL: IVP Academic, 2009.

deSilva, David. *Honor, Patronage, Kinship and Purity: Unlocking New Testament Culture.* Downers Grove, IL: InterVarsity Press, 2000.

Jewett, Robert. *Saint Paul Returns to the Movies: Triumph over Shame.* Grand Rapids: Eerdmans, 1998.

Laniak, Timothy S. *Shame and Honor in the Book of Esther.* Atlanta: Society of Biblical Literature, 1998.

Richards, E. Randolph, and Brandon J. O'Brien. *Misreading Scripture with Western Eyes: Removing Cultural Blinders to Better Understand the Bible.* Downers Grove, IL: InterVarsity Press.

The publications of New Testament scholars David deSilva, Joseph Hellerman, Kenneth Bailey, Robert Jewett, Jerome Neyrey, Bruce Malina, John Pilch and John Elliott often highlight the honor-shame aspects of biblical texts. Though more academic and technical, their works are full of historical and cultural insights.

Notes

1 A WORLD OF SHAME

[1]While all of the stories and examples in this book are based on real people and events, names and identifying details have been altered to protect the privacy of the individuals involved.

[2]Michael Martinez, "Uncle Calls Boston Marathon Bombers 'Losers,'" CNN, April 19, 2013, www.cnn.com/2013/04/19/us/marathon-suspects-uncle /index.html.

[3]Ravi Zacharias, "Testimony: Antidote to Poison," *Christianity Today*, April 2013, 79.

[4]"A New Era Has Arrived," *Dabiq* 1 (2014): 6-9 (emphasis added), http:// media.clarionproject.org/files/09-2014/isis-isil-islamic-state-magazine -Issue-1-the-return-of-khilafah.pdf.

[5]Naomi Eisenberger and Matthew Lieberman, "Why It Hurts to Be Left Out: The Neurocognitive Overlap Between Physical Pain and Social Pain," *Trends in Cognitive Sciences* 8, no. 7 (2004): 294-300; Kipling Williams, Joseph Forgas and William von Hippel, eds., *The Social Outcast: Ostracism, Social Exclusion, Rejection, and Bullying* (New York: Psychology Press, 2005).

[6]C. S. Lewis, "The Weight of Glory," in *The Weight of Glory* (1949; repr., San Francisco: HarperSanFrancisco, 2001), 39.

[7]Ruth Benedict, *The Chrysanthemum and the Sword: Patterns of Japanese Cultures* (Cambridge, MA: Riverside, 1946), 1. Her book sold two million copies in Japan and became a bestseller in neighboring China. This work

spawned a flood of subsequent shame research in both America and Japan, a testament to its explanatory power.

[8]Ibid., 223.

[9]Samantha Power, *Sergio* (New York: Penguin, 2010), 531; John Braithwaite, *Crime, Shame, and Reintegration* (Cambridge: Cambridge University Press, 1989); Kwame Anthony Appiah, *The Honor Code: How Moral Revolutions Happen* (New York: W. W. Norton, 2010); Gershen Kaufman, *The Psychology of Shame: Theory and Treatment of Shame-Based Syndromes,* 2nd ed. (New York: Springer, 1996); Deepa Narayan, *Voices of the Poor* (New York: Oxford University Press, 2000), cited in Steve Corbett and Brian Fikkert, *When Helping Hurts* (Chicago: Moody Press, 2009), 51-54; Stephen Kinzer, *Reset: Iran, Turkey, and America's Future* (New York: Times Books, 2010); Jennifer Jacquet, *Is Shame Necessary? New Uses for an Old Tool* (New York: Pantheon, 2015).

[10]David deSilva, *Honor, Patronage, Kinship and Purity: Unlocking New Testament Culture* (Downers Grove, IL: InterVarsity Press, 2000), 158-63.

[11]Biblical scholars have become increasingly aware of honor and shame, as evidenced by the use of social-science criticism. Prominent Old Testament researchers include Lyn Betchtel, P. J. Botha, Ronald Simkins and Johanna Steibert. For New Testament studies, see publications by deSilva (*Honor, Patronage, Kinship and Purity; The Hope of Glory: Honor Discourse and New Testament Interpretation* [Collegeville, MN: Liturgical Press, 1999]), Robert Jewett (*Romans: A Commentary,* Hermeneia [Minneapolis: Fortress, 2006]; "Paul, Shame and Honor," in *Paul and the Greco-Roman World,* ed. J. Paul Sampley [Harrisburg, PA: Trinity Press International, 2003], 859-901), and members of the Context Group such as Jerome Neyrey (*Honor and Shame in the Gospel of Matthew* [Louisville: Westminster John Knox, 1998]), Bruce Malina (*The New Testament World,* 3rd ed. [Louisville, KY: Westminster John Knox, 2001]), John Pilch, Richard Rohrbaugh and John Elliott.

[12]Aristotle, *Nicomachean Ethics* 4.3.

[13]Cicero, *Epistulae ad Quintum fratrem* 1.1.38, quoted from J. E. Lendon, *Empire of Honour: The Art of Government in the Roman World* (Oxford: Clarendon, 1997), 36.

[14]Dio Chrysostom, *Orationes* 31.37.

[15]David Whitehead, "Philotimia," in *The Oxford Classical Dictionary* (Oxford: Oxford University Press, 2003), 1171.

[16]Lendon, *Empire of Honour*, 35.

[17]DeSilva, *Honor, Patronage, Kinship and Purity*, 23.

[18]We recognize there are limitations to the terms "honor-shame culture" and "innocence-guilt culture." We will discuss those limitations in the next chapter.

[19]The statistics reflected in figure 1.1 summarize results from the Culture Test. The Culture Test was developed primarily as a missions training tool, not a social research instrument, so results are more suggestive than scientific. Nevertheless, general observations regarding global cultural types merit attention in Christian mission today. In this figure, the category "Western" includes Western Europe, the United States, Canada, New Zealand and Australia. Majority World includes the remaining global regions: Latin America, Eastern Europe, Middle East, Africa and Asia.

[20]Jenny Hwangyang, "Immigrants to the US: A Missional Opportunity," in *Global Diasporas and Mission*, ed. Chandler H. Im and Amos Yong (Oxford: Regnum, 2013), 148-57.

[21]Soong-Chan Rah, *The Next Evangelicalism: Freeing the Church from Western Cultural Captivity* (Downers Grove, IL: IVP Books, 2009), 13. For more on the trends of global Christianity, see Lamin Sanneh, *Disciples of All Nations: Pillars of World Christianity* (Oxford: Oxford University Press, 2008); Philip Jenkins, *The Next Christendom* (New York: Oxford University Press, 2002); Dana Robert, "Shifting Southward: Global Christianity Since 1945," *International Bulletin of Mission Research* 24, no. 2 (2000): 50-58.

[22]We use the term *native* not in a colonialistic fashion, but in the sense of "digital native," referring to someone born and raised in such a context.

[23]Jackson Wu, *Saving God's Face: A Chinese Contextualization of Salvation Through Honor and Shame*, Evangelical Missiological Society Dissertation Series (Pasadena, CA: William Carey Library, 2012), 10-12.

[24]Lesslie Newbigin, *The Gospel in a Pluralist Society* (Grand Rapids: Eerdmans, 1989), 144.

[25]Krister Stendahl, "The Apostle Paul and the Introspective Conscience of the West," *Harvard Theological Review* 56, no. 3 (1963): 203-6.

[26]The problem comes when people absolutize this theology contextualized in the West, elevate it to the level of biblical truth and export it internationally, thus leading to a type of theological/cultural colonialism.

[27]The diamond image is from Steve Taylor, "Participation and an Atomized World: A Reflection on Christ as Representative New Adam," in *Proclaiming the Scandal of the Cross: Contemporary Images of the Atonement*, ed. Mark D. Baker (Grand Rapids: Baker Academic, 2006), 104; Mark D. Baker and Joel B. Green, *Recovering the Scandal of the Cross: Atonement in New Testament and Contemporary Contexts*, 2nd ed. (Downers Grove, IL: IVP Academic, 2011). Jayson Georges, *The 3D Gospel: Ministry in Guilt, Shame, and Fear Cultures* (Timē Press, 2014).

[28]Jayson Georges, "From Shame to Honor: A Theological Reading of Romans for Honor-Shame Contexts," *Missiology* 38, no. 3 (2010): 295-307; Georges, *The 3D Gospel*; "Why Has Nobody Told Me This Before? The Gospel the World Is Waiting For," *Mission Frontiers* 37, no. 1 (2015): 6-10.

[29]This includes authors writing from an explicitly Christian perspective such as John A. Forrester, Robert Jewett, Alan Mann and Robin Stockitt, as well as works on shame that are not explicitly Christian by authors such as Brené Brown, James Gilligan and Gershen Kaufman.

[30]Kenneth Bailey, *Poet and Peasant and Through Peasant Eyes: A Literary-Cultural Approach to the Parables in Luke*, combined ed. (Grand Rapids: Eerdmans, 1983). See also Bailey's *Jesus Through Middle Eastern Eyes: Cultural Studies in the Gospels* (Downers Grove, IL: InterVarsity Press, 2008).

[31]Marcos Baker, *¿Dios de Ira o Dios de Amor? Cómo Superar la Inseguridad y Ser Libres para Servir*, 2nd ed. (Buenos Aires: Ediciones Kairos, 2007).

[32]Baker and Green, *Recovering the Scandal of the Cross*.

2 THE HEART OF HONOR-SHAME CULTURES

[1]Timothy Tennent, "Anthropology: Human Identity in Shame-Based Cultures of the Far East," in *Theology in the Context of World Christianity: How the Global Church Is Influencing the Way We Think About and Discuss Theology* (Grand Rapids: Zondervan, 2007), 80.

[2]In addition to resisting the general label "honor-shame culture" because it implies that honor-shame is a dynamic in only some cultures, anthropologist also, helpfully, caution against labels such as "Japanese culture," which

implies they are one, static and universal, rather than dynamic and varie-
gated. We agree with these observations. In this book our prime interest is
the honor-shame dynamic. We use the language of "honor-shame culture"
not to take a stance against the above critiques, but simply to refer to places
where that dynamic is more present than others.

[3]Seneca, *Epistle* 102.8.

[4]Julian Alfred Pitt-Rivers, "Honour and Shame," in *Honour and Shame: The
Values of Mediterranean Society*, ed. John G. Peristiany (Chicago: University
of Chicago Press, 1966), 21.

[5]Julian Pitt-Rivers, "Honor," in *International Encyclopedia of the Social Sciences*, ed. David L. Sills (New York: Macmillan, 1968) 6:505.

[6]Duane Elmer, *Cross-Cultural Conflict: Building Relationships for Effective
Ministry* (Downers Grove, IL: InterVarsity Press, 1993), 138.

[7]The following paragraph draws on Elia Shabani Mligo, *Jesus and the
Stigmatized: Reading the Gospel of John in a Context of HIV/AIDS-Related
Stigmatization in Tanzania* (Eugene, OR: Wipf & Stock, 2011).

[8]Chris Buckley, "Rat Meat Sold as Lamb in China Highlights Fears," *New
York Times*, May 3, 2013, www.nytimes.com/2013/05/04/world/asia/rat
-meat-sold-as-lamb-in-china-highlights-fears.html.

[9]Pitt-Rivers, "Honor," 506.

[10]Michael Martinez, "Uncle Calls Boston Marathon Bombers 'Losers,'" *CNN*, April
19, 2013, www.cnn.com/2013/04/19/us/marathon-suspects-uncle/index.html.

[11]Alexandra Garcia and Sergio Pecanha, "World Cup Despair in Brazil," *New
York Times*, July 9, 2014, www.nytimes.com/interactive/2014/07/09/sports
/worldcup/brazil-losing-quotes.html.

[12]Christopher Flanders, *About Face: Rethinking Face for Twenty-First-
Century Mission* (Eugene, OR: Wipf & Stock, 2001), 121-59.

[13]Michael Herzfeld, "Honour and Shame: Problems in the Comparative
Analysis of Moral Systems," *Man* 15, no. 2 (1980): 339.

3 THE FACE OF HONOR-SHAME CULTURES

[1]"Patron" derives from the Latin *patronus*. Related terms include "benefactor" (Greek), "suzerain" (ancient Near East), "big man" (Oceania tribes)
or "lord" (medieval feudal system with vassals). Russian colloquially uses
"roof" for the patron-like activities of being a protective covering.

²"The Name Game: Business Cards an Essential Part of Operating in China," *New York Times*, January 10, 2011, www.nytimes.com/2011/01/11/business /global/11bus.html.

³Richard Y. Hibbert, "Defilement and Cleansing: A Possible Approach to Christian Encounter with Muslims," *Missiology* 36, no. 3 (July 2008): 344.

⁴George M. Lamso, *The Shepherd of All: The Twenty-Third Psalm* (Philadelphia: Holdman, 1939), 65.

⁵Brian Fikkert and Steve Corbett, *When Helping Hurts* (Chicago: Moody Press, 2009), 51-53.

⁶David Augsburger, *Pastoral Counseling Across Cultures* (Philadelphia: Westminster, 1986), 113-15.

⁷Margaret Visser, *Beyond Fate* (Toronto, ON: House of Anansi Press, 2005), 41.

4 OLD TESTAMENT

¹Jayson Georges, "Missional Harmony," *Mission Frontiers* 37, no. 1 (2015): 10.

²In the last thirty years biblical scholars have made fruitful use of anthropology to explain the social values of biblical cultures. While building on these insights derived from their social-science interpretation of the Bible, our approach will be more theological in orientation. David deSilva, *Honor, Patronage, Kinship and Purity: Unlocking New Testament Culture* (Downers Grove, IL: InterVarsity Press, 2000); Jerome H. Neyrey, *Honor and Shame in the Gospel of Matthew* (Louisville, KY: Westminster John Knox, 1998); Bruce J. Malina and Jerome H. Neyrey, "Honor and Shame in Luke-Acts: Pivotal Values of the Mediterranean World," in *Social World of Luke-Acts: Models for Interpretation*, ed. Jerome H. Neyrey (Peabody, MA: Hendrickson, 1991); Bruce J. Malina, *The New Testament World: Insights from Cultural Anthropology* (Louisville, KY: Westminster John Knox, 1993); Timothy Laniak, *Honor and Shame in the Book of Esther*, Society of Biblical Literature Dissertation Series (Atlanta: Scholars Press, 1998).

³In fact, the English word *shame* originates from the Indo-European word "to hide or cover oneself."

⁴Dietrich Bonhoeffer, *Ethics* (New York: Touchstone, 1995), 20.

⁵Modern theology defines the image of God ontologically, asking which precise quality people share with God (e.g., personality, will, morality,

relationality). New Testament writers speak of the "image of God" as the reason people deserve dignity (1 Cor 11:7; Jas 3:9), or a description of Jesus' glorious preeminence as the resurrected Messiah (2 Cor 4:4; Phil 2:6; Col 1:15; Heb 1:3). The image of God denotes the fundamental dignity and honor accorded to humans by God.

[6]Objective shame comes from the fact that we have failed to maintain God's relational expectations to glorify him. God looks on sinners as shameful (and shaming) children; that is an objective, theological reality beginning in Gen 3. Subjective shame is the subsequent personal emotions of negative self-assessment. This subjective shame, along with other human problems, is rooted in our fundamental disunion with God. Objective guilt occurs when a person is "culpable," deserving blame for doing something wrong. Subjective guilt refers to the affective "remorse" one senses internally. Of course, these are not four neatly demarcated quadrants in a person's spiritual life, but a simple taxonomy for untangling the complexity of sin.

[7]John Piper, "Isaiah 48:9-11 // For My Name's Sake," uploaded by Desiring God, August 8, 2014, 10 min., 45 sec., https://vimeo.com/102945569.

[8]Simon Chan, *Grassroots Asian Theology: Thinking the Faith from the Ground Up* (Downers Grove, IL: IVP Academic, 2014), 44.

[9]As an example, the study note for 2 Sam 12:1-31 in the esv Study Bible says, "David started by breaking the tenth commandment (coveting, Ex. 20:17), then the seventh (adultery, Ex. 20:14), and then the sixth (murder, Ex 20:13), while the Lord silently watched his behavior. Here at last the Lord calls him to account for standing above the law. . . . Nathan apparently asks David to intervene in a legal matter." However, the text of 1 Sam 12 does not portray David's actions in such legal terms.

[10]This translation comes from the esv footnote, which explains the literal Hebrew phrase. Both esv and nrsv translate this Hebrew idiom as "will you not be accepted?" to make the communal and relational dimensions of "face" language more apparent for English readers.

[11]Samantha Power, *Sergio: One Man's Fight to Save the World* (New York: Penguin, 2010), 531.

[12]James Gilligan, *Violence: Reflections on a National Epidemic* (New York: Vintage, 1997), 110–11.

[13]Brené Brown, *I Thought It Was Just Me (but It Isn't): Making the Journey from "What Will People Think?" to "I Am Enough"* (New York: Gotham, 2007), xix.

[14]Frank Moore Cross, "Kinship and Covenant in Ancient Israel," in *From Epic to Canon: History and Literature in Ancient Israel* (Baltimore: Johns Hopkins University Press, 1998), 6-7.

[15]Saul Olyan, "Honor, Shame, and Covenant Relations in Ancient Israel and Its Environments," *Journal of Biblical Literature* 115, no. 2 (1996): 201-18.

[16]This reading that God has chosen Israel for a covenant relationship in order to restore the glory of Adam was common at Qumran as well: 1QS 4.22-23; CD 3.19-20; 1QH 17.14-15; 4QpPs 37 3.1-2.

[17]Gen 12:1-3; 15:5, 14; 17:2-8; 22:16-18; 26:3-4; 35:11-12.

[18]Laniak, *Shame and Honor in the Book of Esther*, 8. The following two narrative patterns and diagrams are adapted from ibid., 7-15.

[19]Ibid., 7-17.

[20]Kenneth Bailey, *The Good Shepherd: A Thousand-Year Journey from Psalm 23 to the New Testament* (Downers Grove, IL: IVP Academic, 2014), 53-55.

[21]Roland Muller, *Honor and Shame* (Philadelphia: Xlibris, 2001), 56.

[22]C. S. Lewis, "The Weight of Glory," in *The Weight of Glory* (1949; repr., San Francisco: HarperSanFrancisco, 2001), 38.

[23]David deSilva, *Honor Discourse* (Collegeville, MN: Liturgical Press, 1999), 98. Aristotle defined the word Greek word commonly translated as "wrath" (i.e., *orgē*) as a longing for revenge for dishonoring slights in his *Rhetoric* (2.2.1, 8).

5 JESUS

[1]Some examples of this use of honor language are Mt 28:18; Jn 1:1-3; 17:5; Acts 13:32-35; Rom 1:3-4; 1 Cor 8:6; Eph 1:20-22; Phil 2:9-11; Col 1:15-17; Heb 1:1-218; Rev 5:1-14.

[2]K. C. Hanson, "How Honorable! How Shameful! A Cultural Analysis of Matthew's Makarisms and Reproaches," *Semeia* 68 (1996): 81-112.

[3]Such a paraphrase relies on the social and exegetical insights of Jerome Neyrey, *Honor and Shame in the Gospel of Matthew* (Louisville: Westminster John Knox, 1998), 164-228. This paraphrase serves not as an "exegetical commentary," but more as an "amplified homily" to capture

Jesus' subversive intentions and the possible effects of his words on a first-century Jew of an honor-shame culture. An exegetical defense of this honor-shame reading can be found in the works of Neyrey and Hanson (cited above).

4N. T. Wright, *Jesus and the Victory of God* (Minneapolis: Fortress, 1996), 432.

5David deSilva, *Honor, Patronage, Kinship and Purity: Unlocking New Testament Culture* (Downers Grove, IL: InterVarsity Press, 2000), 279-304.

6"Floating Hospital of Hope," *CBS Evening News*, February 18, 2013, www .cbsnews.com/videos/the-floating-hospital-of-hope/.

7DeSilva, *Honor, Patronage, Kinship and Purity*, 284.

8Wright, *Jesus and the Victory of God*, 191-92.

9This section is an adaptation of Marcos Baker, *Centrado en Jesus* (Lima: Ediciones Shalom, 2013), 81-88.

10Joel Green states that it is likely that she is not only marginalized as a prostitute but also that she is a prostitute because she was already marginalized or in a precarious position. Perhaps her parents sold her into prostitution in a moment of economic crisis or she was a woman without a husband or other supportive family, and prostitution was one of the few options she had for survival. Joel B. Green, *The Gospel of Luke*, New International Commentary on the New Testament (Grand Rapids: Eerdmans, 1997), 309.

11Kenneth E. Bailey, *Jesus Through Middle Eastern Eyes: Cultural Studies in the Gospels* (Downers Grove, IL: IVP Academic, 2008), 246.

12Ibid., 255.

13Joel Green, *Theology of the Gospel of Luke*, New Testament Theology (Cambridge: Cambridge University Press, 1995), 79.

14Bailey, *Jesus Through Middle Eastern Eyes*, 257.

15Scott Bartchy, "Table Fellowship," in *Dictionary of Jesus and the Gospels*, ed. Joel Green, Scot McKnight and I. Howard Marshall (Downers Grove, IL: InterVarsity Press, 1998).

16Kenneth E. Bailey, "The Pursuing Father," *Christianity Today*, October 26, 1998, 34-40; Bailey, *Poet and Peasant and Through Peasant Eyes: A Literary-Cultural Approach to the Parables in Luke*, combined ed. (Grand Rapids: Eerdmans, 1983), 158-206; Bailey, *The Cross and the Prodigal: Luke 15 Through the Eyes of Middle Eastern Peasants*, 2nd ed. (Downers Grove, IL: IVP Academic, 2005).

[17]Kevin J. Vanhoozer, "The Atonement in Postmodernity: Guilt, Goats and Gifts," in *The Glory of the Atonement*, ed. Charles Hill and Frank A. James III (Downers Grove, IL: InterVarsity Press, 2004), 404.

[18]For instance, in the letter to the Hebrews, written to Jews, the cross is discussed in terms of their sacrificial system. Paul, writing to a more Gentile audience, talks of redemption—borrowing from their familiarity with slaves and the slaves being freed from their bondage. Yet in different letters, in different contexts Paul uses different metaphors and emphasizes different aspects of the saving significance of the cross. In Galatians, in the context of confusion and discord over who is truly part of the family of God he writes of adoption. In Colossians, addressing the relation of Christ to other cosmic powers, philosophies and religions, Paul presents the cross as triumph over the powers (Col 2:15). For an in-depth exploration of the diversity of New Testament atonement imagery, see Mark D. Baker and Joel B. Green, *Recovering the Scandal of the Cross: Atonement in New Testament and Contemporary Contexts*, 2nd ed. (Downers Grove, IL: IVP Academic, 2011), chaps. 2-4.

[19]Works on honor-shame and the atonement include Christopher L. Flanders, *About Face: Rethinking Face for Twenty-First-Century Mission* (Eugene, OR: Pickwick, 2011); Robert Jewett, *Saint Paul Returns to the Movies: Triumph over Shame* (Grand Rapids: Eerdmans, 1999); C. Norman Kraus, *Jesus Christ Our Lord: Christology from a Disciple's Perspective* (Scottdale, PA: Herald, 1990), 205-28; Alan Mann, *Atonement for a Sinless Society*, 2nd ed. (Eugene, OR: Cascade, 2015); Philip D. Jamieson, *The Face of Forgiveness: A Pastoral Theology of Shame and Redemption* (Downers Grove, IL: InterVarsity Press, 2016); Jackson Wu, *Saving God's Face: A Chinese Contextualization of Salvation Through Honor and Shame* (Pasadena: William Carey Library, 2012).

[20]If Rome saw physical pain as the primary aim in capital punishment, they had more painful options than crucifixion. For instance, 2 Macc 7 describes execution by flogging, scalping, hacking off the extremities, cutting out the tongue and then frying the person in heated pans. See Martin Hengel, *Crucifixion* (Minneapolis: Fortress, 1997).

[21]Cicero, *Pro Rabirio Perduellionis Reo* 16; trans. Hengel, *Crucifixion*, 42.

[22]Lactantius, *Divine Institutes* 4.26: "For some one may perchance say: Why, if He was God, and chose to die, did He not at least suffer by some honourable kind of death? Why was it by the cross especially? Why by an infamous kind of punishment, which may appear unworthy even of a man if he is free, although guilty?" The repulsive shame of the cross continues to be a key reason Muslim theologians reject the historicity of Jesus' crucifixion—they refuse to believe Allah would let an honorable prophet bear such shame.

[23]Mt 26:67; 27:28-31, 41, 44; Mk 14:65; 15:16-20, 29-34; Lk 22:63-65; 23:11, 35-37.

[24]We limit the discussion to Paul as a way of containing the discussion to these few pages. Yet we choose Paul with intentionality because his writing about the cross is so central to views of the atonement articulated in a way that coheres with Western guilt-innocence perspectives. Therefore it is especially important to note as well the prominence of the themes of honor and shame in relation to the cross in Paul.

[25]Jewett, *Saint Paul Returns to the Movies*, 128-29.

[26]James D. G. Dunn, *The Theology of Paul the Apostle* (Grand Rapids: Eerdmans, 1998), 93, citing *Apocalypse of Moses* 20.2 and 21.6.

[27]Robert Jewett, "Honor and Shame in the Argument of Romans," in *Putting Body and Soul Together: Essays in Honor of Robin Scroggs*, ed. Graydon F. Snyder, Virginia Wiles and Alexandra Brown (Valley Forge, PA: Trinity Press International, 1997), 265.

[28]For examples of this dynamic and development of the theme of this paragraph, see Mark D. Baker, "Saving Significance of the Cross in a Honduran Barrio," *Mission Focus: Annual Review* 14 (2006): 59-81.

[29]Other examples include the following: "The scripture says, 'No one who believes in him will be put to shame'" (Rom 10:11); "It is my eager expectation and hope that I will not be at all ashamed, but that with full courage now as always Christ will be honored in my body, whether by life or by death" (Phil 1:20 esv).

[30]For a discussion of justification that gives biblical examples and substantiation, see Mark D. Baker, *Religious No More: Building Communities of Grace and Freedom* (Downers Grove, IL: InterVarsity Press, 1999), 97-103. For a more in-depth explanation of this view of justice/justification, see

James D. G. Dunn and Alan Suggate, *The Justice of God: A Fresh Look at the Old Doctrine of Justification by Faith* (Grand Rapids: Eerdmans, 1993); Richard B. Hays, "Justification," in *Anchor Bible Dictionary*, ed. David Noel Freedman (New York: Doubleday, 1992), 3:1129-33.

[31]Paul affirms the faithfulness of God (Rom 3:3), God's truth (Rom 3:4), the righteousness of God (Rom 3:5), and the truth(fulness) of God (Rom 3:7)— all functionally equivalent subjective genitives affirming God's integrity and faithfulness.

[32]The one Greek word *dikaiosynē* is behind the English words "justice" and "righteousness." Although in most English translations of Rom 3 both English words appear in the text, Paul used the one Greek word throughout. In this paragraph we are using "justice" throughout to make the connections to justification clearer. For further discussion of this translating issue and the meaning of *dikaiosynē*, see the works noted above.

[33]Paul clearly sees not seeking revenge and loving enemies as part of the transformed life enabled by the Spirit and God's saving work through the cross and resurrection (Rom 12:1-2, 9-21).

6 SPIRITUALITY

[1]Proceeding paragraphs adapted from Jayson Georges, "Honor-Shame Sub-cultures in the U.S.," *Mission Frontiers* 37, no. 1 (2015): 19. See also Mark D. Baker, *Religious No More: Building Communities of Grace and Freedom* (Downers Grove, IL: InterVarsity Press, 1999).

[2]Ruth Benedict, *The Chrysanthemum and the Sword* (New York: Houghton Mifflin, 1967), 223.

[3]Andy Crouch, "The Return of Shame," *Christianity Today*, March 2015, 38.

[4]Susan Greenfield, quoted in Gary Rivett, "Neuroscientist Susan Greenfield Warns Young Brains Being Re-wired by Digital Technology," *ABC News*, November 20, 2014.

[5]Crouch, "Return of Shame," 34.

[6]Brené Brown, *I Thought It Was Just Me (but It Isn't): Making the Journey from "What Will People Think?" to "I Am Enough"* (New York: Gotham, 2007), 5.

[7]Brown, *I Thought It Was Just Me*.

8John Piper, "Misplaced Shame to Mission Shame," Desiring God, October 3, 1988, www.desiringgod.org/articles/from-misplaced-shame-to-mission -flame.

9Based on Jayson's correspondence with Colin E. Andrews, personal notes, April 10, 2011.

10John Piper, "Faith in Future Grace vs. Misplaced Shame," in *Faith in Future Grace*, rev. ed. (Colorado Springs, CO: Multnomah, 2012), 129.

11Clayborne Carson, *The Autobiography of Martin Luther King, Jr.* (New York: Warner Books, 1998), 95.

12This analysis of 2 Cor 2:14 relies on Scott J. Hafemann, *2 Corinthians*, NIV Application Commentary (Grand Rapids: Zondervan, 2000), 107-9.

13Ibid., 112.

14Story adapted from Baker, *Religious No More*, 148-51.

15Frederick Herzog, *Liberation Theology: Liberation in the Light of the Fourth Gospel* (New York: Seabury, 1972), 79.

16Roberta Bondi, "Becoming Bearers of Reconciliation," *Weavings* 5, no. 1 (1990): 9-10.

17Psychology has analyzed the nature of individual shame as commonly experienced by people in the West. As starting points we recommend Edward Welch, *Shame Interrupted: How God Lifts the Pain of Worthlessness and Rejection* (Greensboro, NC: New Growth Press, 2012); Lewis Smedes, *Shame and Grace: Healing the Shame We Don't Deserve*; Brown, *I Thought It Was Just Me*; Curt Thompson, *The Soul of Shame: Retelling the Stories We Believe About Ourselves* (Downers Grove, IL: InterVarsity Press, 2015).

7 RELATIONSHIP

1Steve Hawthorne, "To Love the Glory of God," *Mission Frontiers* 37, no. 1 (2015): 28.

2David Augsburger, *Pastoral Counseling Across Cultures* (Philadelphia: Westminster, 1986), 112.

3Duane Elmer, *Cross-Cultural Conflict: Building Relationships for Effective Ministry* (Downers Grove, IL: InterVarsity Press, 1993), 80-81. Elmer's entire chapter "The One-Down Position and Vulnerability" examines this channel for conflict resolution.

[4]Darren Duerksen, "The Indian Gift of Honor: Simply Honoring Someone's Presence" (unpublished paper, 2012).

[5]James Tito, "A Lesson from Jose: Understanding the Patron/Client Relationship," *Evangelical Missions Quarterly* 44 (July 2008): 320-27.

[6]Del Chechen, "The Patron-Client System: A Model of Indigenous Discipleship," *Evangelical Missions Quarterly* 31 (October 1995): 46-51.

[7]Ibid., 46.

[8]David deSilva, *Honor, Patronage, Kinship and Purity* (Downers Grove, IL: InterVarsity Press, 2000), 133-34.

[9]Frederick Danker, *Benefactor: Epigraphic Study of a Greco-Roman and New Testament Social Field* (St. Louis: Clayton, 1982).

[10]Bruce W. Winter, "The Public Honoring of Christian Benefactors: Romans 13:3-4 and 1 Peter 2:14-15," *Journal for the Study of the New Testament* 34 (1988): 87-103.

[11]Paul Hiebert, "Clean and Dirty: Cross-Cultural Misunderstandings in India," *Evangelical Missions Quarterly* 44 (January 2008): 90-92.

[12]Gregory P. Whitsett, "Living in Favor with God and Man: Honorable Christian Living in a Theravada Buddhist Context," in *Shame and Honor: Presenting Biblical Themes in Shame and Honor Contexts*, ed. Bruce L. Bauer (Berrien Springs, MI: Department of World Mission, 2014).

[13]Phil Parshall, "Contextualization," in *Toward Respectful Understanding Witness Among Muslims*, ed. Evelyne A. Reisacher (Pasadena, CA: William Carey Library, 2012), 226-27.

[14]"Floating Hospital of Hope," *CBS Evening News*, February 18, 2013, www .cbsnews.com/videos/the-floating-hospital-of-hope/.

8 EVANGELISM

[1]This story is adapted from Mark Baker, "Two Foundational Stories of the Cross: How They Affect Evangelism," *Mission Focus: Annual Review* 15 (2007): 27-39.

[2]Martin Luther King Jr., "A Christmas Sermon on Peace" (sermon delivered in Atlanta, GA, December 24, 1967), www.ecoflourish.com/Primers /education/Christmas_Sermon.html. King's comments on means and ends were spoken to advocate the peaceful, nonviolent means for the ends of civil rights and a peaceful society in the 1960s South.

[3]Michael Medley, *Resilience: The Art of Bouncing Back* (unpublished curriculum).

[4]For the notion of God's common grace extended to all people, see Wayne Grudem, *Systematic Theology* (Grand Rapids: Zondervan, 1994), 657-65.

[5]Joel B. Green, *Theology of the Gospel of Luke*, New Testament Theology (Cambridge: Cambridge University Press, 1995), 86.

[6]James W. Fernandez, *Persuasions and Performances: The Play of Tropes in Culture* (Bloomington: Indiana University Press, 1986); Fernandez, *Beyond Metaphor: The Theory of Tropes in Anthropology* (Stanford: Stanford University Press, 1991).

[7]Quoted in Fernandez, *Persuasions and Performances*, 10.

[8]For more on the theory and process of contextualization, see Paul Hiebert, "Critical Contextualization," in his *Anthropological Insights for Missionaries* (Grand Rapids: Baker, 1985), 171-92; Jackson Wu, *One Gospel for All Nations: A Practical Guide to Biblical Contextualization* (Pasadena, CA: William Carey Library, 2015).

[9]Paul Sadler, "A Japanese Gospel Message," *Evangelical Missions Quarterly* 50 (January 2014): 26-33. Retold with permission from *Evangelical Missions Quarterly*.

[10]For a generic, decontextualized version of this story, see Jayson Georges, "The Bible's Story for Honor-Shame Contexts," *Mission Frontiers* 37, no. 1 (2015): 8-9. The whiteboard movie "Back to God's Village" is also available at http://honorshame.com/videos.

[11]Nabeel Jabbour, *The Crescent Through The Eyes of the Cross: Insights from an Arab Christian* (Colorado Springs, CO: NavPress, 2008), 161-72.

[12]Ibid, 163.

[13]Ibid, 166.

[14]Kwame Bediako, *Jesus And The Gospel In Africa: History And Experience* (Maryknoll, NY: Orbis, 2004), 31-32.

[15]Krister Stendahl, "Paul and the Introspective Conscience of the West," *Harvard Theological Review* 56, no. 3 (1963): 206.

[16]This idea and the following paragraphs were first developed in Jayson Georges, "From Shame to Honor: A Theological Reading of Romans for Honor-Shame Contexts," *Missiology* 38, no. 3 (2010): 295-307.

[17]James D. G. Dunn, *The Theology of Paul the Apostle* (Grand Rapids: Eerdmans, 1998), 334-89.

[18]Robert Jewett, "Honor and Shame in the Argument of Romans," in *Putting Body and Soul Together: Essays in Honor of Robin Scroggs*, ed. Graydon F. Snyder, Virginia Wiles and Alexandra Brown (Valley Forge, PA: Trinity Press International, 1997), 270.

[19]Richard Hays, "'Have We Found Abraham to Be Our Forefather According to the Flesh?' A Reconsideration of Rom 4:1," *Novum Testamentum* 27 (1985): 76-98.

[20]David deSilva, *Honor, Patronage, Kinship and Purity: Unlocking New Testament Culture* (Downers Grove, IL: InterVarsity Press, 2000), 201.

[21]Robert Jewett, *Saint Paul Returns to the Movies: Triumph over Shame* (Grand Rapids: Eerdmans, 1999), 12.

9 CONVERSION

[1]This section is adapted from Jayson Georges, *The 3D Gospel* (Timē Press, 2014), 60-71. Missiological literature often discusses "power-encounter" for tribal/animistic worldviews in which fear and power are the predominant cultural forces. Our proposal of a third form of Christian witness, named "community encounter," is similar to "love encounter" by Doug Hayward in "The Evangelization of Animists: Power, Truth or Love Encounter?" *International Journal of Frontier Missions* 14, no. 4 (1997): 155-59; and "allegiance encounter" by Charles Kraft in "What Kind of Encounters Do We Need in Our Christian Witness" *Evangelical Missions Quarterly* 27 (July 1991): 258-67.

[2]Christopher L. Flanders, *About Face: Rethinking Face for Twenty-First-Century Mission* (Eugene, OR: Wipf & Stock, 2011), 194-200.

[3]Andrew Mbuvi, "African Theology from the Perspective of Honor and Shame," in *The Urban Face of Mission: Ministering the Gospel in a Diverse and Changing World*, ed. Harvie M. Conn, Manuel Ortiz and Susan S. Baker (Phillipsburg, NJ: P&R, 2002), 295.

[4]Timothy Tennent, "Anthropology: Human Identity in Shame-Based Cultures of the Far East," in *Theology in the Context of World Christianity: How the Global Church Is Influencing the Way We Think About and Discuss Theology* (Grand Rapids: Zondervan, 2007), 97-99.

[5]Marten Visser, *Conversion Growth of Protestant Churches in Thailand* (Zoetermeer, Netherlands: Boekencentrum, 2008), 123.

[6]Leith Gray and Andrea Gray, "Paradigms and Praxis, Part II: Why Are Some Workers Changing Paradigms," *International Journal of Frontier Missiology* 26, no. 2 (2009): 63.

[7]Robert E. Brenneman, *Homies and Hermanos: God and Gangs in Central America* (New York: Oxford University Press, 2012), 65.

[8]Another way he was trapped was that his gang would kill him if he quit the gang. Brenneman explains that the only "exception clause" at the time was if a gang member converted and became a true evangelical Christian.

[9]Ibid., 180.

[10]Ibid., 182.

[11]Ibid., 187.

[12]Ibid., 181.

[13]Ibid., 187.

[14]Used with permission from author.

[15]Zeba A. Crook, *Reconceptualising Conversion: Patronage, Loyalty, and Conversion in the Religions of the Ancient Mediterranean* (Berlin: de Gruyter, 2004), 13. At several points this section draws on Crook's thesis as a whole.

[16]Ibid., 14.

[17]This aligns better with the *primary* meaning intended in Rom 3:23, where "all" in the context of Paul's argument in Rom 1–3 refers to "all groups" (Jews *and* Gentiles), not "every individual."

[18]E. Randolph Richards and Brandon J. O'Brien, *Misreading Scripture with Western Eyes: Removing Cultural Blinders to Better Understand the Bible* (Downers Grove, IL: IVP Books, 2012), 120-28.

[19]Ibid.

[20]Frederick W. Danker, Walter Bauer, William F. Arndt and F. Wilbur Gingrich, *Greek-English Lexicon of the New Testament and Other Early Christian Literature*, 3rd ed. (Chicago: University of Chicago Press, 2000), 967-68, lists three definitions of the word: (1) "awareness of information about someth., *consciousness*"; (2) "the inward faculty of distinguishing right and wrong, *moral consciousness, conscience*"; (3) "attentiveness to obligation, *conscientiousness.*" A longer review of the biblical idea is Hannes

Wiher, *Shame and Guilt: A Key To Cross Cultural Ministry* (Bonn: Verlag für Kultur und Wissenschaft, 2003), 36-42.

[21]In chapter two we examined the various sources of shame, and in chapter six we distinguished between misplaced shame and well-placed shame.

[22]Dietrich Bonhoeffer, *Ethics* (New York: Touchstone, 1995), 25.

[23]N. T. Wright, *Jesus and the Victory of God* (Minneapolis: Fortress, 1996), 250-52.

[24]Ibid., 257.

[25]*Pistis* occasionally refers to "that which is believed" (e.g., Acts 6:7). The conversation here discusses the more common usage denoting one's response to Jesus. The phrase *pistis Christou* can be translated as "faith in Christ" (objective genitive) or "faithfulness of Christ" (subjective genitive). While *pistis* is the action of both Christ and the believer, we only discuss the latter in this section on conversion. For more, see Mark D. Baker, *Religious No More: Building Communities of Grace and Freedom* (Downers Grove, IL: InterVarsity Press, 1999), 104-7.

10 ETHICS

[1]This story was reported by Rod Nordland, "In Spite of the Law, Afghan 'Honor Killings' of Women Continue," *New York Times*, May 3, 2014, www .nytimes.com/2014/05/04/world/asia/in-spite-of-the-law-afghan-honor -killings-of-women-continue.html.

[2]Liana Sun Wyler and Kenneth Katzman, "Afghanistan: U.S. Rule of Law and Justice Sector Assistance," *Congressional Research Service*, November 9, 2010, www.fas.org/sgp/crs/row/R41484.pdf.

[3]John Leland and Namo Abdulla, "Honor Killing in Iraqi Kurdistan: Unhealed Wound," *New York Times*, November 20, 2010, www.nytimes .com/2010/11/21/world/middleeast/21honor.html.

[4]Anthony Appiah, *The Honor Code: How Moral Revolutions Happen* (New York: Norton, 2010); Appiah, "Best Weapon Against Honor Killers: Shame," *Wall Street Journal*, September 25, 2010, http://online.wsj.com/news /articles/SB10001424052748703989304575504110702939510. Appiah and other advocates coined the catchphrase "There's no honor in honor killings" to address honor killings.

[5]Joel B. Green, *1 Peter*, Two Horizons New Testament Commentary (Grand Rapids: Eerdmans, 2007), 171.

[6]John H. Elliott, "Disgraced Yet Graced: The Gospel According to 1 Peter in the Key of Honor and Shame," *Biblical Theology Bulletin* 25, no. 4 (1995): 174.

[7]Used with permission from the author.

[8]This phenomenon is often referred to as "high power distance" or "hierarchical," compared to Western cultures where leadership is described as "low power distance" or "egalitarian."

[9]Joseph H. Hellerman, "The Humiliation of Christ in the Social World of Roman Philippi, Part 1," *Bibliotheca Sacra* 160, no. 639 (2003): 332.

[10]Ibid., 336.

[11]Ibid.

[12]John Dickson, *Humilitas: A Lost Key to Life, Love, and Leadership* (Grand Rapids: Zondervan, 2011), 24 (emphasis original).

[13]David deSilva, *Honor, Patronage, Kinship and Purity: Unlocking New Testament Culture* (Downers Grove, IL: InterVarsity Press, 2000), 294.

[14]The rhetorical structure of the household code in 1 Tim 5–6 is particularly significant. Each of the three main sections opens with this injunction to honor, then follows with specific instructions for how that practically works itself out in the community. "Honor" is the primary command in every instance.

[15]Kwame Bediako, *Jesus and the Gospel in Africa* (Maryknoll, NY: Orbis, 2004), 26.

[16]Victor P. Furnish, *Theology and Ethics in Paul* (Nashville: Abingdon, 1968), 233.

[17]Richard Hays, "Ecclesiology and Ethics in 1 Corinthians," *Ex Auditu* 10 (1994): 33.

[18]Ibid., 31-32. The argument of this section on 1 Corinthians relies on Hays's article.

[19]David deSilva, *The Hope of Glory: Honor Discourse and New Testament Interpretation* (Eugene, OR: Wipf & Stock, 2009), 128.

11 COMMUNITY

[1]Bruce W. Longenecker, *The Lost Letters of Pergamum: A Story from the New Testament World* (Grand Rapids: Baker Academic, 2003).

[2]Ibid., 90.

[3]Ibid., 92.

[4]Ibid., 112.

[5]Ibid.

[6]John H. Elliott, "Disgraced Yet Graced: The Gospel According to 1 Peter in the Key of Honor and Shame," *Biblical Theology Bulletin* 25, no. 4 (1995): 173.

[7]For example, Phil 1:27-30; 1 Thess 1:6; 2:13-14; 3:1-4; 2 Thess 1:4-5; Heb 10:32-34; Rev 2:9-10, 13.

[8]David A. deSilva, "Turning Shame into Honor: The Pastoral Strategy of 1 Peter," in *The Shame Factor: How Shame Shapes Society*, ed. Robert Jewett (Eugene, OR: Cascade, 2011), 161.

[9]Ibid., 160-80.

[10]Ibid., 167.

[11]Translation from Joel B. Green, *1 Peter*, Two Horizons New Testament Commentary (Grand Rapids: Eerdmans, 2007), 54.

[12]DeSilva, "Turning Shame into Honor," 164.

[13]Ibid., 170.

[14]Ibid., 172.

[15]Ibid., 179.

[16]Elliott, "Disgraced Yet Graced," 173.

[17]Robert Brenneman, "Vom Töten zum Beten," *Welt-Sichten*, November 2013, 21. English translation by Robert Brenneman.

[18]Christopher Flanders, "Fixing the Problem of Face," *Evangelical Missions Quarterly* 45 (January 2009); https://emqonline.com/node/2208.

[19]Paul G. Hiebert, "Conversion, Culture and Cognitive Categories," *Gospel in Context* 1, no. 4 (1978): 24-29; Hiebert, *Anthropological Reflections on Missiological Issues* (Grand Rapids: Baker, 1994), 107-36. Our diagrams are adaptations of Hiebert's.

[20]For concrete examples and analysis of bounded churches, see Mark D. Baker, *Religious No More: Building Communities of Grace and Freedom* (Downers Grove, IL: InterVarsity Press, 1999), 17-33.

[21]Hiebert, *Anthropological Reflections*, 124.

[22]Ibid., 125.

[23]In this sense a centered church is not the opposite of a bounded church. What Hiebert describes as a fuzzy set is the opposite of a bounded set. When you have bounded church and simply remove or make the boundaries indistinct you get a fuzzy church. A centered approach is a totally different paradigm from bounded or fuzzy. For further description of the differences between the three, see Mark D. Baker, "Learning from Paul: Centered Ethics That Avoid Legalistic Judgmentalism and Moral Relativism," in *Ecclesia and Ethics: Moral Formation and the Church*, ed. Edward Alan Jones III, John Frederick, John Dunne, Eric Lewellen and Janghoon Park (London: T&T Clark, 2016), 55-67.

[24]For more information on the Amor Fe y Vida church, their study of and application of Galatians, see Baker, *Religious No More*.

[25]Tony Webb, "Towards a Mature Shame Culture: Theoretical and Practical Tools for Personal and Social Growth" (PhD diss., University of Western Sydney, 2003).

[26]Howard Zehr, *The Little Book of Restorative Justice* (New York: Good Books, 2014).

[27]John Braithwaite, *Crime, Shame and Reintegration* (Cambridge: Cambridge University Press, 1989), 12.

[28]Although one can find this ceremony described in various places in print and on the Internet, we have not found one without error (for instance, attributing it to a tribe that does not exist, or misplacing the tribe geographically). We were not able to confirm the veracity of the practice. Nevertheless, our focus is on Yurityz's true story of reintegrative shaming.

[29]Yurityz Villasenor shared this story in Mark's class "Global Christian Theologies" at Fresno Pacific Biblical Seminary, December 3, 2015. It is used here with her permission.

[30]Robert Brenneman, email to the authors, May 28, 2015.

[31]Braithwaite, *Crime, Shame and Reintegration*, 163.

[32]Gabriela Profeta Phillips, "Honor, Shame, and the Cross: A Missiological Perspective from a Muslim Context," in *Shame and Honor: Presenting Biblical Themes in Shame and Honor Contexts*, ed. Bruce Bauer (Berrien Springs, MI: Andrews University, 2014), 15.

[33]Andrew Mbuvi, "African Theology from the Perspective of Honor and Shame," in *The Urban Face of Mission: Ministering the Gospel in a Diverse*

and Changing World, ed. Harvie M. Conn, Manuel Ortiz and Susan S Baker (Phillipsburg, NJ: P&R, 2002), 294.

[34]David deSilva, *Honor, Patronage, Kinship and Purity: Unlocking New Testament Culture* (Downers Grove, IL: InterVarsity Press, 2000), 138.

[35]Christopher J. H. Wright, *The Mission of God's People: A Biblical Theology of the Church's Mission* (Grand Rapids: Zondervan, 2010), 209.

[36]Werner Mischke, *The Global Gospel: Achieving Missional Impact in Our Multicultural World* (Scottsdale, AZ: Mission ONE, 2015), 255.

[37]DeSilva, *Honor, Patronage, Kinship and Purity*, 138-39.

[38]Ahmed Ali Haile, *Teatime in Mogadishu: My Journey as a Peace Ambassador in the World of Islam* (Harrisonburg, VA: Herald Press, 2011), 6.

Name and Subject Index

Scripture Index

The website HonorShame.com offers practical tools and training for Christians ministering in honor-shame contexts. You will find free training videos, evangelism resources, recommended books, journal articles and more. New ideas and resources are introduced regularly, so subscribe at HonorShame.com/blog to stay connected. This site was founded by Jayson Georges in 2013, and in 2016 became the digital hub of the Honor-Shame Network.

ALSO ON SOCIAL MEDIA:

Twitter.com/HonorShame
Facebook.com/HonorShame

Finding the Textbook You Need

The IVP Academic Textbook Selector
is an online tool for instantly finding the IVP books
suitable for over 250 courses across 24 disciplines.

www.ivpress.com/academic/